The
Baking
Book

Lloyd Moxon

The Baking

Illustrations: Joseph D'Addetta

Book

Culinary *Arts* Institute
A DIVISION OF DELAIR PUBLISHING COMPANY INC.

To Aida who would have been surprised

Delair Publishing Company, Inc.
420 Lexington Avenue
New York, New York 10170

Manufactured in the United States of America and published siumltaneously in Canada.

ISBN: 0-8326-0634-0

Preface

Why another Bread Book? If all the books published in America on baking bread were lined up on a long shelf, it would be a very long shelf. Since that is true, why do I have the unmitigated gall, the chutzpah, the effrontery to write another book on baking bread?

The answer is simple. I am a graduate microbiologist, a specialist on yeast biochemistry. I am not in agreement with many practices recommended in the bread books on the market. I think that I have a better way of baking. I tested my concepts using laboratory criteria to tell if my experiments were successful. They were and I have written this book to show aspiring bakers how to save money on the use of yeast, how to take shortcuts that do not result in inferior bread and how to make bread rise properly instead of sagging. In the process of compiling and testing the recipes, I found and developed many recipes that will result in great breads, rolls, sweet rolls, desserts and entrees based on bread.

Despite the superabundance of bread books, I feel that I have something to pass on to my readers that is worth learning. In addition to the items mentioned above, I wanted to do a book on Health Food Breads, but not at the expense of ordinary breads. Using the suggestions given in the health food section of this book, most of the recipes in this and in any other book can be converted to the health food standard of good nutrition. In addition to the rules for converting regular recipes, many recipes for Health Food Breads are given. Among these are 100% whole wheat breads that rise well because of special techniques in preparing this bread. Most 100% whole wheat breads are poor risers.

I hope that you will have as much fun baking and eating the breads from these recipes as I had in testing them and writing the book.

Lloyd M. Moxon
Inglewood, California
October 1979

Contents

Anyone Can Bake Bread

If I can bake bread—tasty, wholesome bread—anyone can do the same. Once she (or he) feels that the craft has been mastered, there is a tremendous desire to take a bow, to win the applause and the praise of friends. I was no exception to this desire. I was a little secretive about baking in the beginning, for I only allowed family to taste my efforts. Having gained confidence from their response, I prepared for the crucial test. My turn to host our regular Tuesday night gathering was coming. I spent two weekends getting ready for this test. To describe the results, I'll try to tell it as it happened, to the best of my memory. Of course, the expletives have been deleted as has much of the conversation not pertinent to the baking of bread.

We were seated around the poker table when I told the boys that I had started to bake bread. They laughed at me. Al Feinstein was dealing at the time; he laughed so hard that the cards shot out of his hands and splattered all over the table. John Hall whooped so hard that he put the wrong end of his cigar into his mouth. All of the expletives he uttered at that moment have been deleted. "Where do you get off, Mox, trying to bake bread?" said Robert Gordon, our group's self appointed comedian, "You're such a klutz, you can't even find your way out of the kitchen."

"Actually, Bob," I replied, "the kitchen's just like my laboratory."

"One difference," said Sam Goldman, "you gotta eat what you brew in the kitchen. I wouldn't want to touch anything down at your lab."

"Why this sudden interest in baking?" asked someone. I didn't see who said it, but the voice sounded like Jack Woodward's. "Why bread?" he continued. I saw that my guess was right.

"I really don't know, Jack," I answered, "perhaps my interest in brewing and baking is related to doing yeast cultures, or perhaps it all stems back to one of my aunts. I lived with her while going to high school. She used to bake the greatest Challah I ever tasted. You just couldn't compare store bread or even bakery bread to that Challah. It was so good it tasted like cake."

"My grandmother used to bake bread," said Feinstein, "I remember eating it hot out of the oven."

"My mother baked bread too," said Hall. "It was something else."

"Yeah," said Gordon, "when I first got married, the wife baked biscuits. Thank God she gave up."

Al Feinstein had a funny look on his face. "You know, all these bakers we remember were women. How come, Mox, you want to get out in the kitchen and bake bread?"

"Shad-up already," I said, "Deal. I'll talk about baking later, when we take our snack bread."

The game started again, but they wouldn't let up on me. "Pattycake, pattycake, baker's man," chanted Gordon.

"You'll soon eat your words," I muttered back, but not loud enough for the others to hear. At last the clock stood at 11:30. We would break in fifteen minutes. "Deal me out of this hand," I told the boys and got up to go into the kitchen. I raided the refrigerator and took out the cold cuts, the cheese and the potato salad. While I was in the kitchen, I turned the oven on and popped a few loaves in to warm.

I had expected the reaction my announcement would bring even before I made it. That was why I had spent two weekends baking and freezing. I was going to overwhelm them with variety. I brought the toaster oven into the card room and then put a bowl of freshly whipped cream cheese, a tub of sweet butter and a basket of bagels next to the toaster. The bagels were homemade, of course. By then the oven had worked its magic and I brought a tray of hot cinnamon-apricot swirls into the room. I had baked a San Francisco type sourdough bread, a corn rye bread, a 100% whole wheat bread and a brioche. The breads had been sitting in the freezer until three hours before the game started. Heated they would taste as if they had just come out of the oven.

Everyone attacked the food. As card players, my friends are run of the mill, but ours is not a high stakes game. As trenchermen, these guys are second to none. Replete at last, Robert Gordon turned to me. "That was some spread, Mox, but I see you went to the bakery for the bread."

"You see wrong," I told him. "I did go to the delicatessen for the corned beef, but all of the bread and the sweet rolls, I baked."

"I don't believe you," he said. "Those loaves looked just like the ones we get at the bakery, and the bagel, they were the best water bagels I ever ate."

"Those were egg bagels Bob, I don't use artificial coloring like the bakery does."

The others were all reluctant to believe me too. "Prove it," said Sam Goldman.

"Sure thing, Sam. Come into the kitchen with me and I'll show you that I'm not trying to pull anyone's leg." Expecting doubts, I had set up a sponge before they arrived. The yeast were bubbling away and the sponge had risen in the bowl. While they watched, I added flour, shortening, eggs and salt to the sponge and then kneaded it into a dough. I put the dough into a greased bowl and covered it. "We've got about forty five minutes to wait," I said, "let's play cards."

It was closer to an hour later that we broke again to go into the kitchen. I had slipped away a little before and turned the fire on below a large pot of water. The dough had risen well; I punched it down, rolled it out and cut it into ropes. After rolling the strands, I shaped them into doughnut shapes. I allowed these to rise for a while and then dropped them one at a time into the briskly boiling water. The rings grew in size as the heat of the water expanded the carbon dioxide gas in the dough. After they had boiled long enough, I fished them out and put them on a greased cookie sheet. The bagels, for they were recognizable as such now, were brushed with beaten egg and sprinkled with poppy seed. They were put into the oven to bake; soon they would come out.

I had made my point; they were willing to believe me now. "Why go to all this trouble, Mox?" asked Feinstein.

"Two good reasons, Al," I answered. "Baking your own costs about a third or less than you pay in the store."

"Is money that important?" said Gordon.

"Money is always important. What I don't spend on store bread can be spent on something else. Besides, Robert, where can you get a decent loaf of bread, one that isn't full of preservatives and tastes like a real bread?"

"How about some of the specialty bakers?" asked Hall.

"You're right about them, but I don't want to travel that far or to pay their price. I find the work of baking less than bucking the traffic and the lines. I told you two reasons, but I can think of others too. Price and taste are good reasons, but when you bake, you have the satisfaction of creating something from nothing. You take flour and water and come up with a good bread."

"You write, Mox, don't you?" asked Feinstein.

"Yes, Al, I do write, but it takes at least nine months for me to write a novel. After it's accepted, it can take a year or longer before it's released by the publisher. With bread, I have instant satisfaction."

"Mox," said Sam Goldman, "you said other reasons, but you only gave us one."

"I'm glad that you asked that question, Sam," I answered. "You're a psychologist, so you'll understand what I mean when I say that kneading dough, slapping it around and forcing it into the shape you want is a darn good way to take out your hostilities."

"I agree," said Goldman.

"Yeah, Mox" said Gordon, you keep baking bread, you're going to get fat."

"No, Gordon, you're the one who's going to

get fat from my baking. I have fine, homebaked bread all the time. I no longer have a desire to gorge myself, but when you come over, you're going to have a hard time not taking another bagel or two."

It was now late, but the aroma of the hot bagels baking in the oven filled the air. I opened the door and pulled out the trays. As we passed the hot bagels around, Gordon, always the one who tried to be a funny man, said, "You know, Mox, a bagel's nothing but a hard boiled doughnut."

"You're right, Gordon," I told him. "If I hadn't used all of the dough on the bagels, I'd take some and fry it instead of boiling. Then you'd have a doughnut."

"I give up," said Gordon. "Let me eat this bagel and then it's time to go home."

Tools and Equipment

Basic White Bread

The tools required to bake bread are simple and are probably already in your kitchen. If not, you can purchase them inexpensively or improvise.

Measuring cups. Measuring cups are available in plastic, glass or metal. Some of the metal ones come in a set of quarter, half and full cups; others use an indented line on the metal to indicate the measurement. Glass, plastic and metal cups with markings are available as either 1 cup measures or 2 cup measures. A glass cup with painted lines is the easiest graduated measuring cup to use, but if you wish to improvise any cup can be used if the same cup is used for all measurements.

Measuring spoons. Measuring spoons are sold as sets consisting of an eighth, quarter, half and full teaspoon as well as 1 tablespoon. These are made of metal or plastic, but the ring that holds the set together is usually shoddy. A key ring can be substituted to make sure that the spoons are not separated. A set of measuring spoons is not necessary to bake bread. The teaspoons and tablespoons in your regular dining set will work very well. About half the time I bake, I wind up using these because I can't find the set of graduated spoons.

Rolling pin. A rolling pin is handy and inexpensive, but in an emergency a wine bottle can be used.

Baking sheets. Any flat metal sheet can be used to bake hearth loaves.

Baking tins. Breads can be baked in any metal or pyrex container. If you have pots with metal handles, they will work very well. Do not bake using pots with wooden or plastic handles because the handles can be damaged by the heat. Meat loaf tins, which are usually used for baking loaves are inexpensive. These are found in plain or "Teflon" coated varities. If the pan is greased the plain pan works well. Breads can be baked in empty tin cans too. Coffee cans are available in convenient sizes, but any can may be used.

Razor blades. A sharp knife can be used to slash the tops of loaves, but who has a sharp knife when it is needed? Buy a package of single edged razor blades at the paint store. They are ideal for slashing bread or to groove break-apart rolls and to trim rolled out dough into circular or rectangular shapes. If you have an old cut-throat razor, that will work well too, but single edged blades are cheap and safe to use.

Whisk. A whisk is handy for beating eggs and for beating batter during the preliminary steps. A wooden spoon can be substituted for beating batter. A fork will beat eggs.

Hearth Loaf

Electric mixer. With a dough hook, an electric mixer can be used to knead bread. A plain mixer can be used to beat a batter bread without muscle strain. This is a luxury item. If you own one, use it; if not, don't rush out to buy one.

Pastry cutter and crimper. This tool is handy to crimp dishes like ravioli and knishes. A fork works slower, but does as good a job of crimping.

Wooden spoon. A wooden spoon is an absolute must, especially if you are working with sourdough. Wooden spoons are inexpensive.

Slotted spoon. Every kitchen should already have a spoon with holes to allow liquid to drain. They are used to remove vegetables from water. In baking they are the proper tool to pull bagels from the boiling water.

Rubber tipped spatula. The spatula is most helpful. It is used to scrape batter out of the bowl. I use it to clean my wooden mixing spoon and scrape the bowl for washing. It is also useful to pick loose flour off the board when I am kneading or to move dough that is sticky. Spatulas are cheap, but the cheap ones usually have a plastic or flimsy wooden handle that breaks the first time you use the tool. That should not be a problem. Pull the handle stub out of the rubber pocket with a pair of pliers and then shove a table knife into the pocket. You now have a rubber spatula with an unbreakable handle. Professional rubber spatulas can be purchased from restaurant supply houses. These have sturdy wooden handles and come in several sizes.

Mixing bowls. A large bowl is needed for mixing and to hold the sponge when the sponge method of baking is used. This bowl should be of glass, ceramic, or plastic. Metal bowls conduct heat too well to be used for sponges or for rising, kneaded yeast breads. Metal bowls will react with the acids in sourdough batters and doughs. It is better to use one of the inert materials than to use metal.

Cooling rack. When breads are baked, it is best to cool them on a wire rack. This allows air circulation under the bread and around the bread. If breads are cooled in the baking tins, moisture from condensation can soften the crust. I use the grill of an old electric broiling unit, but refrigerator racks and other wire racks can be used for the job if you do not wish to purchase a cooling rack. Some people lean loaves against a support instead of using a rack.

Pastry brush. A brush is an invaluable tool for brushing egg, honey, shortening, or water over dough. Any clean brush can be used, even a paint brush.

Sprayer. A spray bottle is a handy, efficient way to spray water or salt water on crusts. It works better for this job than a brush. Any spray bottle, even those used to spray window cleaner, can be used. If you use a bottle that once contained something else, make sure that you wash it thoroughly before using it as a spray bottle for baking.

Testing knife. Any thin bladed knife can be used to test for doneness. Some people use a skewer or a toothpick.

Grill & garage scrubber. This useful tool is made by the 3M Company. It is intended for scrubbing floors and grills, but it works like a demon at cleaning off encrusted flour on the bread board.

The Ingredients Used in Baking Breads

Bread is made of flour and water leavened by yeast or by a chemical agent. Shortening, salt, baking soda, milk or eggs can be added. These will all change the taste and the character of the bread baked. In America, breads are usually baked with milk instead of water. The use of milk tends to produce a soft crumb compared to the rather firm crumb texture of water breads. The word crumb, as used here, refers to the inside section of the bread, the part that is left after the crust is sliced off. The crust is the harder, outer layer that surrounds the bread. By choosing the method of baking and the shape of the bread, you can produce a loaf with more or less crust. The texture of the crumb depends on the ingredients you use. A long, thin French baguette has much more crust than the average loaf; it is produced for crust lovers. The crust can be hardened by brushing with water, softened by brushing with melted butter or milk. When you bake your own breads, you can cater to your own taste.

Flour

The choice of flour will affect the bread you bake. Hard wheat flours make the best breads, but are difficult to find in supermarkets. All purpose flour makes a good substitute; the recipes in this book are based on the use of all purpose flour or stone ground 100% whole wheat flour which is milled from hard wheat.

The following flours are available, but some of them may have to be purchased in specialty shops or health food stores.

Hard wheat bread flour.
All purpose bleached and enriched wheat flour.
All purpose unbleached, enriched flour.
All purpose wheat flour (enriched).
100% stone ground whole wheat flour (Graham).
75% Gluten flour (High gluten flour).
Gluten free flour.
Rye flour (usually whole grain).
Rye meal (a coarse rye flour). If rye meal is not available, it may be easily made at home by chopping rye flakes in a blender or grinding rye grain in a food processor. Rye flakes and grain are available in most health food stores.
Buckwheat flour.
Soy flour.
Corn meal (available as degerminated or whole grain in white or yellow)
Corn grits (coarse ground corn meal).
Oat meal (rolled or cut oats.)
Rice flour.

The following flours should **NEVER** be used to bake bread:

Cake or pastry flour. (This is a soft wheat flour that will not rise properly).
Self rising flour. (This contains a form of baking powder. It should never be used to bake a yeast bread.)

Pre-sifted flour. (This is a finely ground mixture of hard and soft wheat. It can be used for baking bread, but is more expensive than all purpose flour.)

Flour varies from brand to brand making exact measurements impossible. The harder the flour, the more water it will absorb. After making a few breads, you will realize that depending on the humidity of the day and the brand of flour used, you will add either more or less flour in the final steps of making the dough. When the proper consistency is reached, the dough will not be sticky. It will pull cleanly away from your hands as you knead.

Leaven—Yeast and Others

Before the accidental discovery of leavening, man baked flat sheets of bread. Such unleavened bread is still baked today. The chupatis of India and the matzoh of the Bible are examples of flat bread. According to most historians, the use of leaven was discovered in Egypt. This was an accidental discovery much like the modern discovery of penicillin. The first leaven was a sourdough. Some unknown and unsung Egyptian allowed his ingredients for bread to sour—they trapped wild yeast from the air. Man also learned that this souring could produce wine and beer, but he still didn't know what produced the change. Although yeast itself was just some mysterious substance found in souring materials that worked a miracle, the sourdough pot had been discovered.

Yeast today is sold in a dehydrated dry form. This is called active dry yeast. It can also be found in moist cakes, but this form is harder to find for the cakes have a limited life. Most of the yeast makers put up their dry yeast in foil packages each containing one measured tablespoon by volume. This is convenient when using an old recipe for one tablespoon of the dry yeast equals one cake of the moist yeast. When the packet is opened, granules of a brown substance are seen. If these are mixed with water the yeast cells become active. When yeast is proved before it is used, the granules are dissolved in about an ounce of water with ½ teaspoon of sugar mixed in. The sugar provides a food source for the yeast which begins to multiply.

The feeding yeast cells produce bubbles of carbon dioxide gas. If a drop of the yeast-water mixture were put on a microscope slide and examined, you would see that the yeast are tiny, one-celled organisms. Biologists classify these as plants rather than animals. It is these tiny organisms that turn grapes into wine, flour into bread, corn into bourbon and barley into beer.

Most recipes, modern recipes, for bread call for too much yeast. Yeast is expensive, if it is wasted. Old fashioned recipes have been proven by use through the centuries. Even though the old time bakers knew nothing about microbiology or chemistry, they appreciated what worked and discarded what did not. Today recipes are crafted by food editors and home economics majors with no idea of either chemistry or microbiology. They also seem to have little appreciation for the empiric truths discovered by trial and error. They discard the time proven ideas and substitute what sounds reasonable and rational to them. Most of the changes are made to speed up the time it takes to produce a loaf of bread. The older way of baking produces a better bread, but sometimes it is necessary to take shortcuts. In the chapter entitled, "Bread In a Hurry", shortcuts are discussed and some that work well are given. The drawbacks of each method are discussed and the results compared to the breads baked by the sponge method.

When I first started to bake, I used a book that gave many of these modern recipes. I actually thought that I was baking good bread. Compared to what I could purchase in the stores, my bread was excellent. Then I tried one of the older methods and baked an even better bread. After this experience, I tried to evaluate the shortcuts in view of yeast and gluten chemistry. Judged that way, I found that I was saving time at the expense of quality. Because my training is in the sciences, I tried a duplicate experiment by using the same dough, half in a shortcut method and half in the conventional method. I proved to my own satisfaction that I could either bake good bread or I could bake great bread.

A knowledge of microbiology is not needed to bake well, but some facts are of interest to the economical production of first quality bread. Many recipes, particularly the modern ones, call for more yeast than is necessary, particularly if the sponge method of baking is used. A rule of thumb is that one package (1 level tablespoon) of yeast is adequate for eight to nine cups of flour in a direct method. If a sponge is set first then that amount can be decreased. Theoretically it would be possible to start with a single granule. With my luck, I would pick a dead granule so to be on the safe side I never use less than one teaspoon of yeast for eight to nine cups of flour. Since a sponge started with a teaspoon takes longer than one started with a tablespoon of yeast, the recipes in the book all call for 1 package of yeast for a two bread recipe. If you're not in a hurry you can use less unless you are baking with 100% whole wheat flour.

The Sponge Method of Baking

Most modern shortcut methods promise to make the baking of bread easier. They do this by eliminating a step. After trying both methods, I find the longer method is actually easier in terms of work. The idea behind the sponge method is to get lots of yeast working away at making carbon dioxide gas. This is done by mixing the yeast with all of the liquid and part of the flour in the recipe and allowing the mixture to stand in a warm place while the yeast cells multiply. I prefer not to add salt and shortening to the sponge because the salt can slow the growth of the yeast. As the yeast cells increase in number they work on the flour in the bowl. Enzymatic action breaks starches into simple sugars and carbon dioxide gas is given off to bubble through the mixture. The sponge begins to rise and since it is filled with bubbles, it looks like a giant sea sponge filled with water. After the sponge has risen it is easier to work in the remaining flour. Many bakers like their sponge to go overnight. This is a convenient way to bake. When working with yeast, the amount of yeast can be decreased if the sponge will stand for at least eight hours.

The addition of 50 milligrams of Vitamin C (Ascorbic Acid) to a sponge will speed up the production of yeast. Vitamin C acts as a catalyst to yeast growth. When the sponge is ready for the next step in baking, it will be well risen and have many bubbles. If Vitamin C is used, it will take a shorter time for the sponge to rise.

Other Leavening Agents

Compressed yeast or dry yeast can be used to bake breads. Other leavening agents include the sourdough pot, the sweetdough pot and the doughball starter. These are described under starters and are actually yeast in a different form than a cake or dry granules. A starter is a living culture of yeast that is kept healthy through your care. The main advantage of a starter is that once it is growing you have no further expense for yeast.

Certain chemical agents can also be used for leavening. These include several products called baking powders or the use of baking soda with an acid. Buttermilk, yogurt, vinegar, or cream of tartar are used to provide acid. A more detailed description of baking powders is found in the chapter on Quick Breads (page 107). The chemistry of these chemical agents is discussed in more detail. Baking powder contains baking soda and an acid producing substance. When baking soda reacts with an acid, carbon dioxide gas—the same gas produced by yeast—is released. This causes the dough to rise. Self rising flour contains a form of baking powder. Biscuit mixes contain baking powder and shortening.

The source of the gas does not matter. A machine that produced carbon dioxide gas was once tried for baking bread on a commercial scale. No yeast or chemicals were used. The machine forced the gas into the dough making it rise. This is similar to the use of steam in the baking of popovers. The steam comes from moisture in the dough.

Other Ingredients

Liquids. The liquid called for in most of the recipes is water. Other liquids can be substituted, but each change will affect the texture of the crumb. The most common substitution is that of milk. Milk softens the crumb. Bread baked with water is firm compared to that baked with milk. Most American recipes call for milk, but most European recipes use water. Both types produce excellent breads. In the section on basic breads, the recipes are all water breads, but all or part of the liquid can be replaced with milk for a different tasting bread. The addition of skim milk powder is an economical way to add milk to these breads. If condensed milk (canned milk) is used the increased amount of shortening in the bread will give a particularly rich texture. If canned milk is called for, whole milk or half and half can be substituted. If skim milk is used in these recipes the texture will suffer unless additional shortening is added. Skim milk is used in the Health Food section to decrease the amount of saturated fat. Some recipes call for the use of fruit juices instead of water or milk as the liquid. The juice can add a distinctive flavor and color to the bread.

Shortening. Many bread recipes call for a small amount of shortening. Any shortening will work, but some work better than others. Butter and lard particularly enhance the texture of the crumb but these are highly saturated fats. Margarine, if a good brand, works almost as well as butter. Margarines are also saturated fats and many of them contain additives and preservatives. If this is of concern, read the label before buying. Some natural margarines are sold even in supermarkets. Hydrogenated cotton seed oil is sold under many trade names. It does not enhance the texture as well as either lard or butter, but it is a saturated fat. Oil can be used. Oil is easy to use but does little to enhance the color or texture of the crumb. There is one good reason to recommend the use of oil despite the fact that it does little for texture. Polyunsaturated oils are available. The use of safflower, corn or sunflower oil reduces the amount of saturated fatty acids. If a solid shortening is used, it is more convenient to melt it and add it as a liquid instead of rubbing it into the flour.

Glazes. The crust can be treated in several different ways. Shortening, melted butter or milk can be brushed over the crust to soften it. Water or salt water can be sprayed on to make a more crunchy crust. Egg white, egg yolk, or a beaten whole egg can be brushed on to give the crust color and to make seeds adhere to the surface.

Greasing. Nothing is as heartbreaking as turning a freshly baked loaf out of the pan and having a large chunk of the bottom remain stuck to the metal or glass. It is necessary to use a substance which prevents sticking. Fats are the usual greasing material. Lard, butter, hydrogenated vegetable shortening and margarine all work well. NEVER USE OIL TO GREASE A PAN. The fatty acids in oils are in shorter chains than those found in saturated fats. These shorter chains can migrate into the bread giving it an oily taste. Non-stick pans coated with "Teflon® " and other plastic coatings also prevent bread from adhering to the surface. For those who would rather not use saturated fats or plastic coatings, there is yet another way to prevent sticking. Liquid lecithin, a pure vegetable product is available. This contains only 113 calories per ounce and absolutely no cholesterol. A drop of the fluid, about the size of a penny, will grease even a large pan preventing bread from sticking. Liquid lecithin can also be used for frying. A more refined form of lecithin is used in several commercial products including "Pam® ". Since the liquid lecithin is not sold as a propellent spray, it is less expensive to purchase it by the pint bottle.

Sweeteners

Dextrose. This sugar is also known as corn sugar. It is used in candy or commercial baked products but is seldom used for home baking. Modern brewers prefer this sugar to table sugar for beer making. Dextrose is a monosaccharide sugar with the chemical formula of $C_6H_{12}O_6$. The formula is used to indicate that there are six carbons in this particular sugar. Six carbon sugars are called hexoses.

Fructose. Although this sugar is also a six carbon sugar like dextrose and is indicated by the same formula, it has different properties. Fructose is the sugar found in honey. It is now available in granulated form. Since fructose is sweeter than sugar, it is used as a substitute when the number of calories in a cake or bread are of concern. Fructose is considered a natural sugar and is accepted in many health food recipes.

Sucrose. This is ordinary table sugar. Sucrose is made up of a molecue of dextrose bonded to a molecue of fructose. In the refined state it is not accepted as a part of a health food diet. Granulated sugar, confectioners sugar (powdered), cubes and refined brown sugar are all sucrose.

Brown sugar. This sugar is not as refined as the pure, white granulated sugar. It has some molasses mixed in which gives it a brown color and a moist texture. It is not accepted as a proper health food.

Raw brown sugar. This is a partially refined sugar that is available in some health food stores. It has a higher percentage of the vitamins and minerals found in molasses.

Molasses. Molasses is extracted from sugar beets, sugar cane and corn. It is used to make rum. Molasses, particularly the blackstrap variety is rich in vitamins and minerals. The lighter the color, the less iron and vitamins.

Sorghum. A syrup made from the grain, sorghum. This is used on pancakes and could be used for baking if desired.

Honey. Honey is a natural sweetner containing fructose. Honey can be substituted for sugar on a one to one basis, but if the recipe calls for one cup of sugar, substituting a cup of honey will change the recipe's flour to liquid balance. When large amounts of honey are used, the flour must be increased in volume or the bread will not be baked in the time called for in the recipe. For more information on honey, see the section on health foods (page 205) where recipes using honey are given.

Definitions and Techniques

Baking pan. Any metal or glass pan suitable for baking a loaf of bread. The most common type is also called a meatloaf pan. A particularly useful pan to bake in is a well seasoned cast iron skillet. Cast iron conducts heat differently than the sheet metal or glass used in ordinary pans and trays. A bread baked in a cast iron pan has a crunchy bottom crust, even crunchier than one baked on a sheet. After baking, the skillet can be wiped clean if it is well seasoned.

Baking sheets. These are also called cookie sheets. Free standing loaves, hearth loaves, are baked on these sheets. Pizza can also be baked on a baking sheet. An old cast iron griddle makes an exceptionally fine baking sheet.

Baking Tiles. Unglazed ceramic tiles can be used instead of a baking sheet to bake hearth loaves. These are used to line one of the wire oven racks. Stone tile has a unique heat conduction that produces as crunchy a bread as that baked in a cast iron skillet.

Crumb. The inner section of a bread.

Crust. The hard, outer layer of a bread.

Filling. What is put inside a filled, baked product. Fillings include jams, poppy seed, cheese, fruits etc.

Finish. The finish is the glaze or other crust treatment that is used in baking. Sweet baked goods are sometimes finished with powdered sugar dusted over them or with a sweet glaze. Glazes and finishes are described with recipes in the section on shaping breads.

Prove. An old term for letting the bread rise after punching down. Hearth loaves should not be proved for longer than 20 minutes. If allowed to stand too long, the bread sags producing a loaf with a low rise.

Prove. This term also refers to proving whether the yeast used is working. To prove yeast place ½ teaspoon of sugar or honey in a bowl. Add one or two ounces of hot water from the tap and then add the yeast granules. Stir the mixture and allow it to stand for about ten minutes in a warm place. If the yeast cells are alive, they will start to multiply and the mixture will look frothy.

Knead. The process of working dough with your hands to improve the glutin and make it capable of rising.

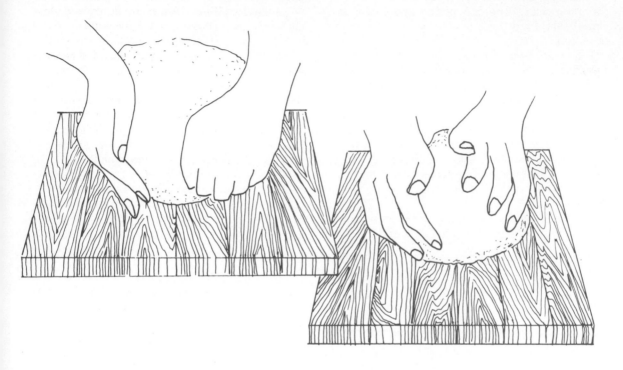

How to Knead

There are two ways to start kneading. The dough can be put onto a floured board in a stiff dough form by working flour into the sponge until it becomes very stiff before dumping it out onto the board. The other way is to work only part of the flour into the sponge and then scrape out the still loose sponge onto a pile of flour. Try it both ways to see which works better for you.

Kneading itself is done after rubbing flour on your hands. Fold the dough toward yourself with your fingers then push it down and away with the heels of both hands. Some people knead with only one hand. I usually squeeze with my fingers as I push. Turn the dough about one quarter and repeat the folding, pushing, squeezing motion until the dough is toughened and the surface appears satin smooth. During this pro-

cess you will find that the dough needs more flour. This is apparent because the new surface you turn up is sticky.

To add more flour, take a small handful of flour and rub it over the sticky surface with the palm of your hand. Continue kneading and rub more flour on each time you come to a sticky surface. (See illustrations on how to knead). A long kneading period toughens gluten and makes the bread rise better. The texture of a well kneaded loaf is fine and smooth. Sometimes a rougher textured loaf, one that does not rise as well and is a heavier bread is desired. One way to produce such a loaf is to limit the kneading. Work in flour by kneading until the dough no longer sticks to your hands. At that point, stop kneading. Place the dough in a bowl and allow it to rise. The bread baked from this dough will be coarser in texture.

Rise. The rise is that period after kneading where the dough is allowed to double in size. This is a crucial step and should not be omitted unless following one of the special shortcut methods. Bread that is not allowed to rise is heavy and doughy.

After kneading, grease a bowl and place the ball of dough into the bowl. Flatten it down and cover. Allow the dough to stand in a warm place. If boiling water is poured into a pan on the bottom of the oven, the oven itself is an ideal place to rise bread. Once the oven door is closed it will be draft free.

Punch down. After the dough has been kneaded and allowed to double, it is struck with the fist or the palm of the hand to force out the carbon dioxide gas that has made it rise. This must be done before the bread is shaped.

Sponge. This term refers to allowing part of the flour to be mixed with all of the liquid and the yeast. It is an extra step, but it gives the yeast a chance to multiply before the bread is kneaded. All methods calling for a starter must follow the sponge method.

Starter. The starter is a culture of yeast cells either wild or commercial. This culture is kept alive and growing in the refrigerator. The starter contains flour and water. Each time a cup of starter is removed from the starter pot, a cup of water and a cup of flour must be put into the pot to replace what was removed. Starters are discussed in detail in the chapter on starters (see page 39).

Basic Breads Baked with Active Dry Yeast

Kneaded breads are leavened by a starter or by yeast. The use of dry yeast instead of a starter saves time, fuss and bother. Convenience is never free; you gain time at the added cost of the yeast. There is an old cliche that says time is money; if you believe the saying, you will be pleased to find that you can speed up your baking if you use yeast instead of starter.

If time is not important and you plan to set up your sponge the evening before you bake, it is possible to cut the amount of yeast called for in the recipe in half. If you're in a hurry and do not set up a sponge, it will be necessary to double the amount of yeast called for in the recipes in this book.

To convert a starter recipe to use with yeast remember that a cup of starter equals one cup of flour plus one cup of water. Place 1 cup of each in the mixing bowl with the yeast and then follow the recipe.

All of the basic breads share a common recipe. Certain ingredients are added or substituted to produce variations in the bread. The shape of the bread and crispness of crust can also be varied.

BASIC WHITE BREAD

The basic bread recipe. This produces 2 large loaves of white bread.

Sponge:
5 cups of flour
3½ cups hot tap water
1 Tablespoon active dry yeast
½ teaspoon sugar or honey
Second Step:
2 Tablespoon sugar or honey
3 Tablespoons oil or melted
  shortening
1 Tablespoon salt
3-4 cups flour

Measure 1 Tablespoon of yeast (1 package) into the mixing bowl and add 1-2 ounces of water hot from the tap. Mix in ½ teaspoon of sugar and allow the bowl to stand in a warm place for about ten minutes.

When the yeast becomes frothy it is said to be proved. Add the remaining 3½ cups of hot tap water and stir in 4 cups of flour, one cup at a time.

Cover the bowl with a towel or plastic wrap and allow it to stand in a warm place until the flour and water mixture rises and is filled with bubbles. This is the sponge and looks exactly like a sponge well filled with water. It is possible to allow the sponge to sit longer if necessary, but when planning to allow the sponge to sit for a long period decrease either the amount of yeast or the amount of flour to prevent running over.

Second Step:

Sprinkle the sugar, salt and oil into the sponge and then stir the sponge down. Add 2 cups of flour and work the mixture into a dough. Put about ½ cup of flour on a bread board and turn the sponge out onto the floured board. Pour 1 more cup of flour over the sponge then flour your hands and start to knead adding more flour as necessary. When you start kneading the dough will feel flabby, but after working it and adding more flour it will become firm and elastic. Knead for about 10 minutes.

Grease a bowl and put the kneaded dough into the bowl. Cover the dough and let it stand in a warm place until the dough has doubled (45 min.-1½ hours). Punch down the dough and knead again for a minute or two to break up any gas bubbles. If the dough feels sticky rub flour over it as you knead. Shape the dough into breads or rolls. Place the shaped breads in a pan or on a baking sheet.

The pans should be greased before baking. Remember to grease the rims of the pans. If corn-meal is sprinkled over the greased pan or sheet before the dough is placed in the pan, the corn-meal will enhance the bottom crust.

It is customary for the shaped loaves to be allowed to rise again at this point. Ignore any other recipes you have read. If a hearth loaf, one on a baking sheet, is being baked, do not allow the dough to rise more than 20 minutes. An excellent bread will be baked with only a 10 minute rise. Too long a rise at this point will result in a middle aged spread. The dough will sag. If the bread is baked in a pan a longer rise is possible for the sides of the pan will support the dough. I bake both pan and hearth loaves after a 10-20 minute rise and have even cut the rise to about 5 minutes.

See the chapter on the shaping of loaves and rolls (page 59). Remember that you do not have to make both breads the same. You can bake 1 pan loaf and 1 hearth loaf. You can bake 1 bread and 1 batch of rolls. Variety in shape prevents boredom. Variety in shape actualy gives a variety in taste for different shapes have more or less crust.

The top crust of the bread should be finished. For a soft crust brush with melted butter or milk. For a crunchy crust brush or spray with cold water. Salt water will produce an even crisper crust. The crust can be brushed with egg white, egg yolk, or a beaten whole egg and then sprinkled with poppy seed or sesame seed. If yolk alone is used add 1 teaspoon of water to 1 yolk and beat before brushing it on. Yolk will produce the darkest color; mixed whole egg is the next darkest. Egg white gives a shiny surface and little color.

After the short rise period the breads are baked at 400°F for 45 minutes. Bake in the center of the oven. Rolls may be baked near the top of the oven and take less time. Test the bread with a knife to be sure that it is done. After testing turn the finished loaf out onto a rack to cool.

Variations on the Basic Bread

The basic bread recipe is not limited to white bread alone. By substitutions and additions a whole galaxy of breads and rolls can be baked from this basic dough. If the shape of the loaves is varied, too, you can have twists, baguettes, cigar shaped loaves, round loaves, and bubble loaves as well as pan breads.

The basic recipe results in a hearty, good tasting loaf that remains fresh for a long time. It is delicious toasted and makes exceptionally tasty French toast. The recipe seems foolproof. Several people using this recipe for their first attempt at a bread produced magnificent loaves. Please note that the flour quantity is not exact because the amount of flour taken up by the water varies with temperature, humidity and the brand of the flour. It may even vary with the mood of the baker.

Brioche

English Bread

The English bread is a white bread similar to the basic white bread, but it is made without any shortening. The recipe and the mixing procedure are identical as is the baking time. English bread is frequently baked as a cottage loaf. Directions for shaping the cottage loaf are in the chapter on shaping bread (page 59). English bread is usually rather salty.

Sponge:
½ teaspoon honey or sugar
4 cups unbleached flour
3½ cups hot tap water
1 Tablespoon (1 package) dry yeast

Second Step:
2 Tablespoons honey or sugar
1½ Tablespoons salt
4 cups additional flour

Prove the yeast by dissolving it in 1-2 ounces of warm water and adding ½ tsp. honey or sugar. Allow to stand until frothy and then add the rest of the water and stir in the 4 cups of flour.

Cover bowl and allow sponge to stand for about 1-2 hours. When the sponge is ready it will have risen and be well filled with bubbles.

Second Step: Mix in the sweetener and salt and then start to stir in additional flour until a dough is formed.

Turn dough out onto floured board and knead for 10 minutes adding more flour as necessary. Place kneaded dough in a greased bowl and cover. Allow dough to rise in a warm place until doubled. This will take about 1-2 hours. Test dough with finger to see if it has doubled.

After kneaded dough has risen, turn it onto a bread board after punching it down in the bowl. Knead again for about 1 minute to force out any gas bubbles and then shape into loaves or rolls. Bake breads at 400°F. for 45 minutes. Rolls should be brown in about 35 minutes at the same temperature.

Basic White Bread with Cornmeal

The addition of cornmeal to the white bread recipe produces a tasty variation. When 1 cup of cornmeal is substituted for 1 cup of the flour in the sponge, the bread has a slightly coarser texture but retains its white color. If two cups of corn meal are added in place of two cups of flour, the bread is now yellow and has a mild corn flavor. Three cups are the maximum that can be substituted and then only if white flour is used. With wheat flour a maximum of two cups can be used. With 3 cups of cornmeal, we have a distinctive corn flavor similar to that of a corn bread.

Sponge
1, 2, or 3 cups cornmeal
unbleached flour-enough when added to cornmeal to make 4 cups.
1 Tablespoon dry yeast
½ teaspoon honey or sugar

Second Step
2 Tablespoons honey or sugar
3 Tablespoons oil or shortening
1 Tablespoon salt
4 cups flour

Prove yeast in 2 ounces of warm water and ½ teaspoon of sugar and honey. When frothy add cornmeal. Stir in enough flour that the total cups of flour and cornmeal add up to four. Cover sponge and allow to stand for about 1 hour or until sponge has formed.

Sprinkle dry ingredients over surface of sponge. Melt shortening and pour over sponge. Stir down the sponge and work flour into it until a dough has formed. Turn out the sponge onto a floured board and knead adding more flour as necessary. Knead about 10 minutes.

Place kneaded dough into a greased bowl and allow to double. Punch down, knead again for 1 minute and shape into loaves or rolls.

Bake at 400°F for 45 minutes. Test with a thin knife to be sure bread is done. Turn finished loaves onto a rack to cool.

Corn grits can be used instead of cornmeal to give a coarser texture and crunchier taste to the bread.

Croissants

Oatmeal Basic Bread

For a bread with a moist taste and an enhanced flavor, substitute 1 cup of oatmeal for 1 cup of flour in the sponge. Follow the basic recipe (page 31). Use rolled oats or steel cut oats. This is the same oatmeal that is used for breakfast. Do not use instant oatmeal.

Buckwheat Basic Bread

The same buckwheat flour that is used to make buckwheat pancakes can be used in bread. Follow basic recipe (page 31). Substitute 1-2 cups of buckwheat flour for 1-2 cups of regular flour in the sponge. If desired, the sugar called for in the recipe can be replaced with 2 Tablespoons of blackstrap molasses. The buckwheat gives this bread a different appearance and taste. This recipe can also be made using wholewheat flour plus buckwheat.

Wheat Germ Basic Bread

The addition of wheat germ to the basic white bread recipe restores much of the nutrition that has been removed in the milling. Wheat germ is substituted for the white flour in the sponge. Replace 1 or 2 cups of white flour with wheat germ. Breads containing wheat germ have a nutty, whole wheat like flavor but this flavor is not as strong as that of a whole wheat bread. Follow the basic recipe after making the substitution (page 31).

Basic Breads with Rye Flour

Part of the white flour can be replaced with rye flour. Up to 50% of the flour can be rye. Do all the replacement in the sponge part of the recipe (page 31). From 1-4 cups of rye flour should be used. Caraway seeds can be added if desired. Delicatessen rye is a sourdough bread. The recipe for that appears on page 150.

50% Whole Wheat Bread

A tasty, wheaty bread can be baked using 4-5 cups of stone ground whole wheat flour to replace part of the white flour called for in the recipe for basic bread (page 31). This is an excellent, nutritious bread. The complete recipe is in the health food section (page 213).

100% Whole Wheat Bread

100% whole wheat bread is the ultimate in nutrition. Because whole wheat flour has less gluten than white flour, special recipes which produce better rising of the dough are given in the health food section (page 213).

Enriched Basic Breads.

All of the basic bread variations listed above except for the English bread can be enriched. English bread, like French sourdough bread is a special type that would be changed into something else by enrichment. The addition of milk or non-fat milk powder to the recipe increases protein. If liquid milk is used, substitute it for the water in the recipe. All or part of the liquid can be replaced by milk, but it is recommended that no more than 2 cups of milk be used. Non fat instant milk powder dissolves quickly and can just be added to the recipe. Use 1-2 cups of the powder. This can be added to the sponge before the flour.

Raisins make any bread a festive bread. Add ½ to 1 cup of raisins to any of these recipes.

Eggs can be added. The egg can be added to recipes where milk has also been added or can be added to a recipe made with water. Breads made with egg have a softer, more cake like crumb. For a two bread recipe it is suggested that 1 large egg or 2 small eggs be added. Most of the recipes will handle a doubling of this amount of egg if you wish, but when eggs are added, the extra liquid will require more flour to be added in the kneading of the bread.

Sourdough Starters

Sourdough, a macho sounding word, evokes pictures of grizzled prospectors in the Yukon, or of round-up cooks beating an iron triangle to summon dusty cowhands to the chow wagon. The picture is true, but sadly incomplete. Soudough bread was baked by women too. Every house in early America kept a sourdough crock bubbling away on the top shelf of the stove where it would be warm. It was possible in that period to keep the sourdough starter without refrigeration because it was used almost every day of the week. Like Aladdin's lamp or the cornucopia, the alcoholic smelling sourdough pot was the source of an unending stream of good things. Biscuits, rolls, waffles, pancakes, coffee cakes, breads and even doughnuts started in the depths of the sour smelling crock.

Sourdough is not uniquely American. It was in common use in all countries of Europe during the nineteenth century and before. Many famous breads are still baked with sourdough instead of yeast. Among these are the delicatessen rye bread which is also called Russian rye or Jewish rye, the German sour pumpernickle and many of the French breads.

Today few people wish to bake every day, but the starter crock can still work its old magic thanks to modern refrigeration. The starter can be stored in the refrigerator with minimal attention. After bread is baked, it too can be frozen and kept fresh in the freezer making it possible to enjoy freshly baked bread that was baked weeks or even months before it is eaten.

Making Your Own Sourdough Starter

A genuine sourdough starter in dehydrated form can be purchased in some shops, but it is easy to make your own. There are many ways to make a starter. Some people start with potato water, others use hops while still others use milk or yogurt. When working with sourdough do not use metal bowls or spoons. The acid in the starter will attack the metal. This will result in a neutralization of the acid and discoloration of the metal. Glass, ceramic, plastic and wood are not attacked by the acid.

Milk Starter

Take one cup of whole milk and place it in a warm place for 48 to 72 hours. In this period the milk will sour. If the glass is covered with cheese cloth and allowed to stand out of doors in warm weather, there is a greater chance of natural wild yeast being trapped. Mix the soured milk with one cup of water and 2 cups of flour and transfer to a plastic container. Cover the mixture and allow to stand for 24 hours in a warm place. This starter is now ready to use. Each time you use the starter you will remove either ½ cup or 1 cup of the starter. After you place the starter you have removed into a bowl to leaven your bread, you must replenish the remaining starter. For each cup of starter removed put back into the starter crock 1 cup of flour and 1 cup of water. Allow the replenished starter to sit in a warm place for 8-12 hours and then refrigerate until the next time you bake. NEVER ALLOW THE REPLENISHED STARTER TO SIT OUT FOR OVER 24 HOURS.

Quick Milk Starter

Take 1 cup of milk and add the contents of 1 capsule of lactobacillus acidopholus to the milk. These capules are sold without prescription in most drug stores and cause the souring of milk. Pull the capsule apart and pour the dessicated bacteria into the milk. Allow the milk to sit in a warm place or out of doors if covered with cheesecloth for 24-36 hours. Add 1 cup of water and 2 cups of flour. This starter is now ready to use. Be sure to replenish the starter each time it is used. See Milk starter (page 39).

Guaranteed Sourdough Starter

Making a sourdough starter from milk does not always work. If wild yeast are trapped your starter will be successful, but if there are no yeasts to trap it will not work. The following starter is sure fire. Add ¼ teaspoon of dry yeast to the soured milk at the same time you add the water and flour. This will work with either of the two milk starters given above. The soured milk will assure the sour flavor while the baker's yeast will assure leavening action. This may not be as glamorous a starter as one made entirely from wild yeast, but it will compare favorably in taste and ability to make bread rise.

Hops Starter

Hops are available from your friendly wine and beer shop, the one that sells homebrew supplies

3 cups flour
2 cups mashed potato
¼ cup hops
½ cup sugar
8 cups water

Boil the water and stir in the hops. Bring gas to simmer and simmer hops for an hour. Strain the water into a glass, plastic, or ceramic bowl and add the sugar, the flour and the mashed potato. Cover bowl and allow to stand in a warm place to ferment for 48 hours.

The starter will be ready to use after 48 hours. Each time a cup of starter is removed, it must be replenished with 1 cup of water and 1 cup of flour.

Yogurt Starter

1 cup milk
1 cup plain yogurt
2 cups flour

Take 1 cup of milk and combine with 1 cup of plain yogurt. Add 2 cups of flour. Cover the bowl and allow to stand for three days to ferment. The yeasts come from the yogurt. Each time starter is used replenish with 1 cup of water and 1 cup of flour for each cup of starter taken out.

Reading something in a book does not necessarily make it true. Since I started to read baking recipes I've found a few chuckles. One of them was in a 1926 Parent Teacher Association cookbook put out in Southern California. They gave a recipe for bread, but omitted flour. As funny as that was, a recipe for a super sourdough starter I found recently struck me as being funnier. The author suggested putting a couple of teaspoons of vinegar into a starter to make it more sour. She probably tried it once and it worked, because vinegar would react with the baking soda used in all sourdough recipes allowing more of the sourness to come through. Where she erred was in replenshing the starter. When this vinegar starter was replenished only half the vinegar would be in the new starter. Each time flour and water was added, the amount of vinegar would be halved. If you want your bread to be more sour, use less baking soda. If you get down to no baking soda and the recipe is still not sour enough, then you can add 1 teaspoon of vinegar to the sponge when you add the rest of the flour. When you reach this point, you had best plan on making a new starter too.

Other Starters

There are many advantages to baking with a starter instead of baking with yeast. The main such advantage is the cost of using a starter. The flour and water put into the starter make up part of the flour and water in the bread. The yeast is self perpetuating. Your only cost is the initial cost of the hops or the milk. Other than that the starter costs nothing. Another advantage of the starter is that you don't run out of yeast. Before I started to buy my yeast in a two pound can, there was always the problem of where were those little packages? I hate rushing off to the store just to pick up a package of yeast.

After baking with both yeast and sourdough starter for a while, I had an idea. Unlike most of my bright ideas, I was unable to find any references to it in any of the books available to me. I'll consider it a new concept until I do. If you can make a sourdough starter, you should be able to make a sweetdough starter.

By sweetdough, I mean one that does not give bread the tangy sour taste of sourdough. What I was looking for was a starter that would produce a bread identical to one baked with dry yeast.

I set up a starter culture and was successful from the first loaf baked. Since the starter contains no milk and is kept covered when not in use, the breads baked using this as the leavening are identical in flavor and texture to those baked with yeast.

Sweetdough Starter

2 cups warm water
2 cups flour
¼ teaspoon yeast
½ teaspoon sugar

Take 2 cups of warm water and stir in 2 cups of flour. Add ¼ teaspoon of yeast and ½ teaspoon of sugar. Mix well and allow to stand in a warm place for 8-12 hours. After standing the starter is ready for use. If you do not use it immediately, refrigerate the crock. Each time a cup of starter is used, replenish with a cup of flour plus a cup of water.

The sweetdough starter will remain sweet for a long time if it is kept covered when not in use. I used such a starter for almost three months before it began to sour. If the starter turns sour, you can either use it all up and then start a new starter or you can keep it going and use it for sourdough.

Using a Sweet Starter

The sweet yeast starter is used exactly as the sourdough starter is used. Follow any sourdough recipe but do not add baking soda. Since the starter is not acid, it is not necessary to neutralize the excess acidity.

All recipes in the sourdough section call for starter but do not specify sweet or sour. Where baking soda is called for it is written 1 teaspoon baking soda (if sourdough starter).

Each time you use a sweet starter, smell the crock. An alcoholic aroma is normal, but if it smells sour, the starter has been contaminated by wild yeasts from the air and you now have a sourdough starter.

Doughball Starters

This is a wild one. I can't claim credit for originating the idea. A friend was talking about the bakery run by his parents in the good old days. He mentioned that his parents used to throw raw dough into the starter pot. I checked further and discovered that the old sourdough bakers frequently mixed their starter with a little flour to make transportation easier.

Bake a bread with either yeast or sourdough. After kneading the dough, break off a small piece. This can be frozen or stored in the refrigerator. A plastic bag is handy to store the dough or you can use a plastic butter dish. The dough contains living yeast organisms.

To use the dough, you can either make a starter from it or use it to make a sponge for the next day's bread. Take 1 cup of hot water from the tap; add 1 cup of flour and ½ teaspoon of sugar. Place the doughball into the solution and let it stand in a warm place for an hour or two. Now add the rest of the flour necessary to make up a sponge; (see any sourdough bread recipe). Let the sponge stand overnight. This sponge can be used to bake a bread or it can be used as a new starter.

The doughball is a handy way to move a starter from one part of the country to another. It is handy to take on camping trips. It is even handier for a bit of legal larceny. Many people claim that each sourdough starter has its own unique characteristics. You can make your own starter, but some of the long established bakeries have outstanding starters. Many of these bakeries will sell raw dough if you come to the bakery. Purchase dough from them. Pinch a small ball, about the size of a ping pong ball, and use it to make up a sourdough starter. The rest of the dough you can bake into a bread or a pizza. To make a starter from a doughball, I usually use 2 cups hot water from the tap plus two cups of flour and ½ teaspoon of sugar. I drop the doughball into the mixture and let it stand over night or sometimes as long as 24 hours. By then the ball has dissolved and the wild yeast are working actively, producing bubbles, gas and that wonderful sourdough aroma.

Taking Care of a Starter

Each time a starter is used it must be replenished. For each cup of starter taken out of the starter pot, put back 1 cup of flour and 1 cup of water. Stir the new flour and water into the starter and then cover the crock and allow it to stand out in a warm place for about 8-12 hours. The starter is now ready to use. If you do not use it immediately, put the crock in the refrigerator.

If you do not use your starter regularly, it is best to stir the starter once a week. If you go three weeks without using the starter, remove the crock from the refrigerator and stir in 1 teaspoon of sugar and leave the starter out for about four hours. If you prefer, you can discard one cup of starter and replenish the starter with 1 cup of water and 1 cup of flour instead of using sugar. If you replenish, allow the starter to stay in a warm place for at least 8 hours. The cup of starter removed can be used to make pancakes instead of throwing out the starter.

When working with sourdough, it is important not to use metal spoons or metal bowls. Do not use tinfoil to cover the bowl. Any metal will react with the acid in the starter, tarnishing the metal and slowing the growth of yeast. Glass, ceramic or plastic are inert and will not harm the starter.

Basic Breads
Baked with Starters

Many different breads can be made using sourdough starter. Similar breads can be made with yeast or with a sweetdough starter, but while these are excellent breads in their own right, they lack the zesty, sour tang of a sourdough bread. The degree of sourness is dependent on the starter itself and on the amount of neutralization you chose to use. Sugar is not used to sweeten a sourdough bread—you sweeten with baking soda. When measuring baking soda for a sourdough loaf, be exact in your measurements. If you do not level the measuring spoon, you will wind up with a less sour loaf than you desire.

Like the recipes for the basic yeast breads, the recipes for the basic sourdough breads are really only one recipe with variations. Other specialized recipes will be given in another section for ethnic breads and specialty breads, but these basic breads represent a large cross section of the available types of bread. Remember that variation of the shape and the crust of the bread will also change the taste.

The basic bread recipes produce hearty, good tasting loaves that remain fresh for a long time. These breads are delicious when toasted and the sourdough makes an exceptionally tasty French toast if sliced thickly. The sourdough recipes are as easy to bake as those made with yeast, but the option of whether to use a sponge or not is not available. All loaves baked with starter have to follow the sponge method.

Basic White Starter Bread — Sweetdough or Sourdough

Since the starter does not work as quickly as yeast, it is convenient to start the bread the evening before you bake.

The Sponge:
  1 cup of starter
  2½ cups hot tap water
  4 cups unsifted unbleached flour.

Replenishing the Starter:
  1 cup unbleached flour
  1 cup hot tap water

Put the starter and the water into a ceramic, glass or plastic bowl. Do not use a metal bowl. Mix in the flour one cup at a time using a wooden spoon or plastic spoon to mix. If the bowl seems too small, you can reduce the flour to 3 cups and add the extra cup in the second step. Less flour will reduce the possibility of the sponge overflowing the bowl. Place the bowl containing the sponge in a warm place after you cover the bowl. I find plastic wrap makes a good cover, but a towel can be used. Heat rises, so a high shelf or the top of the water heater are good places. The oven with only the pilot light is a warm draft free place to keep the sponge. The sponge should sit for 8-24 hours before you go on to the next step. It is usually ready in eight hours, but will not be harmed if allowed to sit longer.

If for some reason you have to get a sourdough bread baked without an eight hour wait for the sponge, it is possible to rush the fermentation by crushing a 50 milligram Vitamin C tablet in the bowl before adding the starter. With Vitamin C acting as a catalyst, the sponge will be ready in 1½ to 2 hours. When a sponge is ready, it will have risen and appear to be filled with bubbles. It looks much like a giant sea sponge filled with water.

Do not forget to replenish the starter after you remove 1 cup to start the bread. The starter crock, after you add 1 cup of water and 1 cup of flour, should be allowed to remain in a warm place for at least 8 hours. When you replenish the starter, be sure to stir it with your wooden spoon before you cover the starter.

The Second Step

The wild yeasts in the starter have been working on the flour and water mixture in the sponge bowl. They have changed the lumpy flour and water mixture to a bubbly sponge. When the plastic is lifted you will smell a sour, yeasty, almost alcoholic aroma if you used a sourdough starter. If you used the sweet starter the sponge will smell yesty. You are now ready to turn the sponge into a bread.

  3½-4 cups flour
  2 Tablespoons sugar
  3 Tablespoons oil or melted shortening (approximately 1 teaspoon of soda if a sourdough starter is used)
  1 Tablespoon salt

Sprinkle the sugar, salt and soda onto the top of the sponge. If the starter was sweet instead of sour do not use soda. Now pour the oil into the bowl and stir down the sponge with a wooden spoon. Add 1 cup of flour to the sponge and work it in with the spoon. You should now have a rather soft dough. Put about ½ cup of flour on a bread board and using a rubber spatula scrape the sponge out of the bowl onto the floured board. Pour another cup of flour over the soft dough and start to work it into the dough using either the spatula or floured hands. The dough will be sticky and need more flour added. Whenever you feel a sticky surface, grab a handful of flour and brush it across that part of the dough with your hand. Continue kneading for about 10 minutes. When the dough is ready it will look satiny and feel firm as if the flabby mess you started with had developed muscles.

Grease a bowl and place the kneaded ball of dough in the bowl. Rub the dough against the sides to pick up some of the grease and then turn it over so that the side that was on the bottom is now on the top. Cover the bowl with plastic wrap or a towel and allow it to stand in a warm place for about 45 minutes. If a pan of boiling water is placed on the bottom of the oven, the dough can be placed in the oven to rise. The heat and moisture given off by the pan of water will assure a maximum rise in a minimum time. Using the oven will assure you of a draft free spot to let the dough rise. Test the dough by poking a finger into the top. When the dough has doubled, the hole will not close quickly. This rising step is of the greatest importance to baking a truly great bread. Recipes that skip this step result in a most inferior loaf.

After the kneaded dough has doubled in size it is ready to be punched down and shaped. Strike the dough in the bowl with your fists or palms to force out the carbon dioxide gas that made it rise. The dough will collapse and return to its original volume. Remove the dough from the bowl and knead it for about 1 minute to remove any gas bubbles not forced out by punching down. If the dough seems sticky, rub a little flour around the outside of the dough ball.

Divide the dough and shape it into loaves or rolls. See the chapter on the shaping of breads. This dough can be made into many different dishes, but for coffee cakes and dessert rolls, I prefer an enriched dough. After the loaves and rolls have been shaped, they should be proved. What a baker means by proved is allowed to rise again. Most recipes call for a long proving period, but I find that only a short period, more of a resting period, will give better results particularly to hearth loaves that are baked without the support of a pan. Too long a second rise will result in a droopy bread that does not rise as high as you would wish. Allow your breads and rolls to prove for a period of 10 to 20 minutes. If rushed, they can be baked after only 5 minutes.

Put the shaped breads that have been allowed to prove for a short time into a cold oven. Turn the heat on to 400°F and bake for 45 minutes. Rolls can be baked at the same temperature, but they should be placed on a higher shelf in the oven. Bake rolls for 30-35 minutes. Before removing from the oven check the color of the crust and test with a thin bladed knife to make sure that the loaves are baked through. Turn the loaf out onto a cooling rack and allow to cool.

If a finish is desired, the loaves should be glazed with water, milk, melted butter or other shortening or with egg before placing in the oven. See the chapter on finishes and glazes (page 79).

Basic White Starter Bread (Summarized)

Sponge:

1 cup starter
2½ cups warm water
4 cups flour

Second Step:

2 Tablespoons sugar or honey
1 teaspoon baking soda if starter is sourdough
1 Tablespoon salt
3 Tablespoons oil or shortening

Mix sponge ingredients, cover and let stand for 8-24 hours. Replenish starter.

Second Step:

Sprinkle dry ingredients over sponge. Pour in oil. Stir down and add flour. Turn out to floured board add more flour and knead while working in more flour.

After kneading, place dough in greased bowl to rise. When doubled, punch down, shape loaves, allow shaped loaves to prove for about 20 minutes. Bake at 400°F for 45 minutes starting with a cold oven. Rolls should be baked for 30-35 minutes. Check for doneness, turn out onto rack to cool.

San Francisco Sourdough Type French Bread

The sourdough breads of San Francisco are famous. Some people say it is the water, others claim that the taste is dependent on the starter strain. Compared to other sourdough French breads, the one from the Golden Gate is different in two ways. It is just a little more sour than most other French sourdough breads. By adjusting the amount of baking soda used in the recipe, the degree of sourness can be controlled. The other difference is the heaviness of the bread. A San Francisco bread is dense and solid. Some commercial breads sold as sourdoughs use yeast in addition to the starter. These breads are lighter and less sour. The recipe below makes a good bread of the San Francisco type. It can be made as a long, cigar shaped loaf, baguettes, rolls, or the traditional round loaf. The main difference between this recipe and that for sourdough white bread is the lack of shortening in the dough and the special crust treatment used to make a more crunchy crust.

Sponge:
1 cup starter
2½ cups hot tap water
The Second Step:
2 Tablespoons sugar or honey
1 Tablespoon salt
½-1 teaspoon baking soda
4-5 cups unsifted flour

Mix sponge ingredients and cover the bowl. Let sponge stand in a warm place for 8-24 hours. Replenish the starter.

Second Step.

Sprinkle the dry ingredients over the sponge and stir down. Add 1 cup of flour. Turn out onto a floured board and pour 1 cup of flour over the sponge. Knead, working in more flour for 10 minutes.

Place the kneaded dough in a greased bowl and cover with plastic wrap. Allow to stand in a warm place until doubled. Punch down the dough, shape into loaves and allow the loaves to prove for 10-20 minutes. Slash hearth loaves—see shaping of loaves.

Before baking, put boiling water into a shallow pan on the bottom of the oven. Using a brush, brush ice water over the loaves or spray them with ice water. Bake at 400°F for 45 minutes. About 10 minutes before loaves are baked, open the oven and brush or spray salt water over the loaves. The salt water is made by mixing 1 teaspoon of salt in 1 cup of water. After the salt water, close the oven and allow the loaves to finish baking.

The treatment with water and the steam from the water pan should produce a crusty, sourdough French bread. To increase the amount of crust, shape breads into long thin flutes called baugettes. If these flutes are slashed deeply with a razor, you will have break apart rolls. See the chapter on shaping breads and rolls (page 59).

Other Basic Breads Baked with Starters

Like the basic white bread, these can be baked with either sour or sweet starters. Only the sourdough French bread must use a sourdough starter, but on the rye variation, the bread baked with the sour starter tastes more like a delicatessen rye than that baked with sweet starter or yeast.

All of the following breads are baked with the recipe for basic white bread. Some of the ingredients are substitutions for a portion of the flour.

Basic Cornmeal Bread

Substitute 1 or 2 cups of cornmeal for flour in the sponge portion of the recipe. Follow the recipe for the rest of the procedure. Cornmeal enhances the texture of the bread and if two cups are used will give the bread a yellow color and a flavor of corn. Do not use 3 cups of cornmeal with a starter. The starter is more limited in its ability to handle ingredients without gluten than yeast.

High Fiber Basic Starter Bread

Substitute 1-2 cups of bran for flour in the starter portion of the recipe. Bran will give a brown color, an interesting texture and is a good source of the fiber deficient in many diets.

Basic Oatmeal Starter Bread

The use of 1 cup of oatmeal in place of one of the cups of flour produces a moist bread of excellent texture and flavor. Use steel cut oats or rolled oats. Do not use instant oatmeal.

Basic 50% Whole Wheat Bread from a Starter

If the sponge is made from whole wheat flour instead of white or unbleached flour, the end product will be about 50% whole wheat. This is an excellent bread whose flavor is enhanced by the tang of sourdough. Use stone ground whole wheat flour.

100% Whole Wheat Bread

It is not recommended that a 100% whole wheat bread be made using a starter. See the recipe in the health food section. If you really want the sourdough flavor for your whole wheat bread, make a sourdough starter using whole wheat flour and use 1 cup of starter in place of 1 cup of flour and 1 cup of water in the recipe for whole wheat bread found in the health food section. This bread will then be baked with both yeast and starter.

The yeast has more rising power and whole wheat breads are hard to make rise. If you absolutely insist on making a whole wheat bread with a starter and no yeast, mix 50 milligrams of Vitamin C in with your starter and make a sponge. Allow the sponge with the Vitamin C to work overnight and then follow the recipe for basic white bread but use whole wheat flour only. This bread will be a little heavier than one baked with yeast, but the boost given to the starter by the Vitamin C will help produce a decent bread.

Basic Starter Bread with Wheat Germ

Wheat germ can be used to restore some of the nutrition removed in the milling of white flour. Follow the basic recipe for white bread but substitute 1-2 cups of wheat germ for the amount of flour. The resultant loaf will be tan colored and have a pleasant wheaty taste.

Basic Starter Bread with Rye Flour

If a sourdough starter is used, the flavor will be closer to the sour rye sold in delicatessens. If you like a dark colored rye bread instead of sugar or honey use blackstrap molasses which will color the bread. Rye flour has some gluten so substitute from 1-3 cups of rye flour for white flour in the basic recipe. The larger amount of rye used the greater the rye bread flavor. Caraway seeds (1 Tablespoon) can be mixed in when the other dry ingredients are added.

Enriched Basic Starter Breads

Any of the breads except the sourdough French can be enriched by adding milk in place of water or using nonfat milk powder. The powder is added in addition to the regular recipe not as a substitution. More enrichment can be had by adding 1-2 eggs to any recipe. Enrichment softens the crumb and makes it taste richer. See the Recipe for Rich Sourdough Bread (below).

This can be baked as a bread, but is the dough used for doughnuts, coffee cakes and other treats too.

All the recipes in this section on starter breads can be made with either sweet or sour starter. Remember that baking soda is used only with sourdough. If you are using a starter made from yeast that has not been allowed to sour, do not add the soda.

Rich Sourdough Bread

This is a special bread, a Sunday go to Meetin' bread that is ideal for company or as a gift when you're invited to dinner at someone's home. If that were the only good thing I could say about this recipe it would be enough to include it in this book, but this dough is ideal for making coffee cakes, sweet rolls, doughnuts and other good things. Cinnamon swirls, apple carousels, apricot target rolls and raisin pinwheels are but a few of the fancy treats that can be made with this dough. The recipe is for a single loaf, but it can be doubled. A sweetdough starter can be used if preferred.

Sponge:
1 cup evaporated milk or whole
  milk
1/2 cup starter
2 cups unbleached flour
Second Step:
1 1/2-2 cups unbleached flour
1/2-1 teaspoon vanilla extract
  (1/2 teaspoon baking soda if
  sourdough starter used)
1 teaspoon salt
3 Tablespoons sugar or honey
1 egg
3 Tablespoons melted butter,
  margarine or oil
1/2-1 cup yellow raisins (for raisin
  bread only)

Sponge. Combine the milk, starter and flour in a bowl. Cover with plastic wrap and let stand in a warm place for 8-24 hours. If whole milk is used instead of canned, it should be heated just to boiling and allowed to cool to a little warmer than body heat.

Second Step.
Sprinkle the dry ingredients over the sponge. Add the raisins. Beat the egg with the shortening and pour in. Stir down the sponge and then work in about 1 1/2 cups of flour. Turn the sponge out onto a floured board and knead for 8-10 minutes adding more flour as necessary. After kneading, place the dough in a greased bowl, cover the bowl and allow to stand until doubled in a warm place. This will take from 45 minutes to 1 1/2 hours.

Punch down the dough and then remove it from the bowl. Knead again for about a minute and then shape into a loaf if a bread is to be baked. If the dough is intended for a dessert, it is now ready. Turn to the chapter on Good Things From Bread (page 83) and using this dough, follow the recipe for the one you select.

If a bread is baked set the oven at 375°F and bake for about 40 minutes. Test with a knife to see if the bread is done and then turn out onto a rack to cool. Raisins are worked into the dough only for a raisin bread. Most of the specialty recipes do not call for the inclusion of raisins in the dough.

PSEUDO SOURDOUGH BREAD

(A sourdough bread made without a sourdough starter)

There are many of us who like the taste of a sourdough, but who do not have a sourdough starter available when they get a craving for that delectable type of bread. As I type this, my starter is not available and I haven't taken the time to make a new one. This does not stop me from enjoying the sour tang of a good sour-dough bread. I had a hot heel straight from the oven just a few minutes ago. Spread with pre-softened sweet butter it was a noble snack. How was I able to bake a bread with this distinctive taste without a starter?

The trick, and it is a trick, is to add 1-2 cups of yogurt to the sponge in place of water. You can use either plain or vanilla yogurt. You can use commercial, but I used my own homemade yogurt. The recipe for making yogurt at home appears in the Miscellanea Chapter (page 240).

Your favorite bread recipe
1-2 cups plain or vanilla
yogurt substituted for
water or milk in that
recipe
Yeast: for an overnight
sponge use 1 teaspoon;
for a 3 hour sponge use
1 Tablespoon; for the
direct method use 2
Tablespoons

I recommend an overnight sponge. The organisms, the culture that makes yogurt sour will react with the flour of the sponge and sour that too, making it like a sourdough starter. A three hour sponge will produce some sourdough tang, but less than an overnight incubation. If you use 2 cups of yogurt with the 3 hour sponge you should get a little more sour taste. When a bread is made by the direct method using yogurt you will get little if any sour flavor, but the yogurt will enrich the crumb of the bread making it similar to one baked with milk.

If 2 cups of yogurt are used with an overnight sponge you may wish to sweeten the flavor with a little baking soda. You'll have to experiment on this one. I prefer an extra sour flavor myself and do not use the baking soda.

I did say to use your favorite recipe, but do use some judgment. I don't think that the world is ready for sourdough Challah and Brioche, but that's only my opinion.

Sourdough Waffles and Pancakes

Having a crock of sourdough starter in your refrigerator is handier than having a box of pancake mix on your shelf. It is almost as handy as having a carton of ready mixed pancake batter. Pancakes and Waffles made from starter are not ordinary fare. They are light, so light you almost have to weigh them down with syrup to keep them from floating off the plate. The flavor is indescribable. The sour tang of sourdough combined with the lightness makes them an experience in good eating.

The best pancakes and waffles are started the night before, but with Vitamin C you can get a batch ready in less than 2 hours. If really rushed, the starter can be used straight from the refrigerator, but these are not quite so light.

The batter is prepared in two steps. First you make a primary batter and let it stand overnight. When you remove the cup of starter from the crock, replenish your starter by adding a cup of water and a cup of flour. Allow the starter crock to remain out in a warm place overnight too.

Primary Batter for Waffles and Pancakes

1 cup of starter
2 cups of flour
2 cups of water
In the Morning:
2 eggs at room temperature
2 Tablespoons oil (4 Tablespoons oil for waffles)
1 Tablespoon sugar
¼ cup milk (room temperature)
1½ teaspoons salt
½ teaspoon baking soda

Primary Batter. Mix the starter with the flour and water and allow it to stand in a warm place overnight. If you're in a hurry, crush a 50 milligram Vitamin C tablet in the bowl before adding the starter. With the Vitamin C, the batter will be ready in about 1½ hours. When the batter is ready for the next step, it will be filled with bubbles. It is an active batter, a batter full of working yeast blowing bubbles of carbon dioxide gas. The next morning, put the replenished starter in the refrigerator for the next time and take the bowl with the primary batter to your work table.

In the Morning. Beat the eggs and stir them into the batter followed by the sugar. Then add the cooking oil and the salt. Stir in the ¼ cup of milk. DO NOT ADD THE BAKING SODA UNTIL YOU ARE READY TO MAKE THE PANCAKES. The soda reacting with the sourdough will produce additional carbon dioxide gas to make the pancakes even lighter. The recipe will make 6 waffles 9 x 9 inch. If that is too many, you can halve the quantity or use the leftover batter to make sourdough rolls.

Sourdough Rolls from Pancake Batter

1½ cups leftover batter
Enough flour to make a stiff dough
½ teaspoon of salt for each cup of flour added.

Work the flour into the batter adding ½ teaspoon of salt for each cup of flour added. When the dough is formed, turn it out onto a floured board and knead for 5-10 minutes, adding more flour if necessary. When the surface of the dough is satin smooth, it is ready. Place the dough in a greased bowl, cover the bowl and allow it to rise for about 1 hour. Punch down the risen dough and knead again. If the dough is still sticky, add a little more flour. Roll out the dough to a ¾ inch thickness and cut circles with a tuna can. Dip both sides of the biscuit in melted butter and place them on a baking sheet. Cover the rounds and allow them to rise for 20-30 minutes. Bake at 375°F for 30-35 minutes.

The Shaping of Breads and Rolls

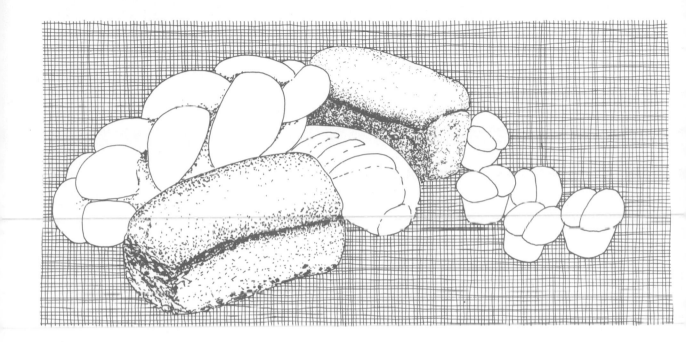

Breads are usually referred to as pan loaves or hearth loaves. A pan loaf is baked in a pan with fairly high sides and conforms to the shape of the pan. Hearth loaves are baked on flat sheets or even on hot stone. The trick to a successful hearth loaf is to make it retain the shape it was given before it was placed on the baking sheet. This can be quite a problem because an unsupported bread will rise to a certain point and then it will start to spread out. To minimize this spreading, I suggest a rise time after shaping that is much less than most other books.

Any shape pan can be used to bake bread. Bread has been baked in empty coffee cans, glass casserole dishes, and special baking pans. Meatloaf pans give a bread of the conventional rectangular shape so handy for sandwich slices. A round pan will produce a round bread; molds can be used to bake a bread in the shape of a fish, a heart or even in a fluted circle. Plain ring shaped baking tins like the one used to make

Bundt cakes will produce a ring shaped bread. This type of pan is used for baking the so called "Monkey Bread."

All pans should be well greased before putting dough into them. **Do not use oil** to grease pans. Oil has a different molecular structure than the solid fats; the fatty acid chains are shorter. Oil will soak into bread while it is baking. This produces an objectionable taste. Most other shortenings can be used to prevent dough from sticking to the pan. Suet and lard, hydrogenated vegetable shortening, butter, margarine and mixtures of the different fats. My personal preference for greasing is to use liquid Lecithin which contains absolutely no cholesterol. This produce is described in detail in the Health Food Section under greasing. Some bakers sprinkle flour or cornmeal on a greased or ungreased pan to help prevent sticking. I prefer cornmeal because the cornmeal becomes part of the bottom crust making it more crunchy.

How to Shape a Pan Loaf

For a rectangular pan, form the dough into an oval. Stretch the top surface of the dough, pulling it around to the bottom where the two sides are pinched into a seam. This stretching gives the top a smooth surface. Place the dough, seam down in the greased pan. The dough should only half fill the pan.

For a round pan, shape the dough into a circle, stretching it as above. This is the same technique described under a round hearth loaf.

To make a ring shaped loaf of bread, roll or pull the dough into a long, thick rope. Place this cylinder into the pan and pinch the edges together where the two ends meet. Water or egg can be brushed on the edges to make a better seal.

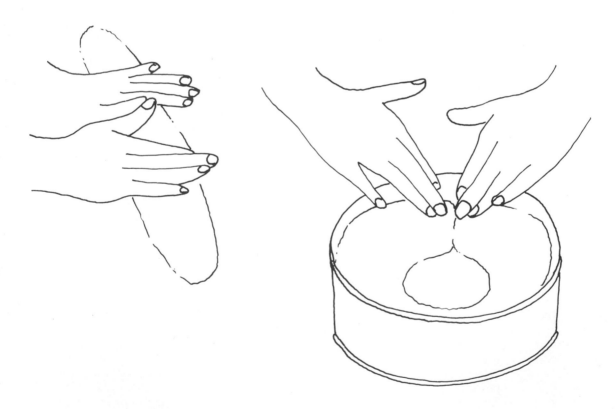

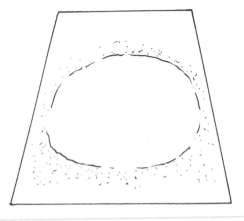

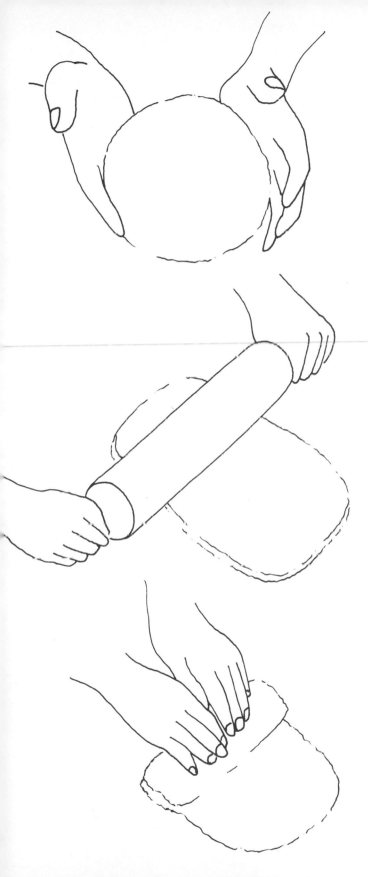

How to Shape a Hearth Loaf

Round hearth loaves are formed by shaping the dough into a roughly circular form. Stretch the top down toward the bottom to give a smooth finish to the upper surface. Pull the stretched portion under the loaf and pinch the edges into a seam. Place the shaped loaf on a greased sheet. Cornmeal is frequently sprinkled on the baking sheet before the loaf is placed there. A greased cast iron skillet can be used instead of a baking sheet. Cast iron conducts heat uniformly and gives a crisp, crunchy crust. If the wire racks of the oven are lined with unglazed ceramic tiles, hearth loaves can be baked directly on the stone instead of using a baking sheet. Breads baked on tile have a crust similar to those baked on cast iron.

Cigar shaped loaves, like the French breads sold in bakeries, can be shaped by rolling the dough out to a rectangle. Shape a cylinder by rolling the long edge away from you toward yourself. Roll the dough tightly and pinch the ends to seal the loaf. The ends can be tapered by placing one hand on each end of the loaf and rocking it on the board. If the final seam is coated with egg or water a better seal will be made. When baking the bread, any bread, always place the seam down on the baking sheet.

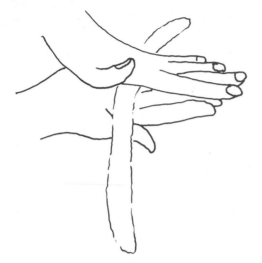

How to Shape a Baguette

A baguette is a thin, cigar shaped loaf. In France, they bake baguettes that are very long, but we are limited by the size of our oven. Before baking, a baguette is about one inch across while a regular French bread is about two inches. Take half the amount of bread you would use to shape a regular loaf and shape it in the same way you would any cigar shaped loaf. A recipe that makes 2 loaves of bread will produce 4 baguettes.

Baguette like loaves can also be made by stretching the dough and rolling it to make a long braided loaves. When rolling, allow the bread to rest between the palms of your hands with any excess hanging free. Roll the dough between your hands, do not roll it on the board. Soft doughs, particularly those rich in oil and egg can almost be pulled out into a long rope.

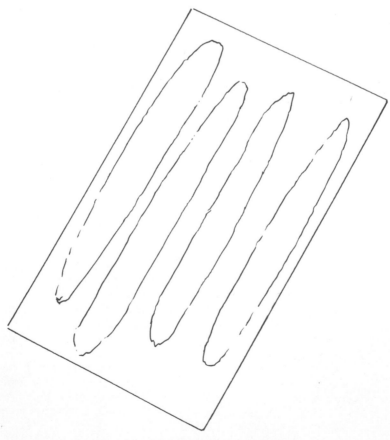

How to Shape a Braided Loaf

Divide enough dough for one loaf into 3 equal portions. Roll or pull the dough into 3 long ropes about 1 inch in diameter. Roll between your hands, not on the board. Taper the ends of the ropes. Most people use three ropes to make a braided bread, but some use more. See illustration on how to braid. I lay the three ropes parallel on my board and then cross them in the middle. It is easier to braid from the middle to the ends than to start at the end. The results are better too. Braid overhand down to one end and then turn the board and braid underhand for the other side. Braiding is easier to do than to write about. If you grab the wrong strand, it is immediately apparent, for you start to unwrap what you've already done. After you complete the braid, transfer it to a greased baking sheet.

How to Shape a Cinnamon Swirl Loaf

This loaf is similar to a jelly roll. Roll the dough out and brush the top with melted butter. Sprinkle cinnamon over the butter and roll up the dough into a cylinder as we did for a cigar shaped loaf. After rolling and pinching the seam, the bread can be made as a hearth loaf or put in a pan.

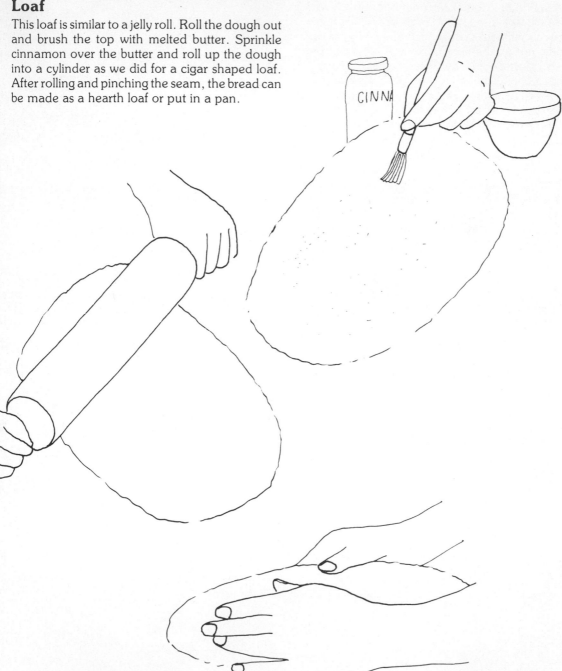

Irish Soda Bread

Bubble Loaves

If a rich dough like that given on page 83 for dessert breads is used, the bread can be made in a ring pan and is called Monkey Bread. With ordinary bread dough, the bubble loaf is best baked on a baking sheet. When baked in a pan, the walls of the pan force the balls of dough to stick together and lose their bubble shape.

After the dough is ready to shape, break off pieces of dough and roll them into balls about the size of ping pong balls. Dip each ball in melted butter and lay it on the baking sheet. When the first layer is complete, start a second layer. If the balls are small, you can use as many as three layers. If larger balls are used, limit the bread to 2 layers. After baking on a sheet, the bread can be broken apart when hot or cold and will not leave crumbs.

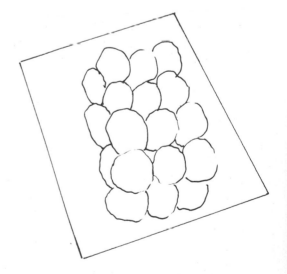

Sourdough Bread

The Shaping of Rolls

Any dough can be used to bake rolls. Whole wheat, rye, sourdough, and even white flours make as tasty a roll as they do a bread. Because they are smaller, rolls are usually baked a shorter time than a whole loaf of bread. Rolls are baked nearer the top of the oven while breads are baked in the middle of the oven.

Breakapart Baguette Rolls

Take any bread dough recipe. For a 2 bread recipe, divide the dough into either 4 or 5 equal portions. Roll or stretch these balls of dough into long ropes about 1 inch in diameter. After the ropes have been formed, lay them on a greased baking sheet that has been sprinkled with cornmeal. Take a sharp razor blade and make a deep slash across each rope every 4 or 5 inches. The cut should be about half way through the rope. After cutting allow the rolls to rise for 15 minutes and then bake them at 400°F for about 30 minutes or until they are nicely browned. The rolls bake best on the top shelf. Test with a thin knife; if the rolls are done, turn them out onto a wire rack to cool. These make crusty rolls with almost any bread recipe. The tops may be left plain, brushed with water, milk, butter or egg. They may be seeded if desired. They may be served as baugettes. Each diner will be able to break off a roll, or they may be broken apart before serving or storing.

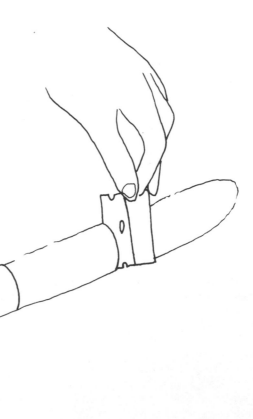

Clover Leaf Rolls

This roll is baked in a greased muffin tin or in individual greased cups. It is the simplest of all rolls to shape. Break off pieces of the dough and roll them into balls about 1 inch in diameter. Dip or brush the balls with melted butter and then drop 3 balls into each cup of the muffin tin. Cover the tin and let the dough rise for ½ to 1 hour. Since the dough is supported by the sides of the tin, a longer rise time is possible. If in a hurry, the rolls can be baked after only a 20 minute rise. Bake at 425°F. for 15 minutes.

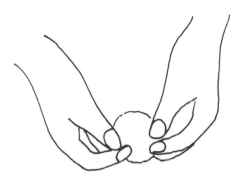

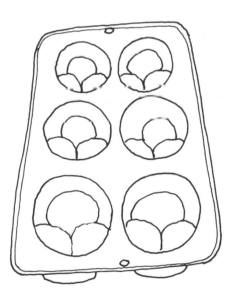

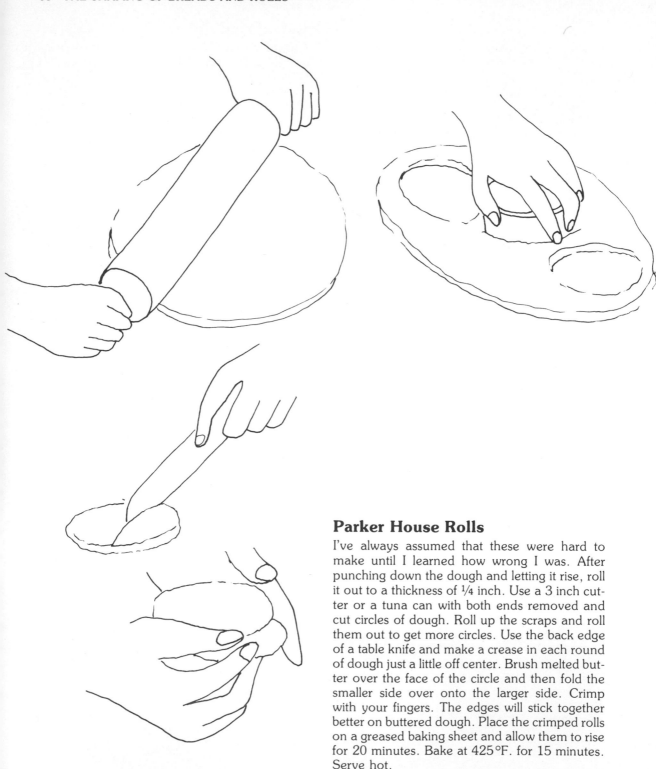

Parker House Rolls

I've always assumed that these were hard to make until I learned how wrong I was. After punching down the dough and letting it rise, roll it out to a thickness of ¼ inch. Use a 3 inch cutter or a tuna can with both ends removed and cut circles of dough. Roll up the scraps and roll them out to get more circles. Use the back edge of a table knife and make a crease in each round of dough just a little off center. Brush melted butter over the face of the circle and then fold the smaller side over onto the larger side. Crimp with your fingers. The edges will stick together better on buttered dough. Place the crimped rolls on a greased baking sheet and allow them to rise for 20 minutes. Bake at 425°F. for 15 minutes. Serve hot.

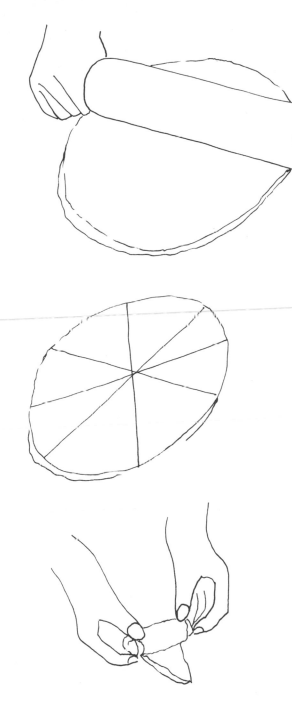

Crescent Rolls And Butter Horns

Piping hot crescent rolls, the croissants that delight gourmets, are a breakfast treat, but do not limit them to breakfast; they are delicious with any meal. Before I started to bake, I thought that it would be most difficult to make these delightfull rolls, but since then, I've learned that these are one of the easiest rolls to shape. Break off a part of any bread dough and roll it into a ball about 4 inches in diameter. Place the ball of dough on a floured board and flatten it with the palm of your hand. You will now have a flat circle of dough. With the rolling pin, roll the dough out so that you have an 8 inch circle about ¼ inch thick. While rolling, keep turning either the board or the dough at an angle of 90° to keep the circular shape. Cut the circle into two halves and then cut each half into two quarters. Cut each quarter in half and you will have eight triangles of dough. The base of these triangles should be about 3 inches long.

Take a triangle and roll up the dough. Start at the broad end and roll toward the point. Seal the tip by coating it with water or egg. If you're making crescents, bend the ends in toward the middle. If you prefer butterhorns, do not bend the roll. Place the rolled dough on a greased baking sheet with the point down. Cover the rolls and allow them to rise for 20 minutes. Bake at 425°F. for 15 minutes.

I prefer to glaze my rolls with an egg wash before baking and I like them best sprinkled with poppy seed.

Crecent rolls bought from a bakery are usually white bread, but any bread dough can be used. They are particularly good with Challah dough. See the illustrations on how to form a crescent roll.

Petite Braids

Small rolls are particularly attractive when braided to form miniature loaves of bread. To make these braids we need thin ropes of dough. These can be formed by rolling, but since they are small, it is easier to roll out the dough to a thickness of ⅝ inch. Cut strips of the dough about ⅝ inch wide and roll the strips between your palms to round them off. You should wind up with a thin rope of dough about ½ inch in diameter. The length of these ropes should be about 15 to 20 inches. Take three strips of this dough and line them up parallel to each other. Now cross them in the center. Braid from the middle, over hand down to the bottom. Turn the board and braid fom the middle to the other hand, but on this section braid underhand. See the illustration.

After braiding the dough, you will have a very long, thin braid. Pinch the ends to seal them and then using a very sharp blade cut the long braid up into 3½ inch segments. After cutting, pinch the top and bottom of each segment and then pull the mini braid from both ends to make it a little longer. Place the petite braids on a greased baking sheet and cover. Allow them to rise for 20 minutes. Bake at 425°F. for about 10 minutes to brown the braids. Before baking the rolls may be glazed by brushing with milk, melted butter, egg yolk, or whole egg wash. They may be sprinkled with poppy seeds or with sesame seeds.

Pan Rolls

Grease a square or round pan with moderately high sides. Roll the kneaded dough into balls about the size of golf balls and lay them in the greased pan so that the sides touch. Make only one layer of balls. Brush all exposed surfaces with melted butter then cover the pan and allow the rolls to rise for 20 minutes or longer. Bake at 425°F. for 15 minutes. The entire pan will be filled making the rolls look like a large bread, but they will pull apart easily when served.

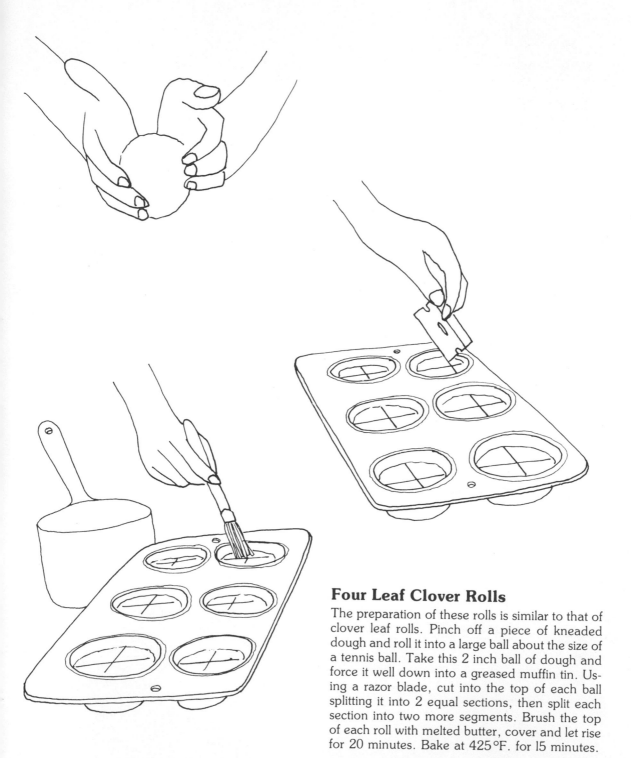

Four Leaf Clover Rolls

The preparation of these rolls is similar to that of clover leaf rolls. Pinch off a piece of kneaded dough and roll it into a large ball about the size of a tennis ball. Take this 2 inch ball of dough and force it well down into a greased muffin tin. Using a razor blade, cut into the top of each ball splitting it into 2 equal sections, then split each section into two more segments. Brush the top of each roll with melted butter, cover and let rise for 20 minutes. Bake at 425°F. for 15 minutes.

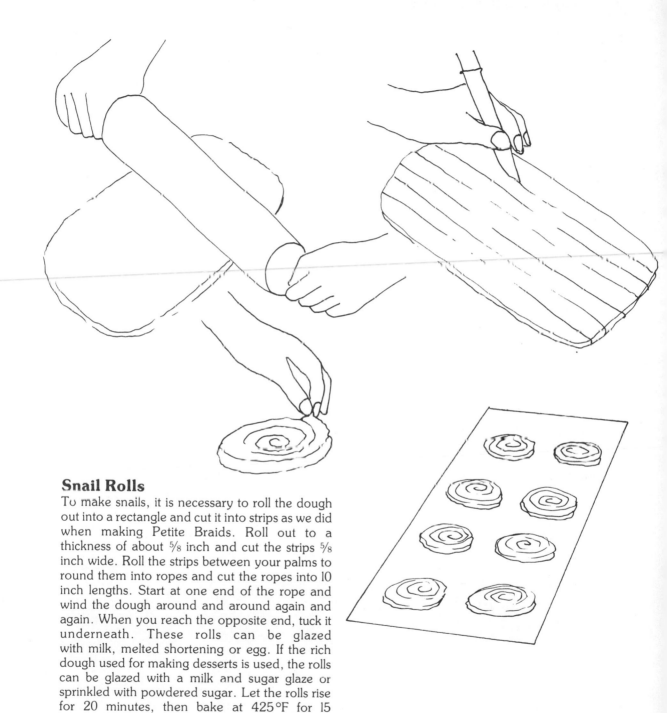

Snail Rolls

To make snails, it is necessary to roll the dough out into a rectangle and cut it into strips as we did when making Petite Braids. Roll out to a thickness of about ⅝ inch and cut the strips ⅝ inch wide. Roll the strips between your palms to round them into ropes and cut the ropes into 10 inch lengths. Start at one end of the rope and wind the dough around and around again and again. When you reach the opposite end, tuck it underneath. These rolls can be glazed with milk, melted shortening or egg. If the rich dough used for making desserts is used, the rolls can be glazed with a milk and sugar glaze or sprinkled with powdered sugar. Let the rolls rise for 20 minutes, then bake at 425°F for 15 minutes.

Long Rolls

After kneading the dough, roll the entire ball out into a large rectangle. The dough should be about ½ inch thick. With a single edged razor blade, cut strips about 3 inches wide and 5 inches long. Roll these up by starting on the short side of the rectangle and pinch as you roll. Brush the last ½ inch of the dough with egg to help seal. Place the seam down on a greased baking sheet. Bake at 425°F. for 15 minutes. Long rolls may be glazed with milk, melted butter or egg.

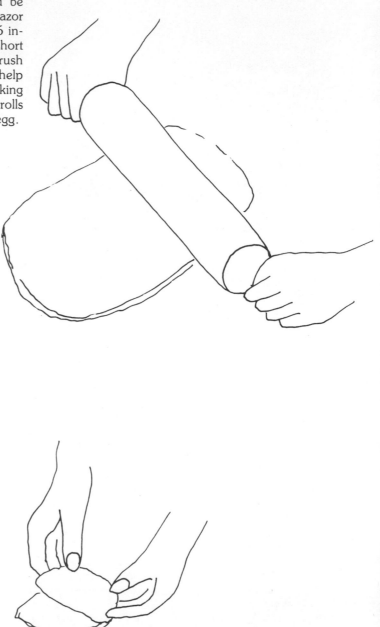

Dinner Rolls

This is an extremely easy roll to shape. Roll the dough out to a one inch thickness. If you prefer to pat the dough to this thickness, you may. Using a tuna can with both ends removed or a 3 inch cutter, cut out circles of dough. Roll the scraps into a ball and flatten the ball to get more rounds of dough. Lay each circle on a greased baking sheet but do not allow them to touch. Take a dinner knife and press the handle down on the center of each round. Press hard, so hard that the dough is almost cut through, but do not actually go all the way. The pressure of the knife handle will force the round into an oval shape. Do not fold the ends against each other, just let them lie there the way they fall after pressing with the knife handle. Bake at 425°F. for about 15 minutes.

Hamburger Rolls

To make a hamburger roll similar in appearance but much better tasting than those sold in the store, roll portions of the dough into tennis ball sized balls. Place each ball on a greased baking sheet and press down with the palm of your hand flattening the roll. For a soft finish, brush the tops of the rolls with melted butter or milk. After baking at 425°F. for 15 minutes check to see if the roll is done. Before using, slice the rolls, grill the hamburgers and prepare yourself for a delightful experience. The dough used for these rolls can be the dough used for any white or wheat bread. Challah dough makes an excellent egg bread type hamburger bun.

Finishes for Breads
and Rolls

These finishes may be applied to any bread or roll. Sweet finishes are discussed in the chapter on Good Things From Yeast Bread (page 83).

Natural Finish

This is the easiest finish of all. Do nothing to the bread after putting it into the pan or on the baking sheet. Even without a finish, the bread will have a nice, rather crunchy crust.

Butter or Margarine Finish

Melt the butter or margarine over low heat. Do not let it burn or blacken. Brush the melted butter over the crust of the unbaked bread with a pastry brush. Some bakers prefer to brush the butter on after baking. Melted butter makes a more tender crust. If used before baking, it helps with the browning of the crust giving it a darker, richer color. Poppy or sesame seeds can be sprinkled on after brushing for the butter will help them adhere to the crust.

Milk Finish

Brush the crust of the unbaked bread with milk. The crust will be crisper after baking than those brushed with butter. Milk also helps with color development.

Egg White Glaze

Beaten egg white is brushed on the crust to give it a shiny look. It should be used either before baking or brushed on when the bread is about 10 minutes from being finished. Color development is only fair with egg white. The crust turns brown. The shiny, glazed look given to a bread by egg white gives it a most professional look. Seeds can be sprinkled on for the egg white glaze will hold them in place during baking. One Tablespoon of water may be beaten in with the egg white to thin it.

Egg Wash Glaze

Beat a whole egg and then brush it onto the crust with a pastry brush. Mixing the yolk with the white gives a deeper color than egg white alone. Seeds will stick to the egg wash. I use this glaze often because I don't have to separate the egg. If I do remember in time to separate the egg, I mix the excess eggs white in with the dough and reserve the yolk until the bread is ready to be glazed. Egg wash can be applied before baking or the loaf can be removed about 10 minutes before it is finished and the glaze applied then.

Egg Yolk Glaze

Separate an egg. Add 1 Tablespoon of water to

the yolk and beat it well with a fork or a whisk. Brush the egg yolk over the surface of the bread with a pastry brush. The color developed will be a darker brown than on a bread brushed with a whole egg wash. Seeds stick very well to an egg yolk glaze. If you use this glaze, be sure to put the egg white in with the flour and liquid. If you forget, you can reserve the white for your next baking. Egg white will freeze.

Water Glaze

If water is brushed or sprayed on a crust, it will make it crisper and crunchier. Ice water works better than water at room temperature. Some French bread recipes call for water to be brushed onto the baking loaf every ten minutes. You can adapt any household sprayer for the job if you wash it thoroughly to remove window cleaner or what ever was originally in the bottle.

Salt Water Glaze

Mix 1 teaspoon of salt in a cup of water. Brush the bread with tap water before baking. Ten minutes before the bread is taken out of the oven, brush the crust with the salt water. This is done to make a hard, crunchy crust.

Steam Finish

When using a water glaze, put a shallow pan on the bottom of the oven. Pour boiling water into the pan before turning on the oven. Steam makes a harder, more crunchy crust, the type of crust favored by Frenchmen.

Sweet Glazes

Recipes for sweet glazes to be used on dessert breads appear in the next chapter. Other sweet glazes will be found in the Health Food section (page 227).

Good Things from Bread

Many sweet breads, coffee cakes, dessert rolls and even doughnuts can be made from the same doughs you use to bake your kneaded, yeast breads. Certain of these doughs produce more delectable confections than the others. I would not recommend a rye dough for a coffee cake. If you are using the dough from the basic recipes, it is suggested that you use the enriched version with eggs and milk. The dough given below is particulary suited to the making of bread-pastries. If you prefer the sourdough or starter version of this dough, it is listed as Rich Sour Dough Bread in the chapter on sourdough breads.

RICH YEAST DOUGH:

Sponge:

*1 cup of evaporated milk
  (whole milk can be used)
2 cups unbleached flour
1 Tablespoon sugar or honey
1 teaspoon of yeast*

The Second Step:

*1½-2 cups unbleached flour
½-1 teaspoons vanilla extract
1 teaspoon salt
1 egg
2 Tablespoons melted butter,
  margarine or oil
2 Tablespoons honey or sugar*

Sponge:
Combine the milk, yeast, sugar and flour in a bowl. If desired, the yeast can be proved with the milk and sugar only for 10 minutes first, but I usually omit that step for this recipe. Cover the bowl with plastic wrap and allow it to stand in a warm place for 1 to 2 hours for a sponge to form. When the sponge is ready, it will be full of bubbles and have risen. If whole milk is used instead of canned, heat it almost to boiling and let it cool to about body heat before using.

The Second Step. Sprinkle the dry ingredients over the sponge. Beat the egg and add it and the shortening. If solid shortening is used, melt it before adding to the mixture. Stir down the sponge and start to work more flour in. After 1 cup of flour has been added, turn the sponge out onto a floured board and knead for 8-10 minutes adding more flour as necessary. After kneading, place the dough ball into a greased bowl; cover the bowl and let the dough rise until doubled. This will take from 45 minutes to 1½ hours in a warm place.

Punch down the dough in the bowl and then knead it again for about 1 minute to remove any gas bubbles. The dough is now ready to use in the following recipes. This dough can also be baked into a rich bread. If you use this recipe for a bread, it is particularly good if ½-1 cup of yellow raisins are added to make a raisin bread. This dough can be made with wheat germ substituted for part of the flour. Use ½-1 cup of wheat germ. Whole wheat flour can be used for up to 50% of the flour in this recipe. See the health food section for a 100% wheat version made with skim milk.

Cinnamon Carousels

½ portion of Rich Yeast Dough (page 83) or Rich Sourdough Dough
2 Tablespoons melted butter or margarine
¼ cup brown sugar or raw sugar
1½-2 teaspoons cinnamon
½ teaspoon freshly grated nutmeg (optional)
More melted butter for dipping — about 3 Tablespoons

After the dough has been punched down, place it on a lightly floured board. Roll the dough out into a rectangle measuring 8 x 16 inches. If your shape is irregular, trim the dough with a single edged razor blade to make a good rectangle. Save the scraps of dough. Using a pastry brush, brush on the 2 Tablespoons of melted butter onto the top surface of the dough rectangle.

Mix the brown sugar and cinnamon and nutmeg together then sprinkle this over the buttered surface of the dough. Roll up the rectangle like a jelly roll, starting with the long surface away from you. Roll the dough toward yourself. Pinch the ends and the long seam shut. If desired, this can be baked as a roll, or it can be used to bake carousels.

Cut the roll into slices at 1¾ inch intervals using a sharp knife or a piece of string or clean dental floss. The roll will make 9 slices. Dip the tops and bottoms of each slice in melted butter and place them on a greased baking sheet or in a large pan. Cover the pan and let the rolls rise for about 30 minutes. Bake at 375°F. for 30-35 minutes. The crust will be a dark gold color when the rolls are finished. Glaze them by brushing on a glaze or sprinkle with powdered sugar. These are outstanding when served hot. Recipes for different glazes appear at the end of this chapter.

Cinnamon Raisin Rings

Cinnamon Carousel Fixings
¼ cup raisins.

This is a variation of the Cinnamon Carousel but has raisins in addition to the cinnamon and brown sugar.

Cinnamon-Apricot-Almond   Swirls   or Cinnamon-Apricot-Walnut Swirls

Cinnamon Carousel Fixings
½ cup slivered almonds or
    chopped walnuts
⅔ cup dried apricots

This is another variation of the Cinnamon Carousel.
Pour boiling water over the dried apricots and allow them to soak for two hours. Drain the water and then chop the apricots in small pieces. Mix the apricots and nuts together.

After the dough has been rolled out, buttered and sprinkled with the cinnamon-sugar mixture, sprinkle the nuts and apricots over the dough. Roll up like a jelly roll and continue with the procedure as outlined in the Cinnamon Carousel Recipe.

Cinnamon Apple Twirls

Cinnamon Carousel Fixings
1 chopped apple

Sprinkle chopped apple over cinnamon-sugar mixture.

Cinnamon Currant Bullseyes

Cinnamon Carousel Fixings
⅔ cup chopped currants

Measure out ⅔ cup of dried currants and pour boiling water over them. Allow to soak for 2 hours. Pour off the water and chop the currants. Sprinkle the currants over the cinnamon-sugar mixture.

Poppy Seed Roll

Poppy seeds cooked with honey make a delicious filling. This is the same filling found in Hamentaschen, the traditional treat served at the festival of Purim by Jewish families. The poppy seed filling goes well in tarts, rolls and other desserts. It can be used with either bread or cookie doughs.

Poppy seed filling is available pre-cooked. It is sold in a #303 can. The only brand I'm familiar with is put out by the "SOLO" company. If commercial filling is used, while you're preparing the dough, open the can and place it in a pot of water. Heat the water which will heat the filling in the can so that it will spread more easily.

Poppy Seed Filling

2 cups poppy seed
1 cup water or milk
¼ cup sugar or ¼ cup brown
   sugar
½ cup honey
⅛ teaspoon salt
1 beaten egg
½ teaspoon vanilla extract (optional)

Pour boiling water over the poppy seeds and let them stand in the hot water until the seeds have all settled. Pour off the water. The seeds will be softer now. If you have a grinder, a blender, or a mortar, grind or pound the poppy seeds. If you can't grind the seeds, you can use them in the recipe after they've been softened.

After grinding or pounding the seeds, combine them with the water or milk, the sugar, honey and salt. Cook the mixture over a low flame until it is thick. Stir frequently while the poppy seeds are cooking. Cool the paste and mix in the raw egg.

Variations of Poppy Seed Filling

1. Before cooking add ½ cup of seedless raisins and grate in about ½ teaspoon of lemon rind. Cook these into the paste.
2. After cooking the paste add ¼ cup of chopped walnuts or chopped almonds.
3. After cooking the paste add ½ cup of grated fresh apple and ¼ cup of chopped nuts.
4. Before cooking the paste add ⅓ cup of chopped dates, or ⅓ cup of chopped dates plus ⅓ cup of seedless raisins.

If after cooking the paste appears too thick, a small amount of water can be mixed in. Heat for a few seconds and stir.

Poppy Seed Roll

½ portion Rich Yeast Dough or
   Rich Sourdough Dough
2 Tablespoons butter or margarine
cinnamon (optional)
sugar (optional)
poppy seed filling
egg
water
powdered sugar or glaze

Take ½ portion of Rich Yeast Dough or Sourdough Dough (see pages 83 and 53) and roll it out on a floured bread board. Roll the dough out to a rectangle of 8 x 16 inches. Trim excess dough off the rectangle.
Melt about 2 Tablespoons of butter or margarine and brush the upper surface of the dough with the melted butter. If desired, cinnamon and sugar can be sprinkled over the dough before the poppy seed filling is added. Make sure the poppy seeds are warm for they will spread better. Spread the filling out over the dough. If there is an excess, save the dough scraps.

After spreading the filling, the dough is rolled up like a jelly roll. Start rolling on the long side away from you and roll towards yourself. Crimp the ends shut. The top seam will stick better if painted with egg or water. Place the roll on a greased baking sheet and cook it for 375°F. for 30-35 minutes. The roll should be well browned. Dust it with powdered sugar or glaze the roll before serving.

Prune Filled Roll

Prune Filling:
1 pound prunes
2 teaspoons lemon juice
    grated rind of 1 lemon

Soak the prunes for several hours. Cook until they are soft. Pit the prunes and chop them. Add the lemon juice and lemon rind. Use this instead of poppy seed filling in the recipe for Poppy Seed Roll.

Doughnuts

Call them sinkers, crullers, underdone bagel, doughnuts or what you will, these delectable fried dough creations are a favorite with everyone not on a diet. To make raised doughnuts and filled doughnuts, we will use the same dough we used to make the coffee cakes described earlier in this chapter. Dough is a very versatile substance. This dough when fried makes heavenly doughnuts, when baked delightful coffee cakes, breads or rolls. If the same dough is boiled, it will make a superlative bagel.

Raised Doughnuts

If desired, the amount of dough can be divided in half and the other half can be used to make another treat.

1 portion of Rich Yeast Dough or 1
    portion of Rich Sourdough
    Dough (pages 83 or 53)
Finish:
½ cup granulated sugar
½ teaspoon cinnamon
Alternate Finish:
½ cup powdered sugar

Divide the dough into 16 equal parts (or half the dough into 8 equal parts). Roll up each piece of dough into a ball then punch a hole through the center of the ball with two fingers. Tug at the dough around the hole to give it a round shape. As each doughnut is shaped, place it on a greased baking sheet. When all the doughnuts have been shaped, cover the sheet and place it in a warm place for about 30 minutes to allow the dough to rise.

Fill a deep fat fryer one third full of fresh cooking oil. If a pot is used instead of a temperature controlled fryer, use a thermometer to check the fat. If you have no thermometer, a cube of bread dropped into the oil will turn brown in 20 seconds if the temperature is 360°F. When the oil has reached 360°F. fry the doughnuts for 2 minutes on each side then remove with a slotted spoon and drain on paper towels.

To finish, mix cinnamon and sugar in a paper bag and then drop the hot doughnuts in the mixture. Toss the doughnuts in the bag. If a powdered sugar finish is used, use powdered sugar only in the bag.

Baked Raised Doughnuts

Although these are not the same as a fried doughnut, they make a good tasting dessert. Use the recipe for fried doughnuts, but after they have risen on the greased sheet, put the sheet in the oven and bake the dough on a high shelf. Bake at 375°F. for 15-20 minutes. When they are brown, they are done.

Jam Filled Doughnuts (Method One)—

There are two ways to make a jam filled doughnut. Method one: Using the same dough we used for raised doughnuts divide them into balls as before. Allow the balls to rise on a greased baking sheet for 20 minutes. Punch a hole in the top center of each ball using either a finger or the handle of a wooden spoon. Place 1/2 teaspoon of jam into the hole and then seal the hole by pinching the dough around the top. Cover again and let rise for another 15-20 minutes. Fry in oil at 360°F. for two minutes, turn and fry another two minutes. Finish by tossing in a bag with cinnamon and sugar or by tossing in a bag with powdered sugar.

Jam Filled Doughnuts (Method Two)—

Take the Rich dough and roll it out until it is no thicker than 1/4 inch. Using a 3 inch cutter or a tuna can with both ends cut out, cut a series of 3 inch circles of dough. Roll the scraps together and with the rolling pin, roll these again and cut out more circles.

Lay a 3 inch circle on a baking sheet and spoon 1/2-1 teaspoon of jam onto the circle. Cover with a round of dough and crimp the edges together well. After all the circles have been used, cover the baking sheet and let the doughnuts rise for 15-20 minutes. Fry in oil at 360°F. for 2 minutes. Turn and fry for another 2 minutes. Remove from the oil with a slotted spoon and allow to drain on paper towels. To finish, toss the doughnuts in a paper bag with cinnamon and sugar or with powdered sugar.

Jam Filled Rolls

These are the same as the jam filled doughnuts, but they are baked instead of fried. Divide the dough according to either Method 1 or Method 2 and fill with jam. Allow them to rise on the greased baking sheet for 15-20 minutes and then bake at the top of the oven. Baking temperature 375°F for 15-20 minutes.

Poppy Seed Filled Doughnuts or Prune Filled Doughnuts

Use the recipe for jam filled doughnuts, but substitute poppy seed filling or prune filling for jam. The recipes for both these fillings are given under Poppy Seed Roll. Fry according to the doughnut recipe.

Poppy Seed Filled Rolls or Prune Filled Rolls

Use the recipe for jam filled rolls, but substitute poppy seed filling or prune filling for jam. These rolls can also be filled with the cheese filling described under Filled Braids.

Poppy Seed Filled Tarts (Hammentaschen)

Hammentaschen is the traditional Jewish tart served at the Purim festival. It is symbolic of the tricornered hat worn by the archvillain Hammen. Hammentaschen is made with either bread dough or cookie dough. The dough used for doughnuts is ideal for this purpose, but a Brioche dough can also be used.

Roll out the dough to a ¼ inch thickness. Cut the dough into 3 or 3½ inch rounds. Place a heaping teaspoon of filling in the center of each round, then pinch the 3 sides together to form a triangle. It is all right if part of the filling shows. Allow the filled tarts to rise on a greased baking sheet for 20 minutes. Bake at 375°F. for 20 minutes or until the tarts are golden brown. Prune filling can be used instead of poppy seed. Although a cheese filling is not a hammentaschen, the tarts can be filled with cheese. They're not traditional, but they're still delectable. The recipe for the cheese filling is given in the section on braids (see Cheese Filled Braid, page 90).

Braids

Another interesting family of dessert breads is the filled braids. They are not as difficult to make as they sound. If your first efforts are a little lopsided, do not despair; this applies to any new shape. The first time I tried to make an English Cottage Loaf, the top knot slid half way off the bottom. That bread reminded me of the way Hildy Johnson wore his hat in the play, *Front Page*. It looked ridiculous, but it tasted just as good as a perfect Cottage Loaf. Practice leads toward perfection.

If you are planning to make a dessert bread, use either the Rich Sourdough Dough or the Rich Yeast Dough Recipe (page 53 or 83). If you are planning to fill the braid with meat, use any of the bread recipes.

To make a single braid, take one quarter portion of the Rich Dough and roll it out to a rectangle measuring 9 x 12 inches. I usually make two to four braids at a time, but you can reserve some of the dough in the refrigerator for a few days or make doughnuts or some other baked dessert if you make less braids.

Once you have the rectangle of dough, position it on a greased baking sheet it so that it runs the long way. Brush the entire upper surface of the dough with melted butter. Take your filling and spread it down the center half of the rectangle allowing one fourth of the dough on either side to remain uncovered by the filling. Using a sharp knife or a single edged razor blade make diagonal cuts about 2 inches apart down both sides. See illustrations (page 90). Start at the top by taking one strip and folding it toward the center. Take the matching strip on the other side and fold it over onto the first strip. Continue down to the end of the rectangle. This crossing gives the braided effect. This is a false or pseudo braid, but a real braid could not be filled. If you wish a more braided effect, cut the strips thinner. After folding over the strips and pinching the bottom and top ends over to seal the ends, cover the braids and allow them to rise for 20-30 minutes. After baking dessert braids can be glazed. See the section on glazes (page 92).

Fillings for Sweet Braids

All braids are shaped in the same manner and all dessert braids should be made with a sweet bread dough. The following recipes are only for fillings. Those fillings whose recipes appear early in this chapter will refer back to the recipe which gives the filling.

Raisin and Apple Braid

2 apples
½ teaspoon cinnamon
⅓ cup raisins
⅓ cup brown sugar
½ teaspoon vanilla extract (optional)

Peel, core and chop the raw apples. Put them into a small pan with the raisins, sugar, cinnamon and vanilla. Cook the apples over a low flame for about 10 minutes or until they are soft. Cool and spread down the center of your rectangle of dough. Cut and fold the braid. Bake at 375° for 25-30 minutes. Cool and finish with a glaze if desired or dust with powdered sugar.

Cheese Filled Braid

The cheese filling can be made with several types of cheese. Hoop cheese, pot cheese, feta cheese, cottage cheese (squeeze out some of the water) or ricotta. My preference among these similar cheeses is the ricotta because I can get it fresh. Hoop and pot cheeses are hard to find. Feta cheese is more expensive. I hate squeezing cottage cheese to force the water out. The ricotta is rich tasting and moist but not too wet. It works well, but any of the others can be used.

12-16 ounces ricotta cheese
1 teaspoon vanilla extract
2 Tablespoons sugar, honey or brown sugar
1 beaten raw egg
1 teaspoon lemon juice (optional)
1 Tablespoon grated lemon or orange peel (optional)

Mix the cheese with the sugar, the egg, lemon juice and vanilla extract; add the grated peel. Spread the cheese down the center of the dough rectangle and make a braid. Bake on a greased baking sheet for 25-30 minutes at 375°F. Glaze the braids when cool.

This is a delectable cheese filling. It is not too rich since it is made with a form of cottage cheese, but the taste reminds me of a cheese Danish filling

Dried Apricot and Apple Braid

2 apples
⅓ cup chopped apricots
½ teaspoon cinnamon
⅓ cup brown sugar
½ teaspoon vanilla extract (optional)
½ teaspoon dried ginger or powdered clove (optional)

Boil water and pour the boiling water over the whole dried apricots. Allow them to stand in the water for 1-2 hours. Drain the water and chop the apricots. Peel and core the apples. Chop the apples and then combine them with the chopped apricots, sugar, cinnamon, ginger or cloves, and vanilla extract in a small pan. Cook over a low flame for about 10 minutes until the apples are soft. Allow the filling to cool and spread over a rectangle of dough. Make the braid and allow it to rise again. Bake the braids at 375°F. for 25-30 minutes. Glaze the braids when cool.

Date Braid

1¼ cups chopped dates
3 Tablespoons lemon or orange juice diluted with water to ⅔ cup.

Dilute the lemon or orange juice to ⅔ cup with water. Pour the diluted juice into a small pan and add the chopped dates. Bring the mixture to boil, stirring continuously. Lower the flame and cook at low heat for about five minutes. Stir occasionaly while the dates are simmering. Allow the date filling to cool and spread over the center of a rectangle of dough. Bake at 375°F. for 25-30 minutes. Glaze the braid when cool.

Poppy Seed Braid

The recipe for Poppy Seed Filling appears under Poppy Seed Roll, page 86. Make the braid in the same way you would make a Date Braid.

Prune Braid

The Recipe for Prune Fillng is given as on page 87. Make the braid in the same way you would bake a Date Braid.

Cinnamon-Apricot-Nut Braid

½ cup chopped walnuts or almonds
⅔ cup dried apricots
½ cup brown sugar
1½-2 teaspoons cinnamon
¼ teaspoon freshly grated nutmeg (optional)

Pour boiling water over the dried apricots and allow them to soak for 1-2 hours. Chop the apricots. Roll the dough out into a rectangle and brush melted butter over the top surface. Mix the brown sugar with the spices and sprinkle part of this mixture over the buttered dough. Spread the chopped apricots over the cinnamon-sugar mixture and make the braid. Brush melted butter over the top of the braid. Take the rest of the cinnamon spice mixture and sprinkle it over the top of the braid as a finish. Allow the braid to rise and then bake at 375°F. for 25-30 minutes.

Cinnamon-Raisin-Nut Braid

This is a variation of the Cinnamon-Apricot-Nut braid. Substitute ⅔ cup of raisins for the apricots and follow the same recipe.

Variations

In any braid not calling for nuts, ½ cup of nuts can be added to the filling.

Sweet Glazes and Finishes

1. *Powdered sugar.* This is dusted over the finished product.

2. *Granulated sugar or granulated sugar plus cinnamon.* This is also dusted over the baked product. If the top of the dessert is buttered with melted butter, the sugar will adhere better. Use ½ cup of granulated sugar to ½ teaspoon of cinnamon. More cinnamon can be used if desired.

3. *Milk finish.* Take a small pan and put 3 Tablespoons of whole milk into the pan. Add ¼ cup of granulated or brown sugar to the milk. Boil this mixture for 2 minutes. Brush over the cooled braid.

4. *Orange juice finish.* 3 Tablespoons of orange juice are boiled with ¼ cup of sugar for 2 minutes. Brush over the cooled braid.

5. *Honey glazes.* (a). Brush honey over the braid. (b). Mix honey with milk or orange juice using 3 Tablespoons of the liquid to ¼ cup of honey. Heat and brush over the cooled dessert.

The Staling of Bread

Green is the color to wear on Saint Patrick's Day, the color of grass, emeralds and traffic lights, but when green is found on bread, it is the color of the enemy. Penicillin, a fungus, finds breads a most hospitable place to stake out a homestead. First the bread breaks out in a smallpox like rash of green pits which is followed by the spreading of the color to the entire surface. When Sir Alexander Flemming discovered the medicinal uses of penicillin, he saved many lives. In a syringe or in a pill, penicillin can be a boon to man, but on a loaf of bread, it is a thief, a robber and a cheat.

Fungi are not the only enemy of bread. Staling is always a threat. Bread is baked from a mixture of flour and water. During the baking, much of the water is driven off into the air as a vapor. If bread is allowed to dry out it becomes hard. To slow this loss of moisture, bread is now kept in plastic bags. Unfortunately, the plastic bag which keeps the moisture from being lost makes it easier for fungi to grow. Molds grow best in a damp atmosphere.

Some people store bread in the refrigerator. Most foods keep better at a cold temperature, but not bread. In the refrigerator, moisture is lost from the bread more quickly than from a bread kept at room temperature. The only sure way to keep bread from staling is to freeze it. It is not necessary to freeze an entire bread. I prefer to freeze half loaves, but if I were living alone, there would be nothing to prevent me from freezing quarter loaves.

Bread can be frozen in foil or wrapped in special freezer paper. I prefer to use the large plastic bags found in the vegetable section of markets. These are large enough for a whole round loaf or a whole pan loaf. Some markets carry extra long bags which will take a whole long loaf. These bags tie shut with a plastic covered or paper covered wire tie.

When removed from the freezer, bread will thaw in about three hours. I usually take them out the evening before and have a fresh bread available for breakfast. Bread stored in foil can be heated without removing the foil, but if stored in plastic, the bread must be stripped before heating. For those who prefer using a whole loaf instead of cutting the loaves before freezing, smaller loaves can be baked. With home baked bread, there is no standard size, shape or weight.

If bread stales without the growth of fungus, there is no need to throw it away. Stale bread does have its uses. If the bread is stale to the taste, but is not yet hard, slice the bread and place the slices on a baking sheet. Place the slices in the oven at low heat and allow the bread to dry out completely. This hard, dry bread can now be ground into bread crumbs in the blender. If you don't have a blender wrap slices in a cloth towel and roll with a rolling pin. After grinding, store the crumbs in the freezer. Crumbs can be used directly out of the freezer without thawing. Plastic bags are awkward. Use a plastic jar or a rinsed, dried empty milk carton to store the crumbs. After filling a half gallon carton, I staple it shut in the middle and end, leaving a spout to pour out the crumbs.

Stale bread can be used to make croutons. Do not slice and dry the bread as you do when making bread crumbs. Cut the staled bread into ½ inch cubes. Place the cubes on a baking sheet and bake for 10 minutes at 300°F.

This produces a plain crouton, but they can be seasoned if you wish. Melt a ¼ cup of butter or margarine in a large frying pan. Add the toasted cubes, tossing them so they will be coated with the butter evenly. These are now returned to the baking sheet and baked again at 275°F, for 30 minutes. To season, mix the seasoning in the melted butter before adding the bread.

Herb seasoning: ¼ teaspoon basil, oregano and thyme.

Herb with onion: ½ teaspoon basil, oregano and 1 teaspoon onion powder.

Garlic: ½ teaspoon garlic powder or 1 crushed garlic clove.

Cheese: 1 Tablespoon Romano or Parmesan cheese.

Cheese plus Herb. Combine herb and cheese.

Croutons like bread crumbs should be stored in the freezer.

Special bread crumbs. My favorite bread crumbs are made by grinding up pretzels. These are already salted and seasoned. If you live near a pretzel factory, you can buy large bags of broken pretzels very cheaply. These broken pretzels can be ground or crushed into an excellent bread crumb. I use these frequently because we seldom have stale bread in our house. We store it frozen in half loaves. These are still fresh when the last slice is gone and a new loaf has been thawed out.

Stale bread can be salvaged by converting it into a dish known as Pain Perdu (lost bread), Poor Knights of Windsor, or French toast. The recipe for this appears at the end of this chapter.

Breads made with honey seem to stale more slowly than those made with sugar or fructose. Honey acts as a natural preservative, but it will not stop the growth of penicillin if the bread becomes moist. The ordinary breads, the basic breads in this book seem to remain fresh for about four to five days if kept in plastic. They of course are less fresh each of those days and after the second day are best toasted. If the bread were stored in a paper bag which allows moisture to escape, the bread would be brick hard in about three days. If bread is allowed to dry out, it can be sprinkled with water and heated. This will restore some degree of freshness.

I have mentioned the storing of bread in plastic bags. These work well, but one note of caution. Do not put hot bread in a plastic bag. As a hot bread cools, it gives off vapors. These will condense in the plastic and drip down on the bread making it wet. Mold would then find the bread an ideal place to grow.

I have little problems with staling because I use my freezer to store bread. My biggest problem with staling comes from baking a new batch and eating the hot bread instead of the one that is on the shelf. If I remember, I place the older chunk of bread back in the freezer. Bread can be frozen, thawed, re-frozen and re-thawed without spoiling. Breads that have been frozen can stale a little quicker than a bread that is bagged and kept on the shelf after baking.

Assorted Rolls

Pain Perdu — Poor Knights of Windsor — French Toast

This recipe is used to rescue bread that has staled. French toast, particularly if made with the bread you bake, is so good, that it should not be limited to stale bread. When I do not have stale, I cut thick slices of fresh bread to make this delicious breakfast.

Several slices of stale bread
eggs beaten with milk
brandy or rum (optional)

Beat the eggs with milk; if rum or brandy are to be used, add 1 ounce of brandy or rum to the egg-milk mixture. Dip the bread in the egg, allowing the bread to soak up the egg. Fry it in a pan greased with butter.

Powdered sugar can be sprinkled on the slices to finish them or they can be served with maple syrup or jam. Many people add cinnamon to the egg before dipping the bread. It may be convenient to slice each piece along the diagonal to make triangles before dipping.

Muffins and Biscuits

Yeast Breads in a Hurry

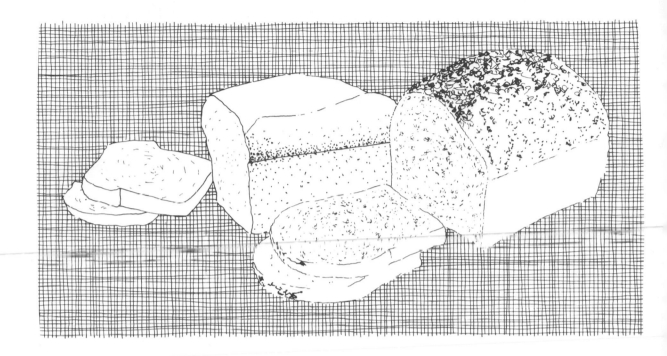

Short Cuts in Baking

There is a time in every bread baker's life that a bread is needed but there is not time to bake a conventional loaf. When company is coming at 7:00 P.M. and you arrive home at 5:30 P.M. to find that there is no bread because your dog snagged the loaf you planned to serve, you are facing a crisis. No, don't get your coat and rush out to the store for a loaf of El Soggo. You can get a bread ready in time for your dinner party if you use a short cut method.

There are many quick breads. Some of them are dessert type breads, but others are ordinary dinner breads. The recipes that follow all work and work well. The breads baked with these recipes are not exactly like those baked by the longer method, but they taste good and will win the approval of your guests.

For years, home bakers have been trying to get a yeast bread baked more quickly. Many bread books give bad advice in this department. They tell you to skip the first rise completely.

Unless special steps are taken, skipping that rise will produce a bread that is heavy and leaden. Don't try to follow an ordinary recipe and leave out the rise after kneading, if you do, you'll be sorry.

Recently a way to skip that rise has been perfected. In fact, there are two ways that work. Yes, Virginia, there is a Santa Claus, and old St. Nick has given us two ways to get bread baked and on the table in less than two hours from the time you open the bag of flour. It isn't black magic, but if this technique were shown to a baker in Salem during the 1600's, you would be condemned as a witch. Let's get to the actual mechanics. Take a bread recipe, any bread recipe that uses dry yeast. If it is one of the recipes in this book, double the amount of yeast called for in the recipe. If your recipe comes from another book use the amount of yeast stated. With this technique you use 1 Tablespoon of yeast for each 4-5 cups of flour.

50 milligrams Vitamin C (ascorbic acid) or a pinch of Ascorbic acid crystals
3½ cups hot tap water
1 Tablespoon salt
3 Tablespoons melted butter or oil
2 Tablespoons honey or sugar
8-9 cups of unsifted flour
2 Tablespoons dry yeast

Method #1. Ascorbic Acid Method

With any bread recipe, add the 50 milligrams of Vitamin C to the recipe. The Vitamin C acts as a catalyst to make the yeast multiply more quickly.

When you are baking bread in a hurry, you will use a direct yeast method and not make a sponge. It is not necessary to prove the yeast before using it unless the yeast is outdated. Take a 50 milligram tablet of Vitamin C, or half a 100 milligram tablet. Crush the tablet in the bottom of a bowl and add 2 Tablespoons of yeast. Add the water, flour, sugar, salt and oil reserving about 2-3 cups of the flour for the kneading. Stir the water-flour mixture into a dough and dump it out onto a floured bread board. Knead for 10 minutes, working in extra flour as necessary. After the dough has been kneaded, allow it to rest for 10 minutes, then shape the dough into loaves or rolls. After shaping allow the breads to prove for 10 minutes. They can go up to 20 minutes, but even 5 minutes would suffice. Bake according to the time and temperature called for in the original recipe. The recipe given above is baked at 400°F. for 45 minutes.

The Vitamin C makes it possible to get a good rising bread without the long period of doubling after kneading. The crust of a bread baked in this manner is treated with the same finishes as a bread baked in the regular manner. The bread is comparable to that baked by the longer method. The crumb should be light and well aerated. Vitamin C is a natural substance necessary to good health and is not injurious, but most of it will be destroyed in the baking.

Method #2. Baking Powder and Yeast Method

The addition of baking powder to any recipe in addition to the yeast makes it possible to skip the rise after kneading. If you are anti-baking powder, you can use one that does not contain alum, or you can substitute baking soda and vinegar for the baking powder. In the quick breads chapter (page 107) baking powders and their substitutes are discussed in greater detail.

1½-2 Tablespoons dry yeast
2 teaspoons baking powder
3½ cups warm water
8-9 cups unsifted flour
3 Tablespoons melted shortening or oil
2 Tablespoons sugar or honey
1 Tablespoon salt

This is a direct method. The yeast is not proved. Place the entire amount of water in a mixing bowl and add the yeast, sugar, salt, oil, baking powder and five cups of the flour. Stir the mixture to a dough and scrape out onto a floured board. Knead for 10 minutes adding more flour as necessary. After kneading shape immediately and bake at the time and temperature called for in the recipe. If using another recipe than the one above, just add 2 teaspoons of baking powder for each 8-9 cups of flour called for in that recipe.

This will produce a bread that rises high and has an excellent flavor and crumb texture. It will taste like a yeast bread not a baking powder bread. This method works even better than the Vitamin C method for producing a bread in a hurry. the rise after kneading was not necessary because this bread was leavened not only by yeast but also by baking powder. Although the crust can be treated with different glazes, I have found that this bread produces a softer, more tender crust than the regular method. I prefer this recipe for making hamburger rolls. If you are a crust lover, an additional 5 minutes of baking time will give you a crunchy crust.

Other Quick Yeast Breads

There is another type of yeast bread that can be baked in a hurry. This bread is a non-kneaded yeast bread, somewhat similar to a batter bread baked with yeast. Since this bread is not kneaded, it is strictly a pan bread, but is as quick to bake as the Vitamin C bread or the yeast bread with baking powder.

2 Tablespoons dry yeast
1 Tablespoon salt
2 cups hot tap water
4½ cups flour
2 Tablespoons oil or melted shortening
1 Tablespoon salt

This is a direct method; it is not necessary to prove the yeast unless it is outdated. Place the yeast in a bowl and add the entire 2 cups of water hot from the tap. Add the flour 1 cup at a time, beating vigorously. Beat by hand for a full 3 minutes or in a mixer for 1 minute after the third cup of flour is added. Add the oil, sugar and salt now and then add the fourth cup of flour. Beat again for a full minute by hand. Work in the last half cup of flour and beat again for at least 1 minute.

The beating is critical. Beat so vigorously you think that your arm is about to fall off. The beating does not have to be continuous. If you get tired, rest and then start beating again. The beating does for this bread what kneading does for a kneaded bread; it conditions the gluten and allows the bread to rise properly.

After beating the batter, put half into a greased loaf tin and the other half into another greased tin. The batter is thick and will not flow. You can bounce the pan on the table but may find it necessary to push the batter into the corners. If the top is smoothed before letting the batter rise, it will make a nicer looking loaf.

Let the batter rise in the baking pans for 20 minutes. Either stand the pans in hot water or place them in a closed oven with a pan of boiling water on the bottom shelf of the oven. Of course, if it is a really hot day neither of these steps will be necessary.

Bake the loaves at 375°F. for 30-35 minutes. Test with a thin knife to make sure they are done. Turn out onto a rack to cool or eat hot.

Variations

¾ to 1 cup of skim milk powder can be added to enrich the bread.

A mixture composed of 1 tsp dill seed, ½ teaspoon dill weed, 1 teaspoon of savory or any other combination of herbs can be added to make a herb bread.

1 egg can be added to enrich the bread.

The recipe for a whole wheat bread by this method will be found on page 213.

Quick Cheese Bread

Do not fill any loaf tin more than half full before baking. The cheese bread variation will make 3 breads instead of 2 because the cheese adds to the volume.

2 Tablespoons (2 packages) dry yeast
2 Tablespoons melted shortening or oil
3 Tablespoons sugar or honey
1 Tablespoon salt
2 cups hot tap water
1 egg
5 cups unsifted flour
2 cups grated cheese

Put the yeast in a bowl and add the 2 cups of water. Add the sugar, salt and oil. Mix in 2 cups of flour and stir until the batter is smooth. Beat the egg and add it to the batter. Grate the cheese and stir it into the batter. Add the third cup of flour and beat hard for 3 minutes by hand. Add the fourth cup of flour and beat again for 1 minute. Add the last cup of flour and beat again for 1 minute. Transfer the batter to three greased baking dishes filling none of them more than half full. Bounce the pans on the counter to spread the batter. If necessary poke the batter into the corners. Allow the batter to rise in a warm place for 20 minutes. On a cold day stand the pans in hot water. Bake at 375°F. for 35-40 minutes. Test with a knife. If done, turn out onto a wire rack to cool.

Quick Breads without Yeast

Baking Powder Breads

Little yeast cells blowing bubbles is not the only way bread can be made to rise. One inventor once patented a machine to blow carbon dioxide gas, from dry ice, directly into the dough; this eliminated not only the yeast, but also the rising time. In the home kitchen we are limited to the use of yeast either as active dry yeast, cake yeast, or sourdough starters or to several chemical means to leaven bread. The best known of the chemical leaveners is a substance we call baking powder.

Back when the twentieth century was just over the horizon, there was a gold rush in the Klondike. The prospectors who looked for the gold had to bake their own biscuits. They could have carried baking powder to make the biscuits rise, but most of them preferred the trouble of toting sourdough starters. There was a reason for their reluctance to use baking powder. At that time there was a superstition prevalent in both the Klondike and the Yukon that baking powder biscuits limited a man's sexual virility, decreased his sexual appetites. They classified baking

powder with saltpeter. Today we know better, but the whole question has become academic. We no longer eat biscuits with every meal; it is a rare day indeed when one eats biscuits unless a tube of those cardboard imitations is removed from the grocer's freezer and taken home.

Although there is no basis in fact for the fear that baking powder will decrease sexual drive, baking powder is made up from chemicals that some people might be reluctant to introduce into their bodies. Since there are several different substances called baking powder as well as a substitute, it would be proper to classify them now to make a choice easier. Read the label when you purchase a can and make sure that you are getting the type you prefer.

All baking powders are made up of a mixture of starch, baking soda and an acid former to liberate the carbon dioxide from the baking soda. The actual leavener is the baking soda, not the baking powder. Tartaric powders are made of cream of tartar, tannic acid, the expected baking soda, and starch. Some leave out the tannic acid because cream of tartar will form tartaric acid when disolved in water. Cream of tartar is extracted from the lees at the bottom of wine barrels: it cannot be made chemically. Phosphate powders contain Calcium Dihydrogen Phosphate to form the acid. Sulfate powders use Sodium Aluminum Sulfate (alum) as their acid forming ingredient.

In all of these powders the acid is liberated by the action of water. The acid reacts with the baking soda to form carbon dioxide gas. They work much like an Alka Seltzer® tablet. In fact, you could use one of these tablets to leaven bread, but if you do, pick the one without asprin. The seltzer tablet and similar products uses citric acid to react with the baking soda.

Double action baking powders usually are a combination of phosphate and sulfate powders. The sulfate powder does not react fully until the temperature is raised. Royal® baking powder uses only Calcium Dihydrogen Phosphate, but the label says it is double action.

As we can see from the formulas of various baking powders, the prime ingredient is baking soda. It is not necessary to purchase a baking powder. Baking soda plus an acid source can be used instead. The most common acid sources available at home are citric acid as lemon or orange juice, vinegar (acetic acid), buttermilk or yogurt. In any recipe calling for a teaspoon of baking powder you can substitute 3 teaspoons of lemon juice plus 1 level teaspoon of baking soda. Vinegar can be used instead of lemon juice. When using buttermilk or yogurt, each cup of the dairy product has the same acid content as one teaspoon of vinegar.

A baking powder can be made using cream of tartar and baking soda, but cream of tartar is very expensive. I should qualify that statement to say that if you buy the one ounce cans at the grocer's it is expensive. I found a fourteen ounce can at a wholesale grocery-restaurant supply house for less than two one ounce cans. Cream of tartar can be used on a one to one ratio with the baking soda.

Baking powder and baking soda are used to bake breads and biscuits because it is a quick way to get hot biscuits, bread or dessert breads to the table. There is no sponge or rising period. Baking powder breads do not taste the same as breads baked with yeast. I think that this difference in taste is because the baking soda is not completely neutralized. I have found that five teaspoons of vinegar will barely neutralize one teaspoon of soda. I like my breads as free from soda taste as possible; to achieve this, my recipes call for more vinegar or lemon juice than recipes found in other books. In fact, when using baking soda, I usually add 3-4 teaspoons of vinegar to the mixture for each teaspoon of baking soda used.

Despite the fact that baking powder biscuits have a different taste than those baked with yeast, I still bake them. They are tasty in their own right and occasionally I prefer that particular taste.

Baking soda is also known as bicarbonate of soda, sodium bicarbonate or even as salterus in old books.

In the section on health food breads, most of the quick breads are baked using baking soda. Tartrate powders and phosphate powders have nothing injurious in their contents, but I am opposed to the use of alum in my food.

Self-rising flour is sold at the grocer's. This product combines flour with a baking powder, usually calcium dihydrogen phosphate. It can only be used in recipes calling for a baking powder. Do not use this flour for yeast breads. I find it as easy to add the baking powder myself and have my flour all purpose. I also think that it is less expensive to use regular flour and baking powder.

Prepared biscuit mixes can be found on the grocer's shelf. None of the recipes in this book call for biscuit mix, but the contents of these convenience products are of interest. If you are tempted to buy one, read the label. The basic mix is made by combining flour, shortening, salt and a form of baking powder. I checked four brands. Three of them used a phosphate powder. The fourth just called it leavening. The type of shortening varies from brand to brand, but it can be either animal, vegetable or a mixture of both. The animal fat is either beef suet or lard, but this is not listed on the label. It is too easy to mix your own; don't use the commercial mixes unless you're fond of animal fat and preservatives.

Quick breads made with either baking powder or baking soda range from those that can only be called, "bread," to some delightful desserts. The recipes are grouped according to the type of bread produced.

Regular Breads without Yeast

50% Whole Wheat Bread

Most breads baked without yeast are baked as batter breads; they are not kneaded. In any batter bread it is important to keep the liquid to flour ratio in balance or the bread will not bake firm in the center. In this bread only a small amount of sugar is used. It can be replaced with either honey or blackstrap molasses without upsetting the balance. If baking soda and vinegar are used instead of baking powder, the 6-8 teaspoons of vinegar should be used to replace that amount of water in the recipe.

1¼ cups hot tap water
2 cups whole wheat flour
2 Tablespoons oil
2 cups unbleached flour
1 Tablespoon sugar or honey
1 teaspoon salt
⅔ cup milk
Leavening agent: either 2 teaspoons baking powder or 8 teaspoons vinegar & 2 teaspoons baking soda (see discussion above)

Dissolve the sweetening agent (honey, syrup, sugar or molasses in the hot water and allow the water to cool to warm. If the vinegar baking soda leavening agent is used, make the vinegar part of the 1¼ cups of water. Mix the dry ingredients together then make a well in the center and add the liquids. Stir well to make a thick, heavy batter.

Turn the batter into a greased loaf tin. (9x5x3 is suitable.) Bake at 400°F for 15 minutes then reduce the temperature to 350°F. and bake an additional 20-30 minutes. Check with a knife to make sure the center of the loaf is done. If the knife comes out dry, cool the loaf by turning out onto a wire rack. Allow the bread to cool upside down. When cool, store in a plastic bag. It is recommended to allow this loaf to stand overnight before slicing.

Variations on above loaf
1. Use 4 cups of unbleached flour for a white loaf.
2. Use 3 cups of unbleached flour and 1 cup of corn meal.
3. Use 3½ cups of unbleached flour plus ½ cup of wheat germ.

Irish Soda Bread

The Irish bake a different bread; it is not leavened with baking powder. They use baking soda and liberate the carbon dioxide gas from the soda with buttermilk or soured milk. Every time I feel like making Irish Soda Bread, I seem to be out of buttermilk, but there are alternate recipes available which will allow you to make the same bread without the sour milk. One recipe I came across not only used baking soda and buttermilk, but also used baking powder. I consider that cheating, for if you use baking powder, you could dispense with both the soda and the buttermilk. To me, a soda bread tastes like a huge baking powder biscuit. To lessen the soda taste, I always add 1 to 2 extra teaspoons of vinegar to my buttermilk.

Irish Soda Bread

1 teaspoon salt
4 cups unbleached flour
1 teaspoon baking soda
1½ cups buttermilk
1 teaspoon sugar
2 Tablespoons butter or margarine
(optional)

Alternate leavening agents.

Use 1½ cups sweet milk plus 1½
teaspoons of lemon juice or
vinegar. or use 1½ cups sweet
milk plus 1 teaspoon of cream of
tartar.

One and one half (1½) cups of
plain yogurt may be used instead
of buttermilk.

Sift the flour, soda and salt together. If sugar is used, sift it in along with the flour, Add the buttermilk (or milk plus vinegar) and mix to a firm dough. If you use the optional shortening, pour the melted butter into the buttermilk. The texture of the dough is critical. If it crumbles, it is too dry; add more buttermilk as needed.

After the dough is ready, shape it into a ball and pull the ends under to give the ball a smooth top. Place the round loaf on a greased pan or in a greased cast iron skillet. Using a razor blade or a sharp knife cut a deep cross on the top of the loaf. The cut should be about ¾ inch deep. Bake the bread at 400°F. until it is a light brown in color. This will take about 40 minutes. Test with a thin knife to make sure that the center of the loaf is done. Turn out onto a rack to cool.

Alternate baking method: Irish soda bread can be cooked on top of the stove. Use a cast iron skillet and cook at medium heat. Turn over when bottom is brown, test to be sure the bread is done.

If you would like less of a soda taste, add 1 to 2 teaspoons of vinegar to the buttermilk. This will neutralize more of the soda.

Vinegar Soda Bread

Since I never seem to have buttermilk in the house when I want to bake a Soda Bread, I use this recipe instead. I have found that it takes at least five teaspoons of vinegar or lemon juice to neutralize one level teaspoon of baking soda. One cup of buttermilk or one cup of yogurt has the acidity of one teaspoon of lemon juice. Vinegar and soda can also be used as a substitute for baking powder. I prefer to use 3-4 teaspoons of vinegar to each teaspoon of baking soda although that does not completely neutralize the soda.

The rule of thumb for substituting vinegar and soda for baking powder is: For recipes calling for baking powder without sour dairy products, for each teaspoon of baking powder in the recipe use 1 teaspoon of soda and 3-4 teaspoons of vinegar or lemon juice. For recipes using buttermilk or yogurt allow two teaspoons of vinegar for each cup of the sour dairy product. An example would be 1 cup of buttermilk plus 2 teaspoons of vinegar to each teaspoon of soda.

If the bread is a batter bread, adding a large quantity of liquid in the form of vinegar will upset the liquid to flour balance. For these breads, decrease the water or milk in the recipe by the number of teaspoons of vinegar or lemon juice used.

Vinegar-Soda Bread

4 cups unbleached flour
3-4 teaspoons vinegar
1 teaspoon baking soda
9 ounces whole milk or skim milk
1 teaspoon salt
1 teaspoon sugar
2 Tablespoons melted butter or
margarine

Sift the flour, soda and salt together into a bowl. Put the vinegar into a measuring cup and add enough milk to make 1½ cups. Add the milk to the flour and mix immediately to a firm dough. If the dough crumbles, add more milk. Shape into a round loaf, pulling at the top and tucking the folds under the loaf. Slash a ¾ inch deep cross on the top of the loaf and bake at 400°F. for 40 minutes or until the loaf is a golden brown in color. Test with a knife. If done, turn out onto a rack to cool.

Variations

Both the Vinegar Soda Bread and the Irish Soda Bread can be made with raisins or currants. Use about 1 cup of the fruit and mix it in when you add the liquid. A whole wheat soda bread can be baked, but a 50% wheat bread will rise better.

If the idea of using vinegar turns you off, there is another alternative, but it is more expensive.

Use 1 teaspoon of cream of tartar instead of the vinegar. Sift the cream of tartar in with the flour.

A Pseudo Soda Bread can be made by using 1½ teaspoons of baking powder instead of vinegar and soda or buttermilk and soda. If you should use buttermilk in this recipe add ½ teaspoon of soda to neutralize the buttermilk.

Sody Bread

This is an old pioneer recipe. Today we would probably call it salt rising bread, but to those that made the westward trek, it was "Sody Bread."

1 teaspoon baking soda
1 cup warm water
2¼ cups flour
1 teaspoon salt

Mix the soda in the water and add the salt. Stir in the flour to form a dough. Knead the dough well for about 8-10 minutes. It may be used immediately or can sit overnight in a warm place. Before baking flatten the dough to a one inch thickness and bake on a greased baking sheet for about 25 minutes at 400°F.

Corn Breads

The grain known to Americans as corn is called maize in Europe. Europeans do not eat corn; to them it is animal food. In America, corn bread has been a longtime favorite.

Mormon Johnnycake

This is an old recipe brought up to date. The pioneers living in the Great Plains area grew corn to fatten hogs. Flour was expensive and hard to come by. Corn was used to stretch the flour.

2 cups yellow cornmeal
½ cup flour
1 teaspoon baking soda
1 teaspoon salt
2 cups buttermilk
2 Tablespoons molasses or
    sorghum

Combine the ingredients and pour the batter into a greased 9 inch pan. Bake at 425°F. for about 20 minutes. A lighter cake can be made by adding 2 beaten eggs and 2 Tablespoons of melted butter. This increases the liquid so it is baked for about 25 minutes at the same temperature. Test the bread with a knife to make sure it is done. Serve the cornbread directly from the baking dish. Notice that this recipe uses 2 cups of buttermilk which will better neutralize the soda and provide more carbon dioxide gas than the modern recipe using 1 cup of buttermilk to one teaspoon of soda.

Easy-Moist Cornbread

Several years ago we used to buy cornbread mixes. Breads prepared from mix are too dry for my taste. We started to make our own using this recipe and found that it was as easy as using a mix, but the taste is superlative. Try this one using a wholegrain cornmeal instead of degerminated corn.

¾ cup unbleached flour
1 cup cornmeal
½ teaspoon salt
1 Tablespoon baking powder
1 cup milk
2 eggs
2 Tablespoons oil or melted butter

Sift the dry ingredients together into a bowl. (If you are using whole grain cornmeal, do not run that through the sifter.) Add the egg, milk and oil. Beat hard until the mixture is smooth and free of lumps. Pour into a greased baking dish either 8 x 8 square or 9 inch round. Bake at 425°F. for 20-25 minutes. Test with a knife. I sometimes use a regular loaf pan for this bread.

This bread can be made with buttermilk and soda plus 1 teaspoon or 2 teaspoons of vinegar instead of using baking powder.

Sourcream or Yogurt Cornbread

This is made by the same recipe as Easy Moist Cornbread, but the cup of milk is replaced with either a cup of yogurt or a cup of soured cream. The change produces a rich, cake-like texture.

Spoon Bread

This bread is usually called Southern Spoon Bread, but it is too good to be limited to a single region. The closest I have ever come to its unique taste is properly made matzoh balls. The recipe calls for 3 eggs, but I frequently use four. In my opinion this is the king of cornbreads. Most recipes call for white cornmeal, but white or yellow it tastes great.

2 cups milk
1 cup corn meal (white or yellow)
2 Tablespoons melted butter or
   margarine
1 teaspoon salt
1 Tablespoon baking powder
3 beaten eggs

Spoon Bread

Warm the milk until bubbles begin to form. Stir in the cornmeal and stir while it cooks until the cornmeal is soft like a mush. Stir in the salt while the cornmeal is cooking and then stir in the melted butter. Allow the corn mush to cool for a few minutes then stir in the baking powder and the beaten eggs. Mix well. The batter is now poured into a greased meatloaf pan or a greased 1½ quart casserole. Bake at 375°F. for about 40 minutes. Test with a knife. The knife should come out of the bread clean.

This bread is served directly from the baking pan. You spoon it out to serve, hence the name Spoon Bread.

How can one describe the indescribable. Most frequently we try by using a comparison, but that does not work too well in this case for too few people have ever eaten properly made matzoh balls. Most matzoh balls taste like bride's biscuits. I could say that spoon bread is indescribably delicious, or I could use hyperbole. The best I can do with hyperbole is, "Spoonbread is sinfully delicious."

Anadama Bread

This is a yeast risen cornbread with much more flour than the usual cornbreads. I have seen at least a dozen different recipes for this bread. Although it is a yeast bread, it could be baked with baking powder if desired. I will show it both ways.

Yeast Anadama Bread

4½ cups unbleached flour
¾ cup yellow cornmeal
1 Tablespoon salt
½ teaspoon sugar
¼ cup molasses
1 package (1 Tablespoon) dry yeast
2 Tablespoons butter
1¼ cups water

Prove the yeast by dissolving in ¼ cup of warm water and adding the ½ teaspoon of sugar. Let it stand until it is frothy. Blend the cornmeal, flour and salt together. Add the yeast mixture and the other cup of warm water and then add the molasses and melted butter. Mix to a dough then turn onto a floured board and knead for about 10 minutes. Place the kneaded dough in a greased bowl and allow it to rise until doubled. Punch down the risen dough then divide into 2 parts and form round hearth loaves. Bake on a greased sheet at 400°F. for 45 minutes. Test with a thin knife and turn out onto a rack to cool.

Baking Powder Anadama Bread

4½ cups unbleached flour
¾ cup yellow cornmeal
1 Tablespoon salt
½ teaspoon sugar
¼ cup molasses
1 Tablespoon baking powder
2 Tablespoons butter
1¼ cups water

Combine the dry ingredients. Add the water, molasses and melted butter. Stir to a dough. Turn out onto a floured board and knead until springy. (10 minutes). Shape loaves immediately after kneading. Bake at 400°F. for 45 minutes. Test with a thin knife to make sure the breads are done. Cool on a rack.

Southern Crackling Bread

This is an interesting quick bread with a different and distinctive taste. It reminds me of Thanksgiving dinner when I stuff myself on a huge dish of turkey stuffing. The bread is delicious toasted and served with butter, but it is equally good served cold from a brown bag lunch or picnic hamper. Havilah Babcock, the author of many outdoor stories wrote a tale about a country doctor in North Carolina. This story appears in *I Don't Want to Shoot an Elephant*. In the story, the doctor says, "I never bite into a pone of Mary's cracklin' without feeling sorry for rich folks." Real Southern crackling bread is baked with pork cracklings, but this recipe calls for bacon. Don't use imitation bacon bits as a substitute. They will give the bread a bacon flavor, but they lose their crunch. If pork crackling is available, it can be used.

Crackling Bread

2 ounces of bacon, fried crisp
  Measure in a measuring cup
  after crumbling. Do not weigh
2 stalks of celery, finely chopped
1/2 cup grated or finely chopped
  raw onion
2 cups unbleached flour
2 teaspoons baking powder
2 Tablespoons bacon drippings
2/3 cup milk
2 eggs
a dash of salt and pepper

Put the bacon on to fry; while it is cooking, chop the celery and grate or chop the onion. Pour off part of the bacon drippings and reserve them for use later. After the bacon is crisp remove it from the skillet and drain it on paper towels. There will still be some bacon drippings in the frying pan. Fry the celery and the onion in the remaining fat until they are soft. This takes about five minutes.

Grease a small cast iron frying pan (6-7 inch) or a small loaf pan. Sift together the flour, salt, pepper and baking powder into a bowl. Add the drippings and rub them into the flour until the mixture looks like bread crumbs. Add the cooked celery, onions, and the crumpled bacon to the flour. Beat the 2 eggs and stir them into the milk. Add the egg-milk mixture to the flour. Stir until a dough is formed. Turn the dough out onto a lightly floured surface and knead for about 2 minutes. Shape the dough and place in the greased pan.

Bake at 375°F. for 1 hour. Check with a knife to be sure that the bread is done. The bread will be firm and can be cooled on a rack.

Other Spoon Breads

I like spoon bread. While this book was in preparation, I ran across some variations that sounded interesting. I tested and changed these recipes to my liking. I hope that you will like them too.

Zucchini Spoon Bread or Zucchini and Cheese Spoon Bread

1/2 pound zucchini squash
1 1/4 cups milk
2 Tablespoons butter
1 teaspoon salt
1 cup corn meal
1 teaspoon baking powder
6 eggs beaten
1/2 cup grated cheese, Swiss or
  Cheddar (optional)

Grate the zucchini. Dissolve the butter in the milk by warming the milk, then stir in the zucchini, salt, cornmeal, and baking powder. Cook the mixture, stirring constantly for about 3-4 minutes until it thickens. Add the cheese if you're making the cheese version. Cook until the cheese melts. Remove from the heat and let it cool for 5 minutes. Stir in the beaten eggs and then transfer the batter to a 2 quart casserole dish. Bake the Zucchini Spoon Bread at 375°F. for 45-50 minutes. Test with a knife blade in the center to make sure it is done. Serve hot.

Onion Spoon Bread

1 cup cornmeal
2 cups milk
3 eggs, beaten
1 cup half and half or canned milk
1 Tablespoon butter
1 1/4 teaspoons salt
1 teaspoon baking powder
4 Tablespoons powdered onion or
  onion flakes

Combine the milk and the cornmeal in a small pot and cook over low heat until you have a cornmeal mush. Remove from the heat and cool slightly, then add the beaten eggs, the half and half, the salt, baking powder and the onion. Mix well and pour the batter in a greased 2 quart casserole. Bake at 350°F. for 50-55 minutes. Test with a knife in the center. Serve hot.

Honey Wheat Bread

This is a nutty flavored wheat bread with the added taste of nature's honey that can reach the table about an hour after you decide to bake a bread.

1 Tablespoon honey
1¼ cups of very hot water
⅔ cup cold milk
2 cups unsifted stone ground wheat flour
2 cups unsifted unbleached flour
1 teaspoon baking powder

Dissolve the honey in the very hot water and then mix in the cold milk. Combining hot and cold will give you a mixture at the proper warm temperature. All of these steps can be done in the mixing bowl to save dishwashing. Add the flour 1 cup at a time to the liquid in the bowl. Use a wooden spoon or a whisk to mix. Mix quickly until you have a thick, runny batter of the right consistency to drop. Turn this batter into a greased loaf tin. A 9x5x3 inch tin is ideal. Smaller tins can be used, but if you do use 2 tins.

Bake at 400°F. for 15 minutes; reduce the temperature to 350°F. and bake an additional 20-30 minutes. Test with a knife. If the bread is done, turn out onto a wire rack to cool. Cool this bread upside down. It is best to bake this bread on a high oven rack like baking rolls. If the bread seems to be browning too quickly, cover it with wax paper or aluminum foil when you have the right shade of brown.

This honey wheat loaf has a tendency to crumble when sliced unless it is saved for the next day. To serve hot, tear off chunks.

Saint Patrick's Day Bread

This is a fine, moist bread that is good any day of the year. This bread is not Irish, but since it is a delicate green in color, it is an ideal dish to serve in honor of Saint Patrick.

2 cups flour
¾ cup buttermilk or yogurt
½ cup sugar
1 teaspoon salt
1 teaspoon baking soda
1 teaspoon baking powder
1 egg
¾ cup nuts (pecans, walnuts or almonds)
1 ripe avocado

Mash the avocado; beat the egg and add it to the avocado pulp. Mix in the buttermilk and chopped nuts. Sift the flour, soda and baking powder into the mixture, adding 1 cup of flour at a time. Stir the mixture lightly as each cup of flour is added. **Do not beat this batter; only stir lightly.** Pour the mixture into a greased loaf tin (8 x 4 inch). Bake at 350°F. for 1 hour. Test the loaf with a knife. If the bread is done, turn onto a wire rack to cool. this bread slices better if it is allowed to stand for 24 hours before serving.

Variations

If you do not have buttermilk, you can use ¾ cup whole milk with a teaspoon of vinegar or lemon juice added. The baking powder can be eliminated by using 1 teaspoon of baking soda. If this is done, add 4 teaspoons of vinegar to the milk. The vinegar milk mixture should be ¾ cup.

Applesauce Bread

This is a fine, moist bread, but not too sweet. I include it in the breads rather than the dessert breads because it uses only ¼ cup of sugar. This bread can be served with coffee if desired for the applesauce gives it a good flavor.

1 cup unsweetened applesauce
2 cups unbleached flour
1 teaspoon salt
¼ cup sugar or brown sugar
1 teaspoon baking powder
1 Tablespoon melted butter
1 Tablespoon warm water
1 beaten egg white
Poppy seeds if desired

Slightly warm the applesauce or use it at room temperature. Pour the melted butter into the applesauce and follow with the salt, sugar and baking powder. Stir in the flour until a dough is formed. Shape the dough into a round or a long cigar shaped loaf. Place the loaf on a greased baking sheet and then slash the loaf with a razor. Brush the egg white (or beaten whole egg) over the crust and sprinkle with poppy seeds.

Bake at 400°F. for 10 minutes then reduce temperature to 350°F. and bake an additional 50 minutes.

This bread can also be baked at 400°F. for 40-45 minutes without changing the temperature.

Test with a knife. If the loaf is done, cool on a rack.

Good Things without Yeast

Baking Powder Dessert Breads

Many dessert breads are baked without yeast; baking powder could be substituted for yeast in many of the traditional recipes, but even without making a substitution, we have many recipes available. Some of the dessert breads could well be called cakes; they are sweet, rich and most satisfying as a dessert.

Carrot Bread – Zucchini Bread – Tomato Bread

Bread made with vegetable pulp has a fine moist texture. With enough sweetener it can be made as sweet as any cake. The recipe below is an all purpose recipe to make 3 different breads.

1 ½ cups flour
1 cup sugar
1 teaspoon baking powder
¼ teaspoon salt
¾ cup vegetable oil or melted shortening
2 eggs
1 ½ cups grated raw carrots or zucchini or 1 ½ cups pulped tomato
1 teaspoon ground cinnamon
1 teaspoon baking soda
2 teaspoons lemon juice or vinegar

Beat the eggs and add the vegetable oil or melted shortening to the beaten eggs. Stir in flour, baking powder, baking soda, salt and cinnamon. Stir in the vegetable pulp. Now add the optional lemon juice or vinegar if you are planning to use it. Stir until mixed well. Pour the mixture into a greased 8 x 4 inch loaf pan. Be sure not to fill the pan more than half full. Allow the batter to rest in the pan for 30 minutes. Bake at 350°F. for 1 hour. Test with a knife to see if it is done and then turn out the bread onto a wire rack to cool.

Lemon juice or vinegar is added to more completely neutralize the baking soda. The vegetables have some acid, but carrots have less than tomato. Complete neutralization of the baking soda gives more carbon dioxide gas and should produce a better rise. Neutralization also removes the soda taste.

Dresden Apple Coffee Crumble

This is a dessert to match any fancy cake. Serve it for company and prepare yourself for either compliments or the question, "Where did you buy that divine cake?"

2 cups unbleached flour
3 teaspoons baking powder
½ teaspoon nutmeg
½ teaspoon cinnamon
¾ cup (packed) brown sugar
1 egg
1 small can evaporated milk or 1
   cup whole milk
½ cup (¼ pound) softened butter
   or margarine
2 cooking apples, peeled, cored
   and sliced
3 Tablespoons (heaping) yellow
   raisins
3 Tablespoons granulated sugar

Sift the flour and baking powder together into a large bowl. Stir the spices and brown sugar into the flour. Although I usually prefer pouring melted butter into the mixture, for this cake we have to crumb the butter into the flour. Take six Tablespoons of the softened butter or margarine and rub it into the flour with a fork until the mixture looks like crumbs. Take ½ cup of the mixture out of the bowl and reserve it for the topping.

The flour, spices, brown sugar and butter have now been combined. To the mixture left in the bowl first add the raisins mixing them in well to ensure even distribution. Beat the egg and add it to the milk; pour the liquid into the dry ingredients. If you wish to make a well in the center of the dry ingredients, you may but that is not necessary. Mix well until the liquid and dry ingredients are blended.

Spoon the batter into a greased, round, spring form pan 9 inches in diameter. Arrange the apple slices on top of the batter in the pan and then sprinkle the reserved crumb mixture over the apples, Two Tablespoons of butter were also reserved; dot the top of the cake with this butter and then sprinkle the granulated sugar over the topping. The cake is now ready to bake.

Bake at 350°F. for about 45 minutes. Test with a knife. If the knife come out clean it is ready to cool. Release the tube and bottom from the pan walls and allow the cake to cool. Serve from the pan bottom. **Do not try to turn this cake out of the pan or the apples will be disturbed.** If you bake in a regular pan, you will have to cool in the baking pan.

Note: most butter cubes and margarine cubes have a scale printed on the paper. This will make it easy to cut off the 6 Tablespoons needed to mix with the flour and leave the 2 Tablespoons for dotting the topping.

Sour Cream Bread

Hidden by a name that does not glorify it, this is a rich tasting dessert bread that is ideal to serve with coffee or tea. Similar breads have been called Sour Cream Coffee Cake. The sour cream enriches the loaf giving it an exquisite flavor. It is possible to substitute yogurt for the sour cream. This bread lends itself to a variety of toppings.

½ cup melted butter or margarine
⅔ cup sugar
3 eggs
2 cups flour
1 teaspoon baking powder
⅔ cup sour cream or yogurt
1 teaspoon vanilla extract
½ cup yellow raisins

Toppings:
Sugar and cinnamon:
½ cup (packed) brown sugar
1 teaspoon ground cinnamon
Nut topping:
½ cup (packed) brown sugar
¼ cup (1/8 pound) softened
   butter
1 Tablespoon flour
1 teaspoon cinnamon
½ cup chopped nuts (walnut,
   almond or pecan)
Streusel topping:
The same as the nut topping, but
   no nuts
Fruit and nut toppings. *Apples, apricots, or raisins can be used to top this cake. These can be mixed with chopped nuts, or whole walnut halves or pecan halves can be laid on top of the batter before baking.*

Melt the margarine or butter. While it is melting, beat the eggs. Mix the melted butter with the eggs and start to blend in the flour one cup at a time. Sift the baking powder in with the flour. After you have worked the flour into the liquid, fold in the sour cream, raisins and vanilla extract. Stir the mixture well and pour into a greased pan. The pan should be large enough that the batter plus the topping will about half fill it. Sprinkle the selected topping over the batter. Bake at 350°F. for 1 hour. Test with a knife and turn the cake out onto a rack to cool. If no topping is desired, the cake is delicious with none or dusted with a mixture of cinnamon and sugar after baking. The glazes mentioned in the chapter on shaping and glazes can also be used to finish this cake.

Honey Raisin Oatmeal Bread

Like a sourdough French bread, this bread uses neither eggs nor shortening.

2 cups all purpose unbleached
   flour
1 teaspoon baking powder
1 teaspoon baking soda
1 teaspoon salt
1 cup rolled oats
½ cup honey
2 Tablespoons molasses
1¼ cups buttermilk
1 teaspoon lemon juice or vinegar
1 cup raisins
½ cup chopped nuts

Sift the flour, baking powder, baking soda and salt into a mixing bowl. Stir in the oats. Add the molasses, honey and buttermilk and beat until the texture is smooth. Stir in the nuts and raisins. Pour the batter into a greased 9 x 5 loaf pan. Allow the batter to sit in the loaf pan for 30 minutes at room temperature; this will allow the rolled oats to absorb moisture and give the bread a better texture.. Bake at 350°F. for 1 hour. This bread is not as sweet as some of the coffee breads, but served warm with butter, it is delicious.

If I have a favorite recipe, it would be one that with variations can produce a multitude of good dishes. Like the yeast dough used for so many dessert dishes in a previous chapter, the coffee cake recipe that follows is as versatile as the drummer in a one man band.

Basic Coffee Cake

1½ cups all purpose flour
½ cup sugar
½ teaspoon salt
2 teaspoons baking powder
1 egg
⅔ cup whole milk
3 Tablespoons melted butter or
    margarine. Oil may be used
Streusel Topping:
¼ cup dry breadcrumbs
¼ cup flour
½-1 teaspoon cinnamon
2 Tablespoons granulated or
    brown sugar
2 Tablespoons of butter or
    margarine

Mix the flour, sugar, baking powder and salt together. They may be sifted if you desire, but it is not necessary. Beat the egg and add it to the milk and melted shortening. Add the liquids to the cake mixture and mix well. Pour the batter into a greased 9 inch square cake pan. A Streusel topping can be used to finish the cake. Bake at 425°F. for about 25 minutes. Test with a knife to see if the cake is done. Cool in the pan and serve from the pan.
Streusel Topping.
This is a different Streusel Topping than the one on page 121. Either may be used.

Cream the butter and sugar together. Add the flour, breadcrumbs and cinnamon. Mix to where the entire topping looks like breadcrumbs. Sprinkle this over the coffee cake before baking.

Variations on the Basic Coffee Cake

These variations are only in the finish. Use the same basic coffee cake dough. The cakes can be made either as conventional coffee cakes with the topping on top or some of them may be made as upside down cakes if you prefer.

Apple Coffee Cake

Make the basic dough and pour it into the pan. Cover the batter with a layer of thinly sliced apples. Sprinkle chopped nuts and brown sugar over the apples.

A richer topping may be made by beating 1 egg with ½ cup of milk or cream and pouring this over the apple topping before baking. Bake at 400°F. for about 40 minutes.

The apple coffee cake without the cream topping may be made as an upside down cake.

Sour Cream Topped Coffee Cake

Bake the basic coffee cake recipe without any topping. About 5 minutes before the cake is finished, remove it from the oven and spread sour cream over the top. The sour cream layer should be about ½ inch thick. Return the cake to the oven and finish baking it. The sour cream should set with 5 minutes baking. Refrigerate before serving.

Sour Cream Apple Coffee Cake

Top the basic coffee cake recipes with apples, nuts (optional) and brown sugar as described in the recipe for Apple Coffee Cake. Bake for about 35 minutes and then remove from the oven. Spread a layer of sour cream over the apple layer about ¼ inch thick. Return to the oven and bake for about 5 minutes longer to set the sour cream. Refrigerate before serving.

Nut Coffee Cake

Separate an egg and add about 1 teaspoon of water to the white. Beat this mixture enough to mix well and use it to glaze the top of the basic coffee cake before baking. This glaze will help hold the nuts in place. Sprinkle thickly with chopped walnuts, almonds or pecans. Bake at 425°F. for 25-30 minutes. Test.

Instead of using egg white, you may use a sugar glaze made by mixing 3 Tablespoons of sugar with 1 Tablespoon of water.

Dutch Apple Coffee Cake

Pour the batter into a shallow pan. A pair of pie pans are ideal. Brush the tops with melted butter and lay the apples slices in parallel lines. Sprinkle with brown sugar and cinnamon. Bake at 400°F. for about 35 minutes.

Prune, Plum or Currant Coffee Cake

Make the basic batter and pour into the pan. Arrange raw currants, canned plums, canned prunes, cooked plums or cooked prunes on top of the batter. Make sure that they are pitted first. Sprinkle cinnamon and sugar over the fruit. Bake at 400°F. for about 30 minutes.

Cherry Coffeecake or Cherry Upside-down Cake

Drain a can of cherries. For an upside down cake place the fruit in the baking pan first and add the batter. For a regular cake use the canned cherries or other canned fruit as a topping. Canned peaches, apricots, or berries make excellent toppings. Reserve all the juice to make jello.

The recipes that follow are similar to the basic coffee cake recipe but they are slightly different.

Fresh Peach Coffee Cake

1½ cups flour
½ teaspoon salt
1 egg
¼ cup sugar
3 Tablespoons butter
½ cup milk
2 teaspoons baking powder
Sliced fresh peaches
  Canned may be used

This cake uses less sugar in the batter.

Mix the flour, baking powder, sugar and salt together. Beat the egg and add it to the milk. Pour the liquid into the dry ingredients and mix together. Place the batter in a baking pan and cover with the sliced fresh peaches. Sprinkle flour and sugar over the peaches and dot the top with additional butter. Bake at 400°. for about 25 minutes. Test with a knife.

For a less sweet coffee cake, this variation with only ½ cup of sugar can be substituted for any of the recipes under basic coffee cake.

Spice Coffee Cake

To either the basic coffee cake recipe or to the less sweet recipe listed as Fresh Peach Coffee Cake, add ½ teaspoon powdered cloves, ½ teaspoon nutmeg and 1 teaspoon cinnamon. Mix the spices directly in with the flour before adding the liquid. If a darker cake is desired 2 Tablespoons of blackstrap molasses can be added with the liquid.

Ethnic Breads

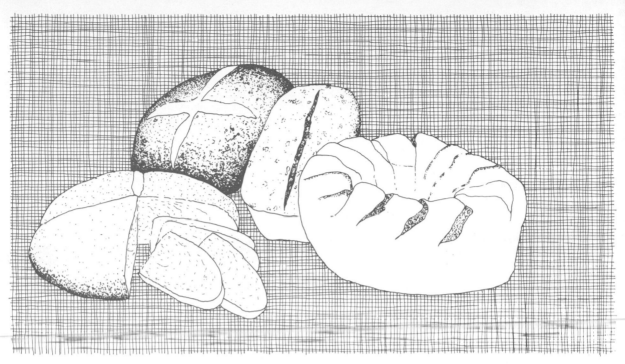

The recipes which appear in the previous chapters of this book are for basic breads, quick breads and desserts. Were we to stop at this point, we would be guilty of discrimination against some very fine breads. The loaves discussed in this section, for the most part, were once ethnic, but in this American Melting Pot, all of them have been naturalized. As the advertising agency claimed, "You don't have to be Jewish to love Levy's rye bread."

To present some type of order to the recipes, I have lumped all of those made with yeast as one group and those made with a sourdough starter as another. The first of our ethnic breads is the bagel. Called by vaudeville comedians, "A hard boiled Jewish doughnut, this is more a roll than a loaf of bread. Bagels are an acquired taste; eat one slathered with butter after toasting and you will have acquired the taste. The bagels you bake at home can be so much better tasting than the frozen atrocities you find in supermarket freezers. Better bagels are sold in bagel baker's establishments and at delicatessens. In my opinion, my bagels are better tasting than those I've purchased at the best bagel company here in Los Angeles. I'm not chauvinistic enough to argue with those who claim that New York City or even Chicago bagels are better than those baked in Los

Angeles. Such argument would be pointless. I'm here and the only bagels available to me are frozen New Yorkers, Los Angeles baked commercial bagels and those I bake myself. Mine cost less and taste better.

There are two main categories of bagels recognized by professional bagel bakers. They call them egg bagel and water bagel. The egg bagel you buy is yellow in color and has some dehydrated egg in the mix. The egg bagel you bake in your home is made from fresh eggs; it may be white or a light yellow in color as contrasted with the deep yellow color given to commercial bagels by dye. At home you do not use artificial coloring to give the impression of a rich egg dough; you use a rich egg dough. Water bagel can be made with either milk or water. Made with milk, they approach the delicacy of a good egg bagel. If you are a purist and wish to capture the hard texture of a delicatessen bagel, substitute water for milk in the recipe listed as Milk Bagel. To really capture the flavor of a bakery bagel, allow them to stale for 24 hours before you eat the bagel. If you are not so much a purist; if you desire ambrosia in the shape of a doughnut, follow the egg or milk bagel recipes exactly and eat the product hot from the oven with sweet butter or cream cheese. At the price of good belly lox, I will not recommend cream cheese and lox on a bagel.

Egg Bagels

Makes about 30 bagels. The recipe can be halved. This recipe for egg bagels produces the finest egg bagels I have ever eaten. The recipe calls for potato water, the water left over after boiling potatoes, but if you substitute tap water you will still produce a superlative bagel so consider the potato water optional. I prefer to bake bagels by the sponge method which uses less yeast. If you are in a real hurry, you can double the yeast and bake by the direct method. The addition of 50 milligrams of Vitamin C will speed up the sponge time to about ½ hour.

Sponge:
1 package (Tablespoon) dry yeast
½ teaspoon sugar
2 cups warm water or warm potato water
4 cups unbleached flour
50 milligrams Vitamin C. (optional)

Second Step:
l egg white
1 egg yolk, reserve for glaze
4 beaten eggs
1 Tablespoon salt
¼ cup oil
1 Tablespoon sugar
About 4 more cups of flour

Sponge. Prove the yeast in about 4 ounces of warm water or warm potato water containing the ½ teaspoon of sugar. In 10 minutes when the yeast becomes frothy, add the rest of the water and stir in 4 cups of flour and the Vitamin C if you are using it. Cover the bowl and allow to stand in a warm place until the sponge shows bubbles of gas. With Vitamin C this will take from ½ hour to 1 hour depending on the temperature. Without Vitamin C the sponge will take about 1½ hours. The warmer the spot where the bowl is kept, the quicker the sponge will be ready.

Second Step.

Add the sugar, salt and oil to the sponge after it has started to bubble. Stir in as much of the remaining 4 cups of flour as the sponge will take. This will be about 3½ cups. This dough is rather oily from the large amount of oil and eggs used. More flour can be forced into the dough by kneading in the bowl. When the dough pulls away from your hand, it is ready to be turned out onto a floured board and kneaded a little more. If you prefer, you can do the entire 10 minutes of kneading in the bowl. As you knead, more flour can be worked in if necessary, but so long as the dough does not stick to your hand, it has sufficient flour.

After kneading, grease a bowl and place the kneaded dough in the bowl. Cover the bowl with plastic wrap or a towel and let the dough stand in a warm place until it doubles. Before punching down give the risen dough the finger test by poking a hole into the dough with your finger. If the hole does not quickly fill in, the dough is ready to use.

When the dough seems almost ready, put a large pot on the stove. Fill the pot about half full of water and put 2 Tablespoons of sugar in the water. Turn the fire on under the pot. While waiting for the water to boil, punch down the dough and turn it out onto a floured board. Knead for a minute or so to pop any gas bubbles and then roll the dough out to a ¾ inch thickness with a rolling pin. Cut strips about 5 inches long. The strips should be a little wider than ¾ inch. Roll these between your palms to form a rope. On your measurements it is best to be generous for we don't want too narrow ropes formed. Curve each rope into a circle and pinch the ends together. The use of water or egg on the ends will make a better seal. As each ring is completed, place it on an ungreased baking sheet or on the bread board. Cover the rings and allow them to rise for 15 minutes.

The water should be boiling now. Drop the raw bagels into the

Baguettes

boiling water one at a time and let them cook in the boiling sugar-water until they rise to the surface. The bagel will grow in the boiling water for the heat expands the carbon dioxide gas trapped in the dough. This makes the boiled bagels float. When they come to the surface, turn them over and boil them for 3 minutes on the other side. Fish the bagels out of the pot with a slotted spoon and place them on paper towels or in a colander to drain. After all the bagels have been cooked and drained, place them on a greased baking sheet. Take the egg yolk you reserved when you made the sponge and beat it with a Tablespoon of water. Brush this egg yolk glaze over the surfaces of the bagel. It will give them that deep, beautiful brown color you expect on a bagel. If you wish to sprinkle poppy seeds or sesame seeds over the glaze, do so before putting the bagels into the oven.

Bake at 425°F. for 20-25 minutes or at 375°F. for about 30 minutes.

The bagel will have a deep brown color when done if the egg yolk glaze is brushed on thickly. About 5-8 minutes before the bagels are finished, check the bottoms. If they are browning more quickly than the top, turn the bagels over and then finish baking.

Variations

Any bread dough can be used to make bagels. The difference between a bagel and a roll is that it is boiled before it is baked. I've even made bagels from sourdough, thinking that it was an original idea at the time I first made them. I soon found out that the idea was not original when I picked up a new book on sourdough baking. Sourdough bagels take a little getting used to for they are not bagels in the traditional sense. They are chewy and tasty, so down with tradition. The recipe used to make all the desserts in the chapter of Good Things From Bread makes a fine bagel. This recipe uses canned milk and eggs.

Whole wheat bread dough can also be used to make bagels. Rye bagels and pumpernickel bagels are sold in most bagel shops. You can either make the dough from the recipes which appear in this chapter for rye or pumpernickel breads or take the egg bagel recipe and make substitutions.

For a rye bagel, substitute 3 cups of rye flour for 3 cups of white flour. Increase the salt to 2 Tablespoons. Decorate the bagel with caraway seeds instead of poppy seeds.

For a pumpernickel bagel, use the same recipe as for a rye bagel but substitute ¼ cup of blackstrap molasses for ¼ cup of the water. For a darker colored bagel add 1 teaspoon of instant coffee powder to the water.

An excellent egg bagel can be made from Challah dough. The advantages of using this dough is that you can bake a loaf of Challah with half the recipe and use the other half to make bagels. The Challah recipe (page 138) uses more shortening than the egg bagel recipe. This produces a very rich, tasty bagel.

Raisin Nut Bagels

This delightful bagel uses the egg bagel recipe as a base. To the regular recipe add 1 cup of chopped nuts and 2 cups of raisins. Grated lemon or orange peel (2 teaspoons) can also be added. The fruit and nuts should be mixed in after the sponge is ready for the second step.

Challah

Salt Bagels

These are regular bagels sprinkled with coarse or kosher salt before baking.

Spice Bagels

These are sweeter than the regular egg bagel so they call for more sugar. Use ¼ cup of sugar and add 2 teaspoons of cinnamon and 1 teaspoon of nutmeg. Raisins and nuts can also be added if desired.

This raisin spice dough can be used to make rolls by eliminating the boiling or will make a delicious doughnut if an additional ¼ cup of sugar (making ½ cup for doughnuts) is added. For Raisin Spice doughnuts form them into rings as you would for bagels then let them rise. Baked doughnuts are baked on a greased baking sheet for 20-25 minutes at 425°F. Finish with powdered sugar or a sugar glaze or cinnamon sugar. See doughnuts on page 87.

For fried doughnuts, after the dough has risen fry the rings in hot oil at 360°F. For more details on procedure and finishing see the section on doughnuts on page 87.

Milk (Water) Bagels

The recipe makes about 18 bagels. The recipe may be doubled. When made with milk, these bagels are as good as the egg bagels.

Sponge:
1 teaspoon (½ package) dry yeast
2 cups flour
1 cup milk (or water)
½ teaspoon sugar
The Second Step:
about 2 cups of flour
1 egg white
1 egg yolk (reserve for glaze)
1 teaspoon salt
1½ Tablespoons sugar
¼ cup (half a cube) melted butter or margarine oil may be used

Sponge:
Warm the milk to tepid; add the yeast and ½ teaspoon of sugar. After the yeast becomes frothy, add 2 cups of flour to the warm milk, mix well and allow to stand in a covered bowl for about 1 -1½ hours or until the mixture looks well filled with bubbles.

Second Step: Separate the egg adding the white to the sponge and reserving the yolk. Melt the butter and pour it into the sponge followed by the salt and the sugar. Stir in some of the remaining 2 cups of flour until a stiff dough is formed. Turn the dough out onto a floured board and knead to smoothness adding more flour as required. The kneading will take about 10 minutes.

Shape the bagels into rings; see previous recipe for Egg Bagels. Allow the rings to rise for 15-20 minutes, then drop them into a pot of boiling water with 2 Tablespoons of sugar added. Cook until the rings rise to the surface and then turn with a slotted spoon. Cook an additional 3 minutes on the other side. Remove the bagel and drain on paper towels or in a colander. Transfer them to a greased baking sheet. Glaze the bagel with egg yolk; beat the egg yolk you reserved with 1 Tablespoon of water and brush it over the exposed surfaces with a pastry brush. Seeds or salt can be sprinkled on after the glaze.

Bake at: 425°F. for about 20 minutes or at 375°F. for 30 minutes.

Raisin Spice Bread

This bread is derived from the recipe for Egg Bagels. It is a good tasting bread with a rich crumb. It is more of a party bread than one for every day meals.

Sponge:

1 package (1 Tablespoon) dry yeast
½ teaspoon sugar
2 cups warm water
4 cups unbleached flour

The Second Step:

4 beaten eggs
1 egg white
1 egg yolk, (reserve for glaze)
¼ cup oil
¼ cup sugar
2 teaspoons cinnamon
1 teaspoon nutmeg
1 cup chopped nuts
2 cups raisins
2 Tablespoons grated orange peel
about 4 cups flour

Milk and Sugar Glaze:

¼ cup sugar
3 Tablespoons milk

Orange Glaze:

confectioner's sugar
orange juice

Sponge. Put about 4 ounces of the water in a mixing bowl and add the yeast and the sugar. Allow this to stand in a warm place until the yeast becomes frothy. Mix in the rest of the warm water and the flour. Cover the bowl and let it stand in a warm place for about an hour for the sponge to form.

Second Step. Add the oil, salt, sugar and spices to the sponge. Stir in the raisins and nuts followed by the beaten eggs and the extra egg white. This bread may be kneaded in the bowl or turned out to be kneaded. Start working in the 4 cups of flour. When the dough no longer sticks to your hands, stop the flour but continue to knead until the dough is firm. Transfer the kneaded dough to a greased bowl and cover the bowl. Allow the dough to rise until doubled or more. Poke a finger into the dough to see if the rising has stopped. If the hole does not close quickly, the bread is ready to be shaped.

Punch down the dough and knead it again for about 1 minute to pop gas bubbles. Remove the dough from the bowl and shape it into two loaves. This bread can be made either as a bubble loaf, a pan loaf, or a hearth loaf. Baking in a ring mold produces a festive bread for a party. If desired, this bread can be made as a Monkey Bread. If two loaves are too many, use part of the dough for bagels, rolls, or even to make dessert rolls.

After shaping, you can glaze the tops of the breads. There was an egg yolk reserved. This can be brushed on and seeds sprinkled over the bread if wanted. If a sweeter dessert bread is desired, bake without a finish. After the bread is removed from the oven brush it with a milk and sugar glaze.

Milk Sugar Glaze. Place the sugar and milk in a small pan and dissolve the sugar under low heat. Bring the liquid in the pan to a boil and boil for 2 minutes. Brush this over the bread.

Orange Glaze. Mix confectioner's sugar and orange juice. Spoon over the bread.

English Cottage Loaf

When made from this recipe, this is a typical English bread with more flour per cup of liquid than the basic breads in the earlier part of this book. This altered flour to water ratio results in a chewy, solid loaf that is a pleasant change of pace. This bread contains no shortening. The shaping of this loaf is also typical English, but any bread can be baked in this form if desired.

Sponge:
2 cups flour
1 cup warm water
½ package (1 teaspoon) dry yeast
½ teaspoon sugar
The Second Step:
1½ teaspoons of salt
2 cups flour

Sponge. Place 4 ounces of the warm water in a mixing bowl and add the yeast and sugar. Allow this to stand in a warm place for about 10 minutes. When the yeast becomes frothy, pour in the rest of the warm water and stir in the 2 cups of flour. Cover the bowl and allow it to stand in a warm place for 1-1½ hours.

The Second Step. Work in the other 2 cups of flour. It is best to stir in the first cup then put part of the other cup on the bread board and scrape the sponge out onto the flour. Start kneading and work in as much of the second cup as you can. Should the dough remain sticky, a small amount of additional flour can be used. Knead about 10 minutes. When the dough is firm and springy, it is ready to rise. Place the kneaded dough in a greased bowl. Cover the bowl and allow it to rise until double. Punch down the risen dough and knead again for 1 minute.

This recipe will make one cottage loaf. Cut off about ⅓ of the dough. You now have 2 pieces. Roll both pieces into balls. **Flatten the top and the bottom of the larger piece but flatten only the bottom of the smaller.** If balls are not flattened, I guarantee that the top ball will slip. Place the small ball on top of the larger ball and center it. Flour your forefinger and push a hole through the center of both balls to tie them together. Place the loaf on a greased baking sheet.

Bake at 450°F. for 30 minutes, then turn down the heat to 375°F. and bake for 20 minutes longer. Tap the loaf; if it sounds hollow, test with a knife. If done, cool on a wire rack.

This loaf is usually baked without a finished top, but the top can be buttered, brushed with milk, or with an egg glaze. It can even be treated with water spray to make a crunchier crust. Warning, this loaf takes practice for the top ball has a tendency to slip. This recipe can also be used to bake regular hearth loaves if you prefer.

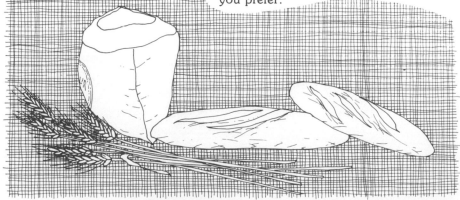

European Peasant Bread (Maslin Bread)

This is a bread baked from mixed whole grain flours. It is called Maslin Bread in England. Several hundred years ago, this was the bread of the common man. Today, it is a health food bread, particularly if the sugar is replaced with honey. In England, they also call this bread granary bread because it is baked from a pre-mixed flour sold as granary flour.

Maslin is a European bread with a high flour to water ratio. For those of you who like your peasant bread dark in color, substitute blackstrap molasses for the sugar. Additional darkening of the color is possible. Add 1 heaping teaspoon of instant coffee powder or of "Postum"® to the water. These additives will not change the flavor of the bread.

Sponge:
1 cup stoneground whole wheat
  flour
l cup rye flour or rye meal
½ package (1 teaspoon) dry yeast
½ teaspoon sugar
1 cup warm water

The Second Step:
about 1 cup rye flour or rye meal
about 1 cup stone ground wheat
  flour
about 1 Tablespoon melted
  shortening or oil

Sponge. Place ½ cup of warm water in a mixing bowl and add the teaspoon of yeast and the ½ teaspoon of sugar. Allow the yeast to prove until it is frothy. Add the other ½ cup of warm water and then mix in 1 cup of whole wheat followed by 1 cup of rye flour. Cover the bowl and allow it to stand in a warm place for 1-1½ hours. When the sponge is ready, it will be filled with bubbles.

The Second Step. Add the shortening and then work in the cup of rye flour. Turn the sponge out onto a board floured with part of the wheat flour and then knead while working in the rest of the wheat flour. Knead about 10 minutes to get a firm, springy dough. Place the kneaded dough in a greased bowl and cover with plastic wrap. Allow the dough to rise for 1 hour then punch down and knead again for 1 minute. Shape the bread into a long or round hearth loaf. Prick the top in several places or slash with a razor blade. Bake the bread without a finish at 400°F. for about 40-45 minutes.

German Beer Bread

This bread is usually baked by the direct method without going through the sponge step. The flour to liquid ratio is lower than the English breads resulting in a rather moist dough. The original recipe came from Munchen and calls for rye meal which is very difficult to find in the United States. Although rye meal is hard to find, it is possible to make your own easily. Whole rye flakes which are used to make an oatmeal like cereal can be purchased at many health food stores. These are made by rolling whole rye kernels under pressure. They contain the rye germ and the rye bran. To convert them to a coarse rye flour, rye meal, place some of the flakes in your blender and blend at a low spead. If you want finer rye, the same flakes can be blended at a higher speed. The coarser flour will give your bread a more authentic peasant texture. I use a medium coarse rye flour which is available, but if you can find the meal, by all means use it.

1½ cups stone ground whole wheat flour
1½ cups rye meal or rye flour
1 package (1 Tablespoon) dry yeast
1 cup dark beer. (Light may be used)
1 Tablespoon salt
1 Tablespoon honey, brown sugar, or molasses

Allow the beer to come to room temperature; flat beer may be used. Mix the yeast and a teaspoon of sweetener into the beer and allow it to stand in a warm place until it becomes frothy. After the yeast has been proved, mix the liquid and dry ingredients together to form a stiff dough. If necessary. more beer or more flour can be added. Knead the dough for about 10 minutes on a floured board. The dough will be rather sticky. DO NOT FORCE TOO MUCH EXTRA FLOUR INTO THE DOUGH. You may dust the outside with enough flour to prevent the dough from sticking to your fingers, but restrain yourself. We want a dough that is sticky on the inside.

Place the kneaded dough into a greased bowl and cover. Allow it to rise for about two hours. A long rise is indicated with a mixed grain dough. Punch down the dough and knead again for about 1 minute or so until the dough is smooth. Shape the dough into a single long or round hearth loaf. Lay the loaf on a greased baking sheet and slash the top of the bread with a razor blade in at least 3 places. Allow the shaped loaf to rise for 20 minutes then bake at 425°F. for 10 minutes. Reduce the heat to 375°F. and bake for another 30 minutes. Test with a knife and turn the finished loaf out onto a wire rack to cool.

If you prefer a pan loaf, this bread can be baked in a 9 x 5 pan. Grease the pan before filling with dough. The top of the loaf can be finished by brushing with water or egg before baking. In Germany, this loaf is frequently sprinkled with either fine oatmeal, coarsely crushed wheat grains or sesame seed. If you wish to follow their practice, brush the top with egg white or whole egg wash before sprinkling the seed or grain.

Beer Bread Variations

Substitute ½ cup of cornmeal, hominy grits or buckwheat grits for ½ cup of the rye flour. The use of these substitutes will give the bread a coarser texture more like a bread baked with rye meal.

Substitute 1½ cups of buckwheat flour for the entire amount of rye flour. Buckwheat flour will give the bread a most interesting taste.

Welsh Barley Bread

Wheat is now the most commonly used flour for bread making, but at one time, particularly in Scotland, Ireland and Wales, barley was used to make bread. Barley flour is found in many health food stores. The bread will be rather heavy and will not rise well for barley flour does not have much gluten. It is a novel bread and makes a good conversation piece when served at a party, for it has an entirely different taste. The recipe is a direct recipe, but if you wish to use the sponge method, decrease the yeast by one half and allow 2 cups of flour to incubate with the yeast and all of the liquid plus ½ teaspoon of sugar for 1-1½ hours before adding the rest of the ingredients.

4 cups barley flour
1 teaspoon sugar
1 package (1 Tablespoon) dry
   yeast
1 Tablespoon salt
1 cup warm water

Put the yeast in a mixing bowl and add the teaspoon of sugar. Allow the yeast and water to stand for about 10 minutes. When the yeast is frothy, add the remaining warm water, the flour, and salt. Mix to a dough with a wooden spoon. It is not necessary to knead this bread for barley flour does not have much gluten. Be sure that the dough is well mixed and all the ingredients are thoroughly blended.

Put the dough in a greased bowl and allow it to rise for about an hour. The dough will not double, but it will rise. Punch down the dough and knead again for about 1 minute. Bake the bread in a round pan. An 8 inch cast iron skillet or a cake pan will work well. Grease the pan and sprinkle the bottom with cornmeal. Bake at 400°F. for about 25 minutes. Test the bread with a knife. If the bread is done, turn it out onto a wire rack to cool. The Welsh name for this bread is Haidd.

Yeast Pumpernickel

Pumpernickel breads are eaten all over Middle Europe. The Scandanavians, the Germans, the Austrians, the Poles, the Russians, the Hungarians and the Rumanians all eat a form of pumpernickel bread. My list though long, has left off several countries that also enjoy this heavy dark bread. The omission is not intended to slight anyone. I only listed as many countries as I did because I cannot pinpoint the ethnic origin of a truly great bread.

There are many breads called pumpernickel. Each country has its own version. The most famous of these breads is the sourdough pumpernickel, but this bread made with yeast is also an excellent black bread. In Europe they bake this loaf with rye meal which is a coarser ground rye flour. Rye meal may be made by chopping whole rye flakes in a blender at low speed. Rye flakes are available in most health food stores.

Pumpernickel (Yeast Version)

Sponge:

*1 package (1 Tablespoon) active
    dry yeast*
2 cups rye flour or rye meal
½ cup blackstrap molasses
*1 teaspoon instant coffee powder
    or "Postum® "*
2 cups hot tap water
2 cups unbleached flour
The Second Step:
1 Tablespoon salt
1 cup rye flour or rye meal
1-2 cups unbleached white flour
1 Tablespoon oil

Sponge. Pour ½ cup of the hot tap water into a mixing bowl and stir in 1 Tablespoon of the molasses. Add the yeast and allow the mixture to sit in a warm place for about 10 minutes or until the yeast is frothy. Using the rest of the warm water, wash the remainder of the molasses into the bowl. Add the teaspoon of instant coffee powder to the liquid and then stir in the 2 cups of rye flour or rye meal and follow that with the 2 cups of unbleached white flour. Cover the bowl with a towel or plastic wrap and allow it to stand in a warm place for at least 2 hours for a sponge to form.

The Second Step. Sprinkle the salt over the sponge and add the oil. Stir down the sponge and start working in the rye flour. When that is stirred in start adding the unbleached flour until a dough is formed. Turn out the dough onto a floured board and knead, adding more flour as necessary. The dough should be firm and springy, but damp on the inside. Shape into loaves. If you wish a pan bread, bake in a 9 x 5 pan. Pumpernickel can be baked as a long hearth loaf, but I prefer the round hearth shape. My preference is based on nostalgia. When I was a youngster, we always bought pumpernickel as a round hearth loaf. Slash the tops with a razor blade and allow the loaves to rise for about 15 minutes before baking.

To get a nice professional, shiny looking glaze, brush the top with egg white. Caraway seeds can be sprinkled onto the loaf. I sometimes use poppy seed or sesame seeds. Bake the bread at 400°F. for 45 minutes. Test with a knife and cool on a wire rack.

Ukrainian Rye Bread

The Ukraine is the bread basket of Russia. This is an unusual recipe because it uses all rye flour. Few breads are baked with 100% rye flour because rye is not rich in gluten. Rye is not completely deficient in gluten, but this bread will be more dense than one baked with wheat and rye flours mixed. To compensate for this lack of rising ability requires a special two step rise. Follow this recipe exactly except for the ingredient marked optional. I added the use of Vitamin C to this bread because I want the yeast to grow more quickly. This bread needs all the push it can get.

Sponge

50-100 milligrams of Vitamin C (optional)

3 cups rye flour or rye meal

1¼ cups of hot water

1 package (1 Tablespoon) dry yeast

¾ cup warm water

2 Tablespoons sugar

The Second Step:

5 cups rye flour or 3 cups rye flour and 2 cups rye meal

1 Tablespoon salt

3 Tablespoon oil or melted butter

Sponge. Put the yeast in a small bowl and add the ¾ cup of warm water, the 2 Tablespoons of sugar and a crushed Vitamin C tablet. While the yeast is proving take a large mixing bowl and pour the very hot, but not boiling, water into the bowl. Beat in the 3 cups of rye flour to form a smooth paste. Cover the bowl with the paste and let it cool. While the paste is cooling, put the ¾ cup of milk in a small pan and heat to boiling. Let the milk cool to warm and then add it to the flour paste. Allow the rye paste and milk mixture to sit for another half hour before adding the yeast and water mixture to the paste. You have now set up your sponge. Allow the sponge to sit, covered for 1 hour.

The Second Step. Add the salt and the oil to the sponge and then work in as much of the 5 cups of flour as you can. When a dough has been formed, turn the sponge out onto a board and knead while working in more flour.

After kneading about 10 minutes, the dough will be firm and springy. Place the kneaded dough in a greased bowl and cover it. Let the bowl stand in a warm place until it has doubled. Since temperature is critical, place the dough in the oven with a pan of boiling water at the bottom of the oven. It will double more quickly in a draft free spot.

Punch down the dough and then put it back in the greased bowl. *Let it rise again* for 1 hour. Punch down the dough for the second time and shape it into 2 pan loaves. Place each loaf in a greased 9 x 5 pan. Put the pans with the dough back in the oven and replace the hot water. Let the loaves rise again until they almost reach the top of the pan. When they reach that point, bake them at 425°F for 45 minutes. Test with a knife and cool the bread on a wire rack after turning the loaves out of the pan.

The lack of gluten in rye flour made the extra rise necessary. Pan loaves are supported by the walls of the pan. Even with this help the bread will be dense and heavy. If you must try a hearth loaf with this recipe, expect it to be even heavier than the pan loaf. For hearth loaves, allow the shaped loaf to rise for only 10 minutes before baking.

Egg Breads

The Queen of all breads is the egg bread. Many cultures have developed noteworthy egg breads. Adding eggs to flour and water enhances the dough beyond description. The first of these super breads is the Challah, a bread of Jewish origin. It was considered so special that a Challah was always served on Friday evening to welcome the Sabbath. If you purchase your Challah at a bakery, it will be a deep yellow; bakers use artificial colors. When baked at home the Challah can vary from a pale yellow to almost white, but that is not the only way it differs from the commercial bread. The taste and the texture are so good that when I was a boy, I thought my aunt's Challah was as good as cake. The recipe here is based on her recipe and contains a little more sugar and more egg than many other recipes. Many books show Challah as being made with milk. That is not the traditional recipe for a bread made with milk could not be eaten with meat by anyone who observed the Jewish dietary laws.

Jewish Challah

Sponge:
1 Tablespoon (1package) dry
   yeast.
2 cups flour.
2 cups hot water.
1 Tablespoon sugar.
The Second Step:
4 Tablespoons sugar.
5 cups unbleached flour.
1 egg white.
1 egg yolk. (reserve for glaze.)
½ cup vegetable oil or melted
   vegetable shortening.
1 Tablespoon salt.
4 beaten eggs.

Sponge. Prove the yeast in about 4 ounces of the hot water mixed with the Tablespoon of sugar. When the yeast is frothy, add the rest of the hot water and the 2 cups of flour. Mix them together, cover the bowl and let it stand in a warm place for 1 -1½ hours. When the sponge is ready it will be filled with bubbles.

Second Step. When making a Challah only vegetable shortening should be used to conform with the dietary regulation of not mixing milk with meat. When made with water and vegetable shortening, the Challah can be served with any dish.

Add the oil and beaten eggs to the sponge then add the sugar and salt and the extra egg white. Beat in the flour 1 cup at a time until a dough is formed. This bread can be kneaded in the bowl for it is rich in oil and eggs. Do not force flour in. Add flour until the dough no longer sticks to your hands. Knead until the dough is firm and springy despite its oily feel.

Place the kneaded dough in a grased bowl and allow it to rise. Challah should better than double so it is important to check the rise by the finger test. Poke an unfloured finger into the dough and see if the hole fills quickly. When it doesn't, the dough has risen enough. Punch down the dough and knead again for about a minute to pop any gas bubbles.

Challah is usually braided, but you can make any shape bread you desire. It is delicious as a pan or a hearth loaf. I particularly like this dough to make crescent rolls.

To make a braided loaf, you first have to decide if you want 1 large or 2 small loaves. For small loaves, divide the dough into 2 portions and then divide each portion into 3 pieces. Form each piece into a rope about 1 inch thick by rolling the dough between your palms or by stretching it out and rolling it. This dough stretches very well and that is the quickest way to form ropes. To make a braided loaf, take 3 of the ropes and cross them at the center of each rope. Start from the middle and braid toward each end. Turn the board and braid the other half loaf. See the section on shaping breads for illustrations.

To make a larger loaf, form ropes that are about 2 inches in diameter or work with six strands instead of three.

Challah is always glazed with egg yolk. Beat the yolk you reserved with a Tablespoon of water and brush it over the exposed surfaces of the bread. Sprinkle poppy seeds over the glaze. After shaping, allow the loaves to stand for about 20 minutes then bake at 350°F. for about 40 minutes for the smaller loaves. The larger ones will take about 50 minutes, but check all loaves about 10 minutes early to make sure the bottom crust is not getting too well done. Test with a knife and cool on a wire rack.

Variations

If you are not following the Jewish dietary laws, 1½ cups of milk (warmed) can be used to replace 1½ cups of the water in making this bread.

Until I typed this recipe for the book, I used a secret ingredient that added much to the flavor. It is not traditional, but it does taste good. My secret, but no longer a secret, is to add 1 teaspoon of vanilla extract to the bread when I add the oil and eggs.

If you want a really rich egg bread, you can modify this recipe by increasing the oil. Use ¾ cup or even 1 cup of oil instead of the ½ cup I called for in the recipe. I prefer to use less, for more oil means more calories. For a special oc-casion you may decide to forget the caloric content and make the bread much richer. You can also increase the sugar content, but do not use more than ¾ cup of sugar.

Since the Challah dough is a great dough, you can play all sorts of games with it. It can be used for rolls, bagels and if you increase the sugar can be used to make desserts. One trick I use occasionally is to roll the dough out and brush it with melted butter. I sprinkle cinnamon over the butter and then roll up the rectangle. Once I have a cylinder formed, I cut pieces of this and use these pieces to form ropes and make a braided, cinnamon Challah. I have also added raisins to the dough for a delightful raisin bread.

Brioche Français

Another renowned egg bread is French in origin; it is called brioche. If you read some bread books, the brioche is a complicated affair to make. They spend much time talking about fancy shapes. I like brioche, but I don't like fussing, so I usually just bake it in a loaf tin. "A rose is a rose is a rose," the poet said. That applies to my brioche. It may look plain, but it tastes fancy. The results are heavenly even if the shape is plebian.

Brioche dough will keep for several days in the refrigerator if you want to ration yourself to just a few muffins at a time. I usually prefer to make a large loaf and freeze part of it. Most recipes call for an overnight refrigeration of the dough before you shape the bread. I'm surprised that those recipes don't suggest that a brioche be baked only when the moon if full. You can make an excellent brioche without bothering to refrigerate the dough. When baking brioche, I don't use the sponge method, but if you would prefer to set up a sponge, just use half the yeast called for in the recipe. Mix 3 cups of flour with the yeast and all of the liquid. Add ½ teaspoon of sugar and let your sponge sit about 1½ hours before adding the rest of the ingredients.

1 teaspoon salt
¼ cup honey or sugar
2 packages (2 Tablespoons) dry yeast
½ cup of hot water
½ cup skim milk powder (optional)
1 cup oil
4 whole eggs
1 egg white
1 egg yolk (reserve for glaze)
5 cups unbleached flour

Brioche Français

In a large bowl, mix the yeast with the hot water and about 1 teaspoon of honey or sugar to prove. When the yeast becomes frothy, mix in the milk powder if you are using it and add the sugar or honey. Beat the eggs and add them to the mix. Do not forget the extra egg white. Start to add the flour. Stir it in 1 cup at a time. When a dough begins to form add more flour until the dough is stiff. KNEAD THE BRIOCHE IN THE BOWL. With all the eggs and oil in this dough, it is rather oily. Do not flour your hands. Knead until the dough no longer sticks to your fingers. At that point stop adding flour but continue to knead until the dough looks wrinkled. Total kneading time is about 10 minutes.

Leave the dough in the mixing bowl, do not grease the bowl. Cover it and allow it to stand in a warm place. In about 1½ hours, the dough should be more than doubled. Test with a finger. The hole should not fill in. Punch down the dough and knead again, in the bowl, for about 1 minute.

Shape the dough and place it in a greased pan. Some sources say that greasing is not necessary, but I prefer not to take a chance. Allow the dough to rise in the pan for about 20 minutes. While the dough is resting in the pan, beat the reserved egg yolk with 1 Tablespoon of water and brush on the glaze to the exposed surfaces of the brioche.

Bake at 350°F. Muffin sized brioches (petites brioches): 20-25 minutes bread sized brioches: 30-40 minutes. Test with a knife and cool on a wire rack.

Shaping Brioche Dough

Brioche can be baked in any pan with fairly high sides. The dough is fairly soft and can almost be used like a batter bread. Just be sure to fill the pan no more than half full and the brioche will pop out of the pan for a brioche rises exceptionally well. If you use a mold or a scalloped pan, you will get a fancy looking brioche. Special shapes known as Petites Brioches are nothing but muffins baked in a fluted muffin tin with a top knot added. Consult almost any other bread book to get this and the other fancy shapes. I'm more interested in content and taste than in shape. Just in passing, a brioche baked in an ordinary bread pan still looks like something out of a fancy bakery.

Variations

Brioche Americain Substitute 1 cup of yellow cornmeal for 1 cup of flour.
Fortified Brioche Substitute 1 cup of wheat germ for 1 cup of flour.
Brioche Au Fromage Mix 2 cups of diced or grated Swiss cheese into the recipe and bake.

Brioche dough can be used for tarts or to cover a Beef Wellington. I particularly like a poppy seed filled tart for the brioche dough is more like a cookie dough in its richness.

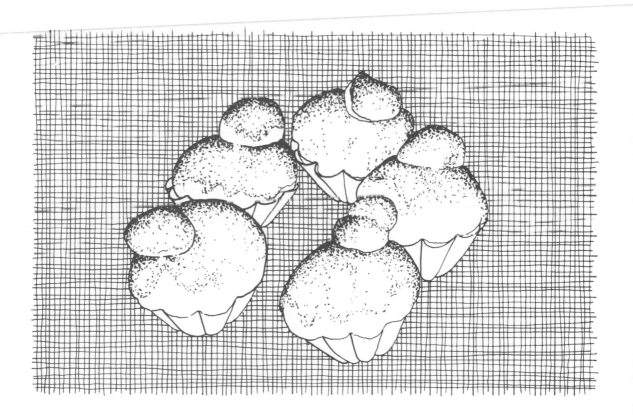

French Bread I

Brioche is not the only bread that emigrated from France to America. The bread we usually call French bread is a yeast bread baked with white flour. Most of these breads have no shortening, but the recipe which follows, French Bread II, is made with shortening. French bread is famous for its crust; to increase the amount of crust, the French bake long, thin loaves they call baguettes. This type of bread stales quickly; in France it is customary to go to the bakery and get fresh bread for every meal. Unlike American cities, bakeries are found on almost every block in Paris. If French bread is stored in a sealed plastic bag, it will stay soft longer than one left open to the air, but the crust may become soggy. The best way to keep this bread fresh is to freeze what is not eaten. If you freeze in aluminum foil, you can put the entire package in the oven to warm the bread. Do not confuse French bread with Sourdough French bread. The taste is entirely different. This recipe is for the direct method. A sponge can be set up if desired.

French Bread (Direct Method)

1 package (1 Tablespoon) dry
yeast
¾ cup warm water
2½ cups unbleached flour
1 teaspoon sugar
1 teaspoon salt

Dissolve the yeast in about 4 ounces of the water and add the sugar. Allow the yeast to stand until it becomes frothy. Place the flour in a mixing bowl and when the yeast is ready pour the yeast solution and the other 2 cups of warm water over the flour. Mix well and knead to a smooth dough adding more flour or more water if necessary. Knead until the dough is springy, about 10 minutes.

Place the kneaded dough in a greased bowl and allow it to double. The rise will take about 1½ hours. Punch down the dough and knead again for 1 minute. Shape the dough into 2 cigar shaped loaves on a floured board. See the next recipe, French Bread II for the proper way to shape the loaves. The shaped loaves should be about 15 inches long and 2 inches wide. Allow them to rise on a greased baking sheet for 15 minutes. At the end of this time take a single edged razor blade and make 3 long, diagonal slashes across the top of the bread. Bake at 475°F. for about 25 minutes. When done the bread will be golden brown. Test with a knife and cool on a wire rack near an open window or under a fan.

For a crustier crust open the oven every 5 minutes and brush or spray the loaves with salt water (1 teaspoon to a cup of tap water). A shallow pan filled with boiling water at the bottom of the oven can also be used to increase the crispness of the crust. The steam produced will harden the crust.

If you have trouble getting the crust crusty enough try letting the loaves remain in the oven for 15 minutes after you turn off the gas. Remove and cool after this period. For those of us that do not have steam injected ovens, this may be the best way to make a real French crust.

The loaves in the recipe are 2 inches wide before baking. They will produce the normal sized French bread. If smaller loaves are shaped, you will have baguettes. Make the loaves only 1 inch wide to get more crust per loaf.

An old European recipe for this bread suggests that 2 Tablespoons of whole wheat flour be mixed in with the white flour in baking this bread.

French Bread II

France is a large country. Unlike the United States where most bread is bought from the grocer, France gives employment to many bakers. Boulangeries are found everywhere you look, for in France, bread is purchased fresh for every meal. Once there was a saying, "Fifty million Frenchmen can't be wrong." I'd like to paraphrase that to, "Fifty thousand French bakers each has his own idea of how to bake a French bread."

Since there are uncounted recipes for the French bread and since this is not a book devoted only to that particular bread, I have limited my selection to two recipes. This one is from France and is entirely different in how the dough is made and handled. It even uses shortening, but it produces a fine crisp loaf of bread. This bread calls for a sponge. I usually make a sponge containing only flour, sugar and liquid, but since this is an ethnic recipe I've given it the way I found it. This sponge includes salt and oil. I prefer to add these later for salt inhibits the growth of yeast. If you do it my way, add the salt and oil the next morning before you add the other ingredients.

French Bread II

Sponge:
4 Tablespoons warm water
1 Tablespoon milk
½ teaspoon dry yeast
½ teaspoon vegetable oil
½ teaspoon sugar
1 teaspoon salt
½ cup unbleached flour
The Next Morning:
½ cup milk (room temperature)
1 cup warm water
1½ Tablespoons vegetable oil
1½ teaspoons dry yeast
1½ teaspoons sugar
4½-4¾ cups unbleached flour
2½ teaspoons salt
1 egg white

Sponge. Mix the yeast with the water and sugar and allow it to sit until it becomes frothy. Add milk at room temperature followed by the salt and oil. Lastly, place ½ cup of flour in a bowl and pour the liquid ingredients into the flour. Mix well, cover the bowl and allow it to sit in a warm place overnight.

The Next Morning. Combine the ½ cup milk with the cup of warm water and add the oil. Combine this with the sugar and 1½ teaspoons of dry yeast. Allow the mixture to stand until the yeast is frothy. Place the dry ingredients in a mixing bowl, Pour the liquid with the yeast into a well in the flour and then add the sponge prepared the previous evening. Stir well to form a soft dough. *Do not knead this dough.* Transfer this soft, unkneaded dough to a greased bowl and cover the bowl. Allow this to stand until the dough doubles in size. This takes about 1 hour in a warm place. *Do not punch down! Do not knead!* Turn the risen dough onto a lightly floured board and divide it into 2 equal portions. With a rolling pin, roll out each portion to form a rectangle about 15 inches long and 10 inches wide. Start on the long side of the dough, away from yourself and roll this dough up tightly. Roll toward yourself, pinching the edges as you roll. When you finish, you will have a cylinder about 15 inches long. Place one hand on each end and roll gently back and forth until the ends are slightly tapered.

Grease a baking sheet and sprinkle it with cornmeal. Place the loaf on the sheet and repeat the process for the second loaf. Slash the loaves diagonally with a razor blade, a shallow slash about 1/8 inch deep. There should be a series of these slashes about 2 inches apart the length of the loaf. Allow the loaves to rise for 1 hour on the sheet. (I prefer a 20 minute rise). Bake at 425°F. for 15 minutes. Reduce the heat to 350°F. and bake for 15-20 minutes longer. Remove the loaves and brush them with the beaten white of an egg. Before beating the egg white, add 1 Tablespoon cold water. Return the glazed loaves to the oven and bake for 5 minutes longer. Test with a knife and turn out onto a wire rack placed next to an open window to cool. In hot weather, place a fan directed at the cooling loaves. The window or the fan helps make a thicker crust.

If you have hard wheat flour instead of all purpose flour, you will get a loaf more like those baked in France.

Parisian Croissants Au Beurre

French croissants are a particular flaky treat unlike the ordinary crescent roll. Crescent rolls can be made from any dough and they are good. I particularly like to make mine from Challah dough which is superlative, but they just ain't the real thing. If you want the ethnic McCoy, the genuine 24 karat croissant, this recipe from France will deliver. It is a direct recipe that does not use a sponge.

2 Tablespoons shortening or oil
3 teaspoons sugar
¾ cup milk
1 teaspoon salt
1 package (1 Tablespoon) dry
  yeast
¼ cup warm water
2½ cups all purpose flour
½ cup butter at room temperature

Melt the shortening and combine it with the milk and the sugar. Add the warm water and the dry yeast. Allow this to stand for about 10 minutes and then work in the flour and salt. Knead about 5 minutes to get a soft but smooth dough. Place the dough in a greased bowl and allow it to rise until doubled. Punch down the dough and knead lightly, then return it to the bowl. Cover the bowl and place it in the refrigerator to cool.

After 20 minutes remove the chilled dough from the refrigerator. The butter should be about the same consistency as the dough. If it is too soft chill it for a few minutes. If it is too hard mash it with a fork to make it easier to spread.

Roll out the dough to form a thin rectangle about 5 inches by 15 inches. Divide the butter in thirds and spread one third of the butter over the top ⅔ of the dough. Now fold the dough by bringing up the unbuttered section and then folding the top down to meet it. Position the seam to the right and the fold to your left and then seal the edges by pressing with a finger.

Roll out the folded up dough again to a strip 5 x 15 inches. Butter the top ⅔ and fold again. Roll out and repeat this process. You have now used up all the butter. After buttering the dough, and the butter is the secret of the croissant, cover it and place it back in the refrigerator for 30 minutes. You can place the folded up dough in a plastic vegetable bag if that is convenient, or better yet wrap it in aluminum foil. The dough in this condition can be frozen in the foil and used by thawing overnight in the refrigerator.

After the 30 minutes remove the dough from the refrigerator and fold it again 3 times, rolling out between each folding. Wrap it again and return it to the refrigerator. It can be stored there up to 3 days if necessary. You can use part of the dough and store the rest. If you are planning to bake the same day, keep the dough in the refrigerator for another 30 minutes.

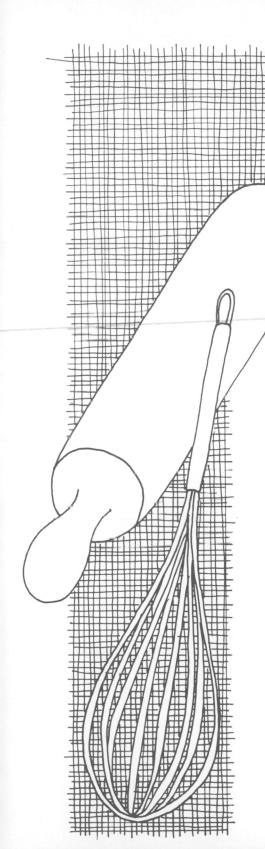

There are 2 ways to shape the croissants. You can roll the dough into a ball and roll it out to a circle of 8-10 inches. Divide the circle into 8 parts with a razor blade and roll up each of the triangles starting at the thick end. This is the method given in the chapter on shaping crescent rolls. There is another way to form these rolls. Take the refrigerated dough and roll it out to a rectangle 10 x 15 inches. The exact size is important so it would be best to make a larger rectangle and trim it to size. Divide the rectangle by a single cut of a razor blade to form 2 strips 5 x 15 inches. Divide each strip into three 5 inch squares. To make small crescents cut each square on the diagonal to form 2 triangles and roll up the triangle starting on the broad end. For a larger croissant, use the whole square and start on one corner and roll it up to the opposite corner, twisting to form the crescent shape. Curve the ends after forming the rolls, place them on a greased baking sheet and allow them to stand for about 20-30 minutes. Brush the rolls with an egg wash before baking.

Bake at 425°F. for 5 minutes then reduce the temperature to 375°F. for 15 minutes or until the rolls are golden brown. Cool on a wire rack and enjoy.

The recipe for Croissants au Beurre is a lot of fuss and trouble. I prefer just taking a good dough like the Challah dough and making a crescent roll. If you have a special occasion and can justify the folding, chilling and fussing, there's nothing like the real thing.

Bulgarian Boiled Bread Rolls

This first cousin to a bagel comes from Bulgaria. Shaping these rolls is much simpler than shaping bagels. You can use any bagel dough, any bread dough or the Bulgarian recipe given here.

1½ teaspoons dry yeast
¾ cup warm water
5 cups unbleached flour
1 teaspoon sugar
½ teaspoon salt
1 Tablespoon melted butter or oil
1¼ cups lukewarm milk

Place the ¾ cup of warm water in a mixing bowl and stir in the yeast and sugar. In 10 minutes the yeast will be frothy. Place the other ingredients in the bowl and stir into a dough. Turn out the dough on a floured board and knead for 10 minutes adding more flour if necessary. Place the kneaded dough into a greased bowl and cover; allow it to stand in a warm place for 1½ hours or until it has doubled.

Punch down the dough and knead again for about 1 minute. Divide the dough into 30 equal portions. It is convenient to roll out the dough before dividing it. Roll each portion into a ball.

Fill a pot with water and add 2 Tablespoons of sugar to the water. Bring the water to a boil. Reduce the heat so the water is kept simmering and drop balls of dough in a few at a time. When the balls rise to the surface, remove them with a slotted spoon and allow them to drain on paper towels or in a colander. After draining, place the balls on greased baking sheets and slit the top of each ball with a single slit. Use a single edged razor blade or a sharp knife. Allow the balls to rest for about 5 minutes and then bake them near the top of the oven at 425°F. for about 15 minutes. The balls can be glazed with egg like a bagel and seeds can be sprinkled on. If you prefer a softer crust brush melted butter over the balls before baking.

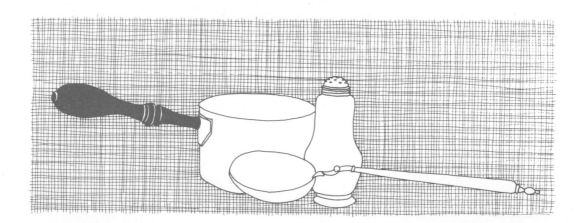

Middle Eastern Pita Bread

A most interesting form of bread is the pita bread baked in the Middle East. This bread is baked in the form of a pocket which is most useful if you wish to make steak in a bag or falafel. No special pan is needed to form the bread into pockets, nor is there any particular trick to doing so. The temperature and the shape of the dough placed in the oven handle the job automatically.

Pita Bread (Direct Method)

4 cups white or whole wheat flour
   (optional. Substitute ¾ cup of
   high gluten flour for the regular
   flour. This produces a better
   rising Pita)
1 package (1 Tablespoon) dry
   yeast
1¼ cups warm water
½ teaspoon sugar or honey
1 Tablespoon salt

Place the yeast in the mixing bowl and add ¼ cup of water. Mix in the sugar and allow the yeast to stand for about 10 minutes. When the yeast is frothy, add the other cup of water, the salt and the 4 cups of flour. Mix to a stiff dough and knead adding more flour if necessary. In about 10 minutes the dough will be springy. Place the dough in a greased bowl and cover the bowl. Allow the dough to rise for about 1½ hours to double. Punch down the risen dough and knead again for 1 minute. Divide the dough into 6 equal parts. Shape each of the 6 pieces into a ball.

Cover the balls with a towel and allow them to stand for about 10 minutes. Roll or flatten each ball into an oval about ½ inch thick. Flattening with the palm of your hand works very well. Place 2 ovals on each baking sheet and bake on a low shelf in a very hot oven at 475°F. If you use the lowest rack, the pita will be baked in about 15 minutes. If you place your baking sheets on the bottom of the oven they will bake in 5-7 minutes. After baking, if the pita are pale-colored, they can be browned quickly in the broiler. Leave the bread in the broiler for only a few seconds or it will burn.

On baking, the ovals puff up and form a pocket of dough. Pita bread is usually cut in halves and filled with interesting foods. One of our local greasy spoons makes a pita burger. They slide a broiled hamburger patty into the pocket and top it with salad greens. The substitution of ¾ cup of high gluten flour for either white or wheat flour will give a much better rising pita bread.

Sourdough Ethnic Breads

Other ethnic breads are made with sourdough starter instead of yeast. The sourdough gives a unique, tart tang to the bread that makes it distinctive and an enjoyable change of pace. Any recipe for a yeast bread can be converted to sourdough if you remember that the cup of starter you use to start the sponge already has 1 cup of liquid and 1 cup of flour in it.

All sourdough breads must be made by the sponge method and it is a slow sponge taking from 8 hours to overnight to develop properly. If you keep a sourdough starter in your refrigerator, it can be used for any of these breads, but some people prefer to make up a special starter for rye or whole wheat breads. All of the recipes in this section can be used to make any shape of bread or roll. Sourdough bagel and sourdough Challah might take a little tolerance on the part of your taste buds, but I won't tell you not to experiment.

Some people think that the only sourdough bread is the French sourdough, but they are wrong. The recipes in this section are for sourdough breads that are baked in Europe and in America. Only one of them is a French sourdough.

Vollkornbrot from Germany

There are many different Vollkornbrots baked in Germany. Some are sourdough, others are made with yeast. The name itself means a whole grain bread. This particular bread is a mixture of rye and whole wheat flours, but if you prefer a lighter bread unleached flour can be substituted for part of the whole wheat. If you have no regular sourdough starter in your refrigerator, you may wish to replenish what is left of this starter and save it for the next time. This is a rye starter.

Special Rye Starter:
1/2 teaspoon dry yeast
2 cups warm water
2 cups rye flour or rye meal
1 slice onion
2 Tablespoons caraway seeds
   (optional)
Sponge: 1 cup starter
3 1/2 cups warm water
2 cups rye flour or rye meal
1 cup stone ground whole wheat
   flour
1 teaspoon sugar
The Next Morning:
1 Tablespoon salt
1 cup rye flour or rye meal
1 1/2 cups whole wheat flour
The white of one egg for glaze

Rye Starter. Place the water in a ceramic or plastic bowl and mix in the flour, yeast and caraway seeds. Stir until smooth and then add the slice of onion. Cover the bowl with plastic wrap and place in a warm spot for 3-4 days. The starter will be bubbly and have an alcoholic aroma when it is ready. The yeast is added to make sure the starter will work, for you cannot be sure of trapping wild yeast. After using the starter, replenish it by adding 1 cup of rye flour and 1 cup of water for each cup of starter used. Allow the replenished starter to stay in a warm place for 8-24 hours and then refrigerate. For information on the care of starters, see the chapter on sourdough starters.

Sponge. Remove the onion from the starter and discard it. Place 1 cup of starter in a plastic or ceramic mixing bowl. The starter then can be replenished, see above. To the cup of starter in the bowl, add 3 1/2 cups of warm water and stir in 1 cup of rye flour and 1 cup of whole wheat flour using a wooden spoon. *Do not use any metal spoons or bowls.* Add the teaspoon of sugar and mix the sponge well. Cover the bowl and let it stand for 8 hours to overnight in a warm place.

The Next Morning. Sprinkle the teaspoon of salt over the sponge and stir it down. Add 1 cup of rye flour and mix to form a dough. Add part of the remaining cup of whole wheat flour and when the dough is formed, turn it out onto a floured board and knead for 10 minutes working in more of the whole wheat flour as required. This dough will be moist on the inside, but as soon as it feels stiff and is dry on the outer surface, it is ready to rise. *Do not force too much flour in.*

Place the kneaded dough in a greased bowl, cover it and let it rise in a warm place until doubled. Punch down the dough and knead again to squash any gas bubbles. Shape into cigar shaped or round hearth loaves and place the bread on a greased baking sheet. Glaze the top with egg white which has been beaten with a Tablespoon of water. Sprinkle caraway seeds over the glaze. Bake at 400°F for 45-50 minutes. Test with a knife and cool on a wire rack.

If a darker bread is desired, 1 teaspoon of instant coffee powder can be added to the sponge. This is a firm coarse bread that goes well with ham and cheese. Slather it with mustard and build a sandwich that will feel like a meal.

Variations

For those bakers in a hurry, the overnight incubation of the sponge can be eliminated by adding 1 package (1 Tablespoon) dry yeast to the sponge. Allow the sponge to work for 1 1½ hours and then continue with the next day procedure. The starter must be used even if yeast is added for the starter gives the sourdough flavor.

This bread is a rather sour bread. If it is too sour for your taste, try to add from ½ to 1 teaspoon of baking soda to sweeten it. Add the soda to the sponge when you add the other ingredients on the second day.

European 100% Black Rye Bread

This bread is baked from the same recipe as the sourdough Vollkornbrot, but it used all rye flour or rye flour plus rye meal. If you have rye meal (see page 21) use 2½ cups. Otherwise follow the Vollkornbrot recipe and use rye flour wherever it calls for whole wheat. Since rye rises poorly add 1 package (1 Tablespoon) of yeast to the starter. The black color comes from 1 or more teaspoons of gravy browning, commercial carmel, instant coffee powder, or "Postum"® . BAKING INSTRUCTIONS ARE THE SAME AS FOR THE VOLLKORNBROT.

Sourdough Rye Bread

There are many rye breads, but there is only one Rye Bread. It is a sourdough rye known by many names. It is called Delicatessen Rye, Jewish Rye, Russian Rye, Corn Bread or Sissel Bread. This paragon among rye breads has a hearty sourdough taste. The Corn or Sissel version is coarser than the others. When this bread is spread with sweet butter it is a taste delight. With ham and Swiss or corned beef, it is an epicurean's dream.

Delicatessen Rye Sponge:

1 cup starter
2 cups water
2 Tablespoons sugar
2 cups rye flour or rye meal
2 cups unbleached flour

Corn Rye Sponge:

1 cup starter
2 cups water
2 Tablespoons sugar
1 cup rye flour or rye meal
1 cup rye meal or corn meal If you have rye meal use 1 or 2 cups. If rye meal is not available use 1 cup rye flour and 1 cup corn meal for texture.
2 cups unbleached flour

The Next Day:

¼ cup vegetable oil
½ teaspoon baking soda
3 teaspoons salt
2 cups rye flour
1-1½ cups unbleached flour
1 Tablespoon caraway seeds

Sponge: Place the starter in a mixing bowl and add 2 cups of warm water, the sugar and all of the flour. Mix well, cover the bowl and let it stand overnight.

The Next Day. (For both Corn Rye and Delicatessen Rye) After the sponge has been allowed to work for at least 8 hours, sprinkle the 3 teaspoons of salt over the surface, add the ¼ cup of oil and the caraway seeds. Sprinkle the baking soda on next and stir down the sponge. Start to work in the rest of the flour, adding the rye flour first then the unbleached until a dough is formed. Scrape the dough out onto a floured bread board and start to knead adding more unbleached flour as required. Knead 10 minutes. This should be a rather moist dough, do not force too much flour.

Grease 2 baking sheets and sprinkle them with cornmeal. Shape the loaves into cigar shaped hearth loaves or round hearth loaves. There should be enough dough for 3 long breads or 2 round breads. Before allowing the breads to rise for 20 minutes, slash the tops with a diagonal cut about ½ inch deep in 3-4 places. To thicken the crust spray the tops with water. I prefer to brush them with diluted egg white and drop more caraway seeds on the glaze. For a really brown crust, use a whole egg glaze instead of egg white.

Bake at 375°F. for 40-45 minutes. Test with a knife, cool on a wire rack.

Rye flour in the United States is usually sold as medium coarse ground flour. In Europe where these peasant type breads originated a coarser flour know as rye meal is available. I make my own rye meal by putting rye flakes into a blender and chopping at low speed. Rye flakes, flattened rye grain is available at most health food store. It takes only a few minutes to chop the flakes into an extra coarse meal that gives an authentic texture to a rye bread.

Middle European
Sour Pumpernickel

Sourdough Pumpernickel is baked in Eastern Europe. It is found in Russia, Poland, East & West Germany. It is also found here in the United States where it emigrated along with the huddled masses to be greeted by the Statue of Liberty. Sour Pumpernickel, as the name implies, is a sour, peasant bread with a robust flavor. To compare it with regular pumpernickel would be like trying to compare a San Francisco Sourdough French Bread with an ordinary French bread or with an Italian bread. They are totally different. To make such a comparison would be like trying to add apples to oranges, or to square the circle. Each bread is good in its own right, but each is different.

Like the Delicatessen Rye, the Sour Pumpernickel would be even better if rye meal were available to replace part of the rye flour. If it isn't don't despair; a bread baked with rye flour alone is almost too good to destroy by eating. In making this bread, you can use any sourdough starter, but if you have a rye starter like the one described on page 148, use it.

Sour Pumpernickel

Sponge:

1 cup starter
*3 Tablespoons blackstrap
   molasses*
*¼ cup vegetable oil or melted
   shortening*
1 cup rye flour or rye meal
2 cups whole wheat flour
1 cup white or unbleached flour
2 cups water or milk
The Next Day:
½ teaspoon baking powder
1 teaspoon salt
½ cup rye flour or rye meal
1-1½ cups white flour
1 Tablespoon caraway seeds

Sponge. Mix the starter ingredients together in a ceramic or plastic mixing bowl. Cover the bowl and let it stand for 8 hours or overnight.

The Next Day. Sprinkle the caraway seeds, salt and baking soda over the sponge and then stir it down. Stir in the ½ cup of rye flour and about ½ cup of the white. Spread about ½ cup of white flour on the bread board and scrape the sponge out onto the flour. If more flour is necessary, rub it into the dough. This is a moist bread, *Do not force flour* into the dough after it can be handled.

For an extra heavy bread, do not let it rise before shaping. If you prefer a lighter, less coarse texture, after kneading for 5-7 minutes, place the dough in a greased bowl, cover it and let it stand until the volume is doubled. If allowed to rise, punch down before shaping.

Pumpernickel can be made as a cigar shaped, long loaf or as a round loaf. I prefer the round shape, but the long one is better for sandwiches. Grease 2 baking sheets and sprinkle them with cornmeal. Shape the loaves, place them on the sheets and slash the tops in several places. There is sufficient dough for 3 loaves. Slash deeply and let the shaped loaves rise again. If you gave the dough a pre-shaping rise, let them rise for 10 minutes. If you omitted the pre-shaping rise, let the shaped loaves rise for ½ hour before baking at 375°F. for about 40 minutes.

Before putting the loaves in the oven, brush the crust with

water or salt water. Ten minutes before they are due out, remove the loaves and glaze with an egg yolk beaten with a Tablespoon of water. After brushing on the glaze, sprinkle the top of the loaves with caraway seeds.

For a darker color, mix 1 teaspoon of instant coffee powder in with the water when setting up the sponge. After glazing, place the loaves back in the oven for about 10 minutes, test with a knife and cool on a wire rack.

Sourdough French Bread

There are many recipes for a sourdough French bread. This recipe is from France. Use any sourdough starter made from wheat flour. See the chapter on Starters (page 39).

Sponge:
1 cup starter
1 cup warm water
2 cups flour (unbleached)
1 teaspoon sugar
The Second Day:
2 cups unbleached flour
1 Tablespoon salt

Sponge. Make the sponge at least 8 hours before you plan to start the bread. Overnight incubation is most convenient. Mix together the cup of starter, 2 cups flour, 1 cup warm water and 1 teaspoon sugar. Cover the plastic or ceramic mixing bowl and allow the sponge to sit overnight.

The Second Day. Sprinkle the salt over the sponge and stir it down. Start adding the 2 cups of flour, mixing as you add. When a dough is formed, flour a board with part of the remaining flour and scrape the sponge out onto the board. Knead the bread for 10 minutes working in additional flour if necessary. When the dough is no longer flabby, place it in a greased bowl and allow it to rise for about 1½ hours or until the dough has doubled.

Punch down the dough and knead again for about 1 minute, then shape it into 2 cylinders. Taper the ends by holding a palm over each end and rocking the loaf on the board. Grease a baking sheet and sprinkle it with cornmeal. Place the loaves on the sheet and allow them to rise for 15-20 minutes. If allowed to rise too long, the loaves will spread. While the loaves are proving, heat water in a teakettle. When the kettle begins to boil, place a shallow pan on the bottom of the oven and pour the boiling water into that pan.

Slash the loaves with a diagonal cut in 3-4 places. Make the slashes about ¼ inch deep. Brush the loaves with water and bake at 400°F. for 40-45 minutes. Test with a knife and cool on a wire rack before an open window or circulating fan. Round loaves can be baked if preferred to the long loaf. You can make a single large loaf or 2 regular sized loaves. On round loaves I usually slash a square on the top.

Quick Sourdough Breads

These are not quick breads. It is possible to speed up the baking of a bread and still have it keep the sourdough flavor. Take any of the sourdough recipes and put 1 Tablespoon of yeast into the sponge. Let the sponge stand for 2 hours instead of overnight. Then bake the bread according to the Second Day step of the recipe. If 50 milligrams of Vitamin C are added along with the yeast, the sponge will be ready in 1 hour. Vitamin C added without yeast will get the sponge ready in 2 to 2½ hours.

You gain time with these tricks, but the breads baked with the added yeast are lighter and highter than those baked with the starter alone or the starter with Vitamin C added. To me, the heavy texture helps the bread say, "Sourdough." When yeast is added, you are baking with yeast; the sourdough starter is only for flavoring. I mention all of the tricks, because you should have a choice. If I'm in a hurry I'd bake a yeast only bread, not a sourdough. If I had to make sourdough, I would use the starter with Vitamin C and no added yeast.

Biscuits, Muffins and Crumpets

Biscuits

Years ago biscuits were a staple addition to any meal. Hot biscuits to sop up egg yolk at breakfast started the day right. Biscuits are quick and easy to make—easier than a bread. Grandmother knew what a treat they were, but modern dietary habits ignore the hot biscuit. It's a shame that good biscuits are seldom made today for those cardboard imitations you find in the grocer's freezer case just can't fill the gap.

When biscuits are baked today, they are apt to be made from a biscuit mix. Mrs. Rasmussen, one of the characters in **Suds in Your Eye,** said, "You can't hardly buy the ingredients as cheap," but that was back during World War II. I've priced biscuit mixes, even the off brand ones, the plain label specials, the store brands. Today, it is a lot cheaper to buy the ingredients. I don't like biscuit mixes for three good reasons. One of those

reasons is the cost; I find it cheaper to use baking powder, shortening and flour. My second reason for disliking mixes is the type of shortening used. All the biscuit mixes I examined were coy about the shortening. Most said a mixture of animal and vegetable fats. The vegetable fat is usually palm oil, the animal fat a mixture of lard and suet. I prefer to pick my own shortening, thank you. I prefer to use vegetable fats or oil that is not saturated. My third reason for not using mixes is the presence of preservatives to prevent the fats from turning rancid. Although I do not list it as a reason, I feel cheated when I use a mix for it is really not that much time saving or labor saving compared to making the biscuits from scratch. The recipes which follow are for baking powder biscuits. The whole series is based on the basic recipe. These are all easy and quick to make.

Basic Baking Powder Biscuits

2 cups unbleached flour
2 teaspoons baking powder
1 teaspoon salt
4 Tablespoons melted shortening or oil
2/3 cup liquid. (water, milk or juice)

Place the dry ingredients in a mixing bowl. You may sift them in if you prefer. Add the liquid shortening and then the liquid. Mix lightly with a fork until a dough is formed. If the mixture is too dry, add a little more liquid. Turn the dough out onto a lightly floured board and knead it for ½ to 1 minute. Roll out or pat out the dough until it is ½ inch thick. Use a biscuit cutter or a tuna can with both ends removed to cut out rounds of dough. If you prefer rectangular biscuits, you can cut them out with a razor blade. Place the biscuits on a greased baking sheet and bake at 450°F. for 12-15 minutes. The tops of the biscuits can be brushed with milk or melted butter before baking. Do plan to put these in the oven just before eating to have hot biscuits.

Variations on the Basic Biscuit

Drop Biscuits. Increase the liquid in the biscuit recipe to 1 full cup. This will give you a thick batter instead of a dough. Use a teaspoon to drop the batter on a greased baking sheet. Bake at 450°F. for 12-15 minutes.

Fried Biscuits. These are drop biscuits and made by the same recipe as the drop biscuits above. Fried biscuits are not baked, the batter is dropped into a hot, greased pan and cooked on top of the stove. Turn when brown and fry the other side. Serve them hot from the pan. These are delicious if you can handle fried food.

Filled Biscuits. Make a basic biscuit dough and roll out the dough to ¼ inch. This is much thinner than we rolled it for the basic biscuits. Cut out rounds or rectangles of this thin dough. Place jam, chopped meat, cheese, or any interesting leftover on one round and cover it with a second round. Crimp the edges together and brush with melted butter or milk. Bake at 450°F. for 12-15 minutes.

Flavored Biscuits. There are several of these, all made with the basic biscuit dough. Most of them have extra ingredients added to give the flavor, but a few of them substitute one ingredient for another.

Mint Biscuits. Add ¼ cup chopped mint leaves to the dry ingredients before adding the liquid.

Nut Biscuits. Add ½ cup of chopped nuts.

Fruit Biscuits. Add ½ cup chopped dates, figs, prunes or raisins. The raisins may be added whole.

Cheese Biscuits. Add ¼ cup grated cheese to the dry ingredients.

Chive Biscuits. Add ¼ cup chopped chives.

Orange Biscuits. Add 1 Tablespoon grated orange peel.

Lemon Biscuits. Add 1 Tablespoon grated lemon peel.

Shortcake Biscuits. To the basic mix, add 1 beaten egg and 2 Tablespoons of sugar. Increase the shortening to 6 Tablespoons. Use these biscuits for Strawberry Shortcake.

Peanut Biscuits. Substitute ½ cup chunky peanut butter for the shortening. Cut the peanut butter into the flour before adding the liquid.

Cream Biscuits. Use 1 cup of cream instead of milk or water. Do not add shortening.

Bran Biscuits. Substitute 1 cup of bran for 1 cup of flour.

Whole Wheat Biscuits. Substitute wheat flour for both cups of white flour.

50% Wheat Biscuits. Use 1 cup of white flour and 1 cup of whole wheat flour in the basic biscuit recipe.

Buttermilk Biscuits. Use buttermilk for the liquid and add ½ teaspoon of baking soda. When making buttermilk biscuits reduce the baking powder to 1 teaspoon for the buttermilk and soda will provide the leavening action of the other teaspoon of baking powder.

Biscuits without Baking Powder

If you wish to bake biscuits without baking powder, you may use 1 teaspoon of baking soda and 2-3 teaspoons of vinegar. Reduce the liquid by 2 teaspoons to keep the volume constant or add a little extra flour to compensate for the vinegar if you do not reduce the liquid.

Baking Powder Biscuits as a Base for Desserts

The dough used for biscuits can be used to make desserts. Roll it out to a rectangle and then proceed as shown in the chapter entitled Good Things from Yeast Dough. Use your imagination. I won't use this dough for desserts for I prefer the rich dough texture of the special dough given in the chapter on desserts. Making them from biscuit dough would be like trying to make bagels from that dough. You would get doughnut shaped, boiled biscuits, not bagels.

Muffins

In many ways, a muffin is much like a biscuit but it is usually made from a looser dough and has more sugar. The texture of muffin dough is that of a drop biscuit, but muffins are baked in a muffin tin or in paper muffin cups. The basic recipe has many variations. If you are making dessert muffins, increase the sugar beyond what the recipe calls for, but do NOT use more than ½ cup of either brown or white sugar when playing with the basic muffin recipe. The use of brown sugar will give the muffin an entirely different taste. Fructose can be used; if it is, use only half the amount of fructose that you would sugar. Since only half as much is used, the calories are reduced.

Basic Muffins

2 cups sifted flour
2 teaspoons baking powder
½ teaspoon salt
2 teaspoons sugar
1 cup milk
1 beaten egg
3 Tablespoons oil

Sifting gives a lighter texture to the muffins, but is not mandatory. Sift the baking powder, sugar, salt and flour into a mixing bowl. Beat the egg and add it to the oil and milk. Pour the liquid into the dry ingredients and stir gently until those dry ingredients are moistened. *Do not beat* this batter. Drop the batter formed into greased muffin tins filling each hole about ⅔ full. Bake at 425°F. for 20-25 minutes. The recipe will produce 1 dozen 2 inch muffins.

Variations on the Basic Muffin

These variations are baked by substituting for some of the ingredients in the basic muffin or by adding other ingredients to that recipe.

Bran Muffins. These are everyday bran muffins. Substitute 1 cup of bran for 1 cup of flour. Bran muffins are best if bran rather than a bran cereal is used. Bran can be found in most health food stores. Raisins, bits of apple or pieces of pineapple can be added to enhance the flavor.

Cheese Muffins. Add ½ cup of grated cheese to the batter.

Corn Meal Muffins. Substitute 1 cup of corn meal for 1 cup of flour in the basic recipe.

Nut Muffins. Add ½ cup of chopped nuts.

Dried Fruit Muffins. Add ½ cup chopped dates, figs or raisins.

Orange Muffins. Grate 1 Tablespoon of orange rind into the basic batter.

Lemon Muffins. Grate 1 Tablespoon of lemon rind into the basic batter.

Cherry Muffins. Add ¾ cup chopped cherries. Fresh or canned may be used.

Apple Muffins. Add 1 cup of chopped fresh apple plus ½ teaspoon of cinnamon. One quarter teaspoon of nutmeg may be added too.

More Muffin Variations

To any of the above variations, substitute 1 cup of either sour cream or yogurt for the cup of milk.

Add 1 teaspoon of vanilla to any of the basic muffin variations for a delightful taste highlight.

Special Dessert Muffins

These are sweeter muffins for special treats. This recipe produces delightful, rich muffins. It does not use baking powder, but depends on the reaction between the yogurt or sour cream and the baking soda to leaven the muffins.

1 cup sour cream or yogurt
½ cup salad oil
1 egg
1 teaspoon vanilla
1 cup all purpose flour
1 cup bran. (not cereal)
½ cup brown sugar
¾ cup raisins
1 diced apple
½ teaspoon salt
1 teaspoon baking soda
12 dates, halved and pitted (optional)

Add the oil, beaten egg, and vanilla to the sour cream and beat until they are combined. Put the dry ingredients in a large bowl and mix them together. Add the liquid to the dry and mix to form a batter. Drop the batter into greased muffin tins or muffin papers and then lay half a date across the top of each muffin. Bake in a pre-heated oven at 350°. for 20-25 minutes. The recipe makes two dozen muffins

Spice Muffins

2 cups all purpose flour
1 teaspoon ginger or dry mustard
1 teaspoon nutmeg
1 teaspoon cinnamon
2 teaspoons baking powder
1 teaspoon salt
1 beaten egg
½ cup sugar, brown or white
½ cup oil
1 cup milk

Sift or mix the flour with the spices, baking powder and salt into a mixing bowl. Combine the oil, egg and milk and add them to the dry ingredients. Beat until the mixture is smooth. Fill greased muffin tins ⅔ full. Bake at 425°F. for 15-20 minutes.

Poppy Seed Roll

English Muffins

Have you ever wondered how English muffins get all those nooks and crannies? They're not put there by Mr. Thomas; they belong there. English muffins are made from a yeast dough. After kneading, the dough is rolled out and cut in circles. Then it is allowed to rise again. While it is rising, all of the yeast cells are busy blowing bubbles of carbon dioxide gas. When the muffin is placed on a hot griddle to cook, the bottom becomes hot while the rest of the muffin is cool. The heat striking the underside makes the bubbles of gas near the bottom rise quickly. As they rise, they expand and then burst when they reach the cooler dough near the top. The burst bubbles produce all of those handy nooks and crannies that are so convenient for melted butter when you eat the muffin.

Not all commercial English muffins are made on a griddle. It is easier for some bakeries to run them through an oven, but in the oven, heat reaches all the surfaces of the muffin evenly. Since the top is as hot as the bottom, there is no uneven expansion of gas and darn few nooks and crannies. These muffins, the baked ones, look like pale hamburger buns instead of like English muffins.

My favorite English muffin is the sourdough version, but a good muffin can also be baked with yeast. Both recipes are given.

Sourdough English Muffins

1/2 cup sourdough starter
1 cup milk
about 2 1/2 cups flour
1 Tablespoon sugar or honey
1 teaspoon salt
1/2 teaspoon baking soda

Combine the milk, the starter and the 2 cups of flour in a mixing bowl. Add the sugar and allow the bowl to stand, covered, overnight in a warm place. The next day, add the salt, the soda and 1/2 cup flour to the sponge and stir well. Turn the stiff dough out onto a floured board and knead for 3-5 minutes. If necessary, a little more flour can be added at this time. Stop kneading and adding flour when the dough no longer feels sticky.

Do not let the dough rise after kneading. Roll it out immediately. Roll to a thickness of 3/4 inch and then cut out 3 inch circles with a pastry cutter or a tuna can with both top and bottom removed. If you want a larger muffin, a pineapple can or the larger sized tuna can, can be used. Sprinkle a greased baking sheet with cornmeal as you cut them out. Sprinkle more cornmeal on top of the rounds of dough and then cover the baking sheet with a towel and allow the muffins to rise for 30-45 minutes.

Bake on a griddle or in a frying pan. Set electric griddles at 275°F. Gas fed griddles and frying pans should be prewarmed and set on moderate. The griddle should be greased before warming. Cook the muffins for 5-8 minutes per side, then turn and cook the other side 5-8 minutes. For best results, muffins should only be turned once.

Split, butter and enjoy your muffin. This recipe will make 1 dozen 3 inch muffins, if you salvage the scraps and roll them out again. Home baked muffins can be kept in the refrigerator or in the freezer just like the ones you buy at the grocer's but they don't taste like them; they taste much, much better.

Strudel

Yeast English Muffins

English muffins do not have to be made with sourdough. Muffins leavened with yeast will still have the necessary nooks and crannies if they are baked on a griddle.

English Muffins (Direct Yeast Method)

1 package (1 Tablespoon) dry
   yeast
2½ cups flour
1 teaspoon salt
2 Tablespoons sugar
3 Tablespoons melted butter or oil
2 cups warm water
1 egg

Prove the yeast by mixing it in a bowl with about 2 ounces of warm water and the 2 Tablespoons of sugar. When the yeast becomes frothy, add the rest of the warm water. Beat the egg and add it and the melted shortening to the water. Stir in the flour 1 cup at a time until a dough is formed. Scrape the dough out onto a floured board and knead it for 5 minutes. Place the kneaded dough in a greased bowl, cover it, and allow it to rise for 1-1½ hours or until it has doubled. Punch down the dough, knead it for a minute and then roll it out to about ¾ inch thickness. Cut the dough in 3 inch rounds using a pastry cutter or tuna can. Place each round on cornmeal and then sprinkle more cornmeal over the muffins. Cover the baking sheets and allow the muffins to rise for 45 minutes. Bake on a greased electric griddle set at 275°F. or on a gas fed griddle at moderate heat. Cook about 7 minutes per side and then serve.

This is an entirely different muffin from the one we baked from sourdough starter. If you prefer to use the sourdough recipe to bake a yeast muffin, simply add ½ cup warm water and ½ cup more flour. Prove the yeast and then follow the sourdough recipe remembering that the extra flour and water will take the place of the starter. Also omit the baking soda for there will be no sourness to neutralize.

Variations on English Muffins

These variations will work with both yeast and sourdough recipes.

Wheat Germ Muffins. Substitute ½ cup wheat germ for ½ cup flour.

Cornmeal Muffins. Substitute ½ cup cornmeal for ½ cup flour.

Oatmeal Muffins. Substitute ½ cup oatmeal for ½ cup flour.

Wheat Muffins. Substitute 1 cup of whole wheat flour for 1 cup of white or unbleached flour.

Whole Wheat Muffins. Use all stone ground whole wheat flour.

Raisin Muffins. Add ½ cup raisins to any of the muffins or variations.

Other Recipes for English Muffins

English muffins can be made from any bread dough. It is not necessary to use either of the recipes given. If you were to take a recipe that made two loaves of bread and divide it into two portions, you could make a bread with half the dough. Roll out the other half to a thickness of ¾ inch and cut circles from the dough with a tuna can. Bake half the circles on a greased baking sheet in the oven. The other half cook on a griddle. You would wind up with a bread, rolls and English muffins.

I've made English muffins from many bread doughs. I particularly like those made with Challah dough. These are an exceptionally rich muffin and taste better if raisins, cinnamon and nutmeg are added to the dough.

Crumpets

I hate to give a recipe for crumpets. I think that they are nasty things to make even if they are delicious to eat. Crumpets, when baked, are very similar to English muffins, even to having all those nooks and crannies we hear about on television. Crumpets are made from a batter just like a pancake. The trick in making a crumpet is to get the batter piled up thickly and to hold a predetermined size and shape. To accomplish this, you cook the crumpet in a crumpet ring or an empty tuna fish can. Old Alaskan prospectors are said to have made sourdough crumpets in cutout Copenhagen snuff tins.

To make a crumpet, prepare a thin batter similar to the batter used for pancakes. Place the rings on a hot griddle or in a pre-heated frying pan. Fill the rings with batter and then start cooking. After about 7 minutes, turn the crumpet over, the whole crumpet including the ring. Cook the other side and remove the ring and its contents from the griddle. If you're lucky, the crumpet will slide out of the ring, but mine always stick and make it necessary to scour the ring before using it again. Since the finished product looks like, and tastes like an English muffin, I'll bake English muffins and not have to fuss with a liquid batter.

The batter used for the sourdough crumpet is identical to the primary batter used to prepare Sourdough Pancakes and Waffles.

Crumpets

Sponge:

1 cup sourdough starter
2 cups hot tap water
2 cups unbleached, whole wheat
  or buckwheat flour
*Replenish your starter by adding 1
  cup of flour and 1 cup of water to
  the starter pot. Allow to stand
  overnight in a warm place*

The Next Morning:

½ cup flour
2 teaspoons salt
½ teaspoon baking soda

Sponge. Mix the ingredients together in a large bowl; cover the bowl and allow it to stand in a warm place overnight. If you don't have a starter, mix ½ teaspoon of yeast with ½ teaspoon of sugar. Add 3 cups of flour. Allow this to stand overnight. If you use this yeast batter, do not add the baking soda in the morning.

The Next Morning. Mix the flour, salt and baking soda into the batter. Prepare the crumpet rings or tuna cans with both ends removed by greasing them and then pre-heat the griddle. Spoon the batter into the rings and cook for 5-7 minutes. Turn the ring containing the crumpet over with a spatula and cook the other side for 5-7 minutes. Remove the crumpets from the heat and then slide them out of the rings. You may have to use a knife to dislodge the crumpets from the rings.

For a richer crumpet, substitute ¾ cup of milk for ¾ cup of water when making the crumpet batter. For an even richer tasting crumpet, add 4 Tablespoons of oil to the recipe.

Nonbreads

Man does not live by bread alone. There are dishes made from grain that cannot be called bread by any stretch of the imagination. Some of these nonbreads are well worth making, especially for company. A few are included in this section only because I felt like including them, for if I were inclined to be conventional, they would have no place in a book on breads. Many of these nonbreads, like the recipes in the following chapter, are for entrees. To be of any value to the reader, I must not only tell how to make the nonbread, but also tell how to serve it. If that makes this section more cook book than bread book, I have no apology.

Many years ago, a good friend who was of Italian descent, gave me a recipe, his Grand mother's recipe, for what he called "banana noodles." These were to be used in making cannelloni or manicotti. At the time he gave me the information, I only went into the kitchen to get a cup of coffee or to raid the refrigerator, but despite the fact that I had no use for that recipe, I put it in a safe place. When I finally did take a good look at the banana noodle recipe, I found that it was a crepe. Crepes are made from flour, water and egg. Because they contain egg, they do not freeze as well as ordinary breads, but some crepes can be frozen filled. Unfilled crepes are fragile in the freezer if they are not placed in some type of container that will protect their edges. The recipes that follow are for minimal number of crepes to avoid the problem of freezing the leftovers. If you expect company, double the recipe. The batter will keep for several days in the refrigerator.

There are many crepe recipes, but they share one thing in common. All crepes are made with a large number of eggs in proportion to the amount of flour used. Some are made with whole eggs plus extra egg yolks. Since this is not a book on crepes, I will give only two recipes followed by a series of fillings. Either of these crepe recipes can be rolled tightly and then sliced into long strips to form a good egg noodle.

Banana Noodles (An Italian Crepe)

¼ teaspoon salt
½ cup flour
3 small or 2 extra large eggs
1 cup milk

Mix the ingredients to form a thin batter. If batter does not look thin, add a little more milk. For best results, chill batter in the refrigerator for 1 hour before use. Use a crepe pan or a 6-8 inch frying pan. Cook like a pancake, but swirl the batter in the pan to cover the entire surface. Use only enough batter to make a thin layer.

Rich All-Purpose Crepe

2 large eggs
¼ teaspoon salt
1 cup flour
2 cups milk
¼ cup (1 cube) butter or
   margarine

Beat the ingredients together after melting the butter. Refrigerate batter for 1 hour. If batter appears too thick, add 1-2 tablespoons of milk to thin. Cook in a crepe pan or small frying pan, coating the pan with a thin layer of batter.

Although crepes can be eaten like pancakes, they are at their best when filled. Crepes can be filled with almost anything, but the following are time tested dishes.

Manicotti

½ pound ground meat
½ chopped small onion
a pinch of garlic powder
1 Tablespoon butter or margarine
¼ teaspoon salt
5 ounces cooked, chopped
   spinach (½ frozen package)
½ cup bread crumbs
⅛ cup Parmesan or Romano
   grated cheese
1 beaten egg
¼ teaspoon dried basil
6 crepes
a pinch of black pepper
2 cups of spaghetti sauce

Cook and chop the spinach or use frozen. Saute the onion with the garlic powder in butter and then add the ground meat to brown. Pour off the excess grease; remove from the heat and then stir in the cooked, chopped spinach, the salt and the grated cheese.

Fill crepes with the mixture and fold. Pour sauce into the bottom of a shallow baking dish and place the filled crepes in the pan. Pour more sauce on top of the crepes. If you wish, a layer of sliced mozzarella cheese can be placed over the crepes to melt. Bake the crepes for 20 minutes at 350°F.

Sauce. Use any of the prepared marinara sauces or make your own sauce. A simple sauce can be made by taking 2 cups of tomato sauce plus ¼ cup of either Romano or Parmesan cheese. Add ¼ teaspoon of basil and ½ teaspoon of ground oregano. After adding the spices and cheese, cook the sauce for 30 minutes at a low heat before using it.

A more complicated sauce is given in the next chapter under pizza.

Cheese Blintzes

You have a choice of several cheeses to use when making blintzes. Hoop cheese or farmer's cheese is called for in the traditional recipes, but cottage cheese with the water squeezed out will work as will fetta cheese or ricotta. I have trouble finding either hoop or farmer's cheese, so I usually use ricotta.

1 cup ricotta, fetta or farmer's
   cheese
1 egg yolk
1 Tablespoon sugar
1 teaspoon lemon juice
2 Tablespoons melted butter for
   frying
6 cooked crepes

Place the cheese in a bowl. If cottage cheese is used, drain it first. Mix the egg yolk into the cheese and then stir in the lemon juice and the sugar. Spoon the filling into the center of the crepe and fold to make a pocket. Fold the bottom, then both sides and then the top. Melt the butter in a skillet and brown the blintz on both sides. Blintzes are usually served with sour cream and jam. They can be sprinkled with powdered sugar before serving.

Cannelloni—An Italian Cheese Blintz

1 cup ricotta cheese (feta,
farmers, hoop or drained cottage cheese can be substituted.)
2 Tablespoons melted butter or
margarine
2 Tablespoons parsley (optional)
1 beaten egg
1 Tablespoon chopped onion or
chopped green onion
a pinch of salt
8 crepes
2 cups sauce
½ cup grated Romano or
Parmesan cheese

To make the filling, combine the cheese, melted butter, chopped parsley, beaten egg, chopped onion and salt. Place 3 Table-spoons of the cheese mixture into each crepe and fold. Place a layer of the sauce in a baking pan and put the filled crepes in on top of the sauce. Pour the remainder of the sauce over the crepes and sprinkle with the grated cheese. Bake at 350°F. for 20-30 minutes.

Sauce. Any prepared spaghetti sauce can be used. Recipes for homemade sauces are given under Manicotti and Pizza in this book.

Greek Cookies

An interesting nonbread form of baking is the cookie. There must be at least 14,757 cookie recipes in existence, give or take a few thousand. With this wealth of possible recipes, I have chosen to include only one in this book. There are at least two reasons for my choice to limit myself. The Greek cookie is not only extremely easy to make, but it is also one of the finest oookies I have ever tasted. They make an ex-cellent gift to take along when invited to dine out or are ideal to serve at a party. Another reason for including this particular cookie is that I have used the cookie dough as a base for a pie crust that is as easy to make as it is delectable.

Greek Cookies

4 cups flour
1 pound unsalted butter or
margarine
3 heaping Tablespoons sugar or 5
Tablespoons honey
1 shot (1 ounce) vanilla extract
1 shot (1 ounce) ouzo or anise
extract (optional)
1 shot (1 ounce) Greek or other
brandy

Melt the entire pound of butter in a double boiler and blend it with the flour, sweetener and liquor. An oily looking dough should be formed. Roll out 1 inch balls; place the balls on a greased baking sheet and flatten them slightly. Bake the cookies at 350°F. until golden brown, (about 30 minutes.) Cool and then toss in a bag with powdered sugar.

Variations

Instead of ouzo or anise extract, use rum, bourbon or sherry. Other liquors can also be substituted for the "Metaxa"® brandy.

An Easy, One Crust Pie Crust

1¼ cups flour
1 teaspoon sugar
1 teaspoon salt
1 cube (¼ pound) butter,
　margarine or ½ cup cooking oil
2 Tablespoon whole milk
½ teaspoon vanilla extract. (op-
　tional)
1 teaspoon sherry, rum, brandy or
　other liquor (optional)

This is based on the Greek cookie recipe.

Mix the ingredients together to form an oily dough. If using a solid shortening, it should be melted before mixing with the flour. Transfer the dough to a 9 inch pie pan and pat the dough into the shape of a pie shell. This is much like working with a mud pie, but since the dough is oily, it will not stick to your fingers.

The pie shell can be baked at 375°F. until it turns brown, about 20-25 minutes. Then it can be filled with your favorite fresh fruit recipe or cream pie recipe. It can also be used for a baked pie by filling the shell before baking the pie.

Pennsylvania Dutch Apple Pie

1 unbaked pie shell (see Easy Pie
　Crust)
Filling:
2 Tablespoons corn starch (or
　flour)
⅔ cup granulated sugar
1½ teaspoons cinnamon
4 sliced, peeled, cored apples
　(about 4 cups)
½ cup yogurt or dairy sour cream
　or sour cream substitute
Topping A:
½ cup brown sugar
1 teaspoon cinnamon
¼ teaspoon nutmeg (optional)
2 Tablespoons flour
Topping B:
½ cup brown sugar
1 teaspoon cinnamon
¼ teaspoon nutmeg (optional)
¾ cup flour
¾ stick (⅓ cup) softened butter or
　margarine

Filling. Combine the apple slices and other ingredients and place in the unbaked pie shell. The pie is now ready for the topping.

Topping. Choose either Topping A or Topping B. If B is used, cut the butter into the mixture of sugar and flour by using 2 knives or rub it into the mixture using your hands. When the flour looks like bread crumbs, the butter has been cut in. Sprinkle either topping over the pie. Bake at 350°F. for 40-45 minutes. The topping should be golden brown.

Indian Pudding & Hasty Puddin'

"Father and I went down to camp,
Along with Captain Goodwin.
And there we saw the men and boys,
As thick as hasty puddin'.

Yankee Doodle keep it up.
Yankee Doodle dandy.
Mind the music and the step,
And with the girls be handy."

Hasty Puddin' and Indian Pudding are both made with cornmeal, but even in colonial times, there was a world of difference. Hasty Puddin' is corn meal mush. Indian Pudding is a gastronomic delight that has been a favorite of

Bostonian gourmets for generations. The recipe for Hasty Puddin' (cornmeal mush) should be on your box of cornmeal; if not, small loss. The recipe for a mouthwatering, culinary delight known as Indian Pudding is below.

Bostonian Indian Pudding

¼ cup sugar
½ cup molasses
¼ cup yellow cornmeal
2 cups cold milk
2 cups scalded milk
1 teaspoon salt
1 teaspoon cinnamon
½ teaspoon nutmeg
½ teaspoon ginger (optional)
4 Tablespoons butter
2 Tablespoons rum

To prepare the pudding, place the cornmeal in the top half of a double boiler, Add half the cold milk and mix well. Slowly add the still hot, scalded milk and mix that in. Place the top of the double boiler into the bottom half which should be filled about half full of boiling water. Cook the mixture of milk and cornmeal until it is thick. This takes about 20 minutes. Mix in the molasses, salt, sugar and spices.

Pour the pudding into a buttered pudding dish (casserole) and then pour the rest of the cold milk and the rum over the top. Place the pudding dish in a pan of hot water and bake the pudding for 3 hours at 250°F. Remove the dish from the oven and allow it to cool for ½ hour. Serve topped with whipped cream, artificial whipped cream or vanilla ice cream.

This is a soft pudding, but it has a smooth texture and delightful flavor. The recipe originated shortly after the Pilgrims arrived in America, but it has been modernized a bit. In this form, the recipe is unchanged from the late nineteenth century.

Strudel

1½ cups of flour; more may be needed when working the dough
1 Tablespoon butter or unsalted margarine
1 egg
⅛ to ¼ teaspoon salt (pinch on older recipes)
3 Tablespoons cold water (ice water preferred)
1 cube (¼ pound) butter or unsalted margarine

Strudel dough preparation. Place the flour in a bowl and make a well in the center of the flour. Add the beaten egg, the water, and the 1 Tablespoon of butter plus the salt to the well and work the ingredients into a dough. After the dough forms, work it into a ball. The dough should not be sticky. Flour a bread board and place the ball of strudel dough on the board. With a rolling pin, roll out the dough to form a rectangle 8x16 inch or larger, the exact size of this rectangle is not important. Take the cube of butter out of the refrigerator and slice it into thin slices, distribute the slices of butter over the surface of the rectangle. Starting at one of the narrow ends of the rectangle, fold up the dough past the middle leaving about one third of the top uncovered. Fold down this top and then fold in the sides to form a very small rectangle again. Start to roll out the dough again to work the butter into the dough. The butter may ooze through the dough making it sticky. If it does, sprinkle flour over the envelope to absorb the butter. Use enough flour to prevent the dough from sticking to your fingers and continue to roll out until you once again have a rectangle about the size of the original. Fold this again and roll out again. If necessary add more flour. Repeat this procedure until the dough had been rolled out at least 6 times. Fold up the dough again and wrap it in aluminum foil and place the dough in the refrigerator over night.

Strudel Dough the next day. Remove the foil wrapped dough from the refrigerator. Take the dough out of the foil and roll out to form a rectangle. Repeat this process until the dough has been rolled out 5 times. Fold up again and divide the dough into 2 portions. Roll out each portion to as large and thin a rectangle as possible. Do not tear the dough. It is easier to roll out the dough on waxed paper and for the last rectangle wax paper is highly recommended. Spread the filling out over the dough and then roll up the dough like a jelly roll starting at the long end away from you and roll toward yourself. Pinch the ends away from you and roll toward yourself. Pinch the ends as you roll to prevent the filling from oozing out while baking. Place the strudel roll on a greased baking sheet and then prepare the 2nd strudel roll. If you wish to only make one roll, the dough may be kept in the refrigerator for several days or frozen and kept for several weeks. Bake the strudel rolls at 350°F. for approximately 1 hour or until strudels are browned. If desired, the rolls can be basted with melted butter while they bake, but this step is not necessary. When removed from the oven, powdered sugar can be sprinkled over the rolls to enhance appearance. Slice the rolls after they cool a bit and serve either hot or cold. If there are any left-overs, store in the refrigerator.

Filling for Strudel

5 large apples
½ cup raisins (white or brown)
½ cup chopped walnuts, almonds or pecans (do not use salted nuts)
2 teaspoons cinnamon
2 Tablespoons bread crumbs or toasted bread crumbs
1-4 Tablespoons sugar or honey (for sweet apples use 1-2 Tablespoons—for tart apples use 3-4 Tablespoons—even more sugar can be used if a very sweet apple filling is desired)

Grate the apples directly onto the rectangle of dough after sprinkling the bread crumbs on the dough. Spread the apples over the entire surface of the dough and then sprinkle on the cinnamon and sugar. Cinnamon and sugar can be mixed together first before adding them to the apples. Shake the ground nuts and the raisins over the apples and then roll up the strudel starting at the long end away from you and rolling toward yourself. Pinch the ends as you roll to prevent the apples from leaking out. Bake at 350°F. for about 1 hour. Remove the strudels from the oven and allow to cool. Slice and serve either warm or cold. Rolling of strudel is easier if the dough is rolled out onto a cloth or waxed paper before the filling is added.

Noodles and Rice

Homemade Noodles

Noodles can be made at home, but until recently I thought them too much work to bother with. I remember my aunt making noodles. The dining room table was extended with all the leaves and then the dough was rolled out, cut into strips and allowed to dry. She made so many noodles that it was like living in a pasta factory. If we produce on a smaller scale, I've found that it is not that much trouble. Besides, the noodle dough is just right for won ton, kreplach, ravioli and other great things to eat.

Quick Egg Noodles. Take a crepe and roll it up tightly. Cut slices off the roll and shake them out. Allow them to dry for at least 20 minutes and then serve them in soup. See the recipe for Banana Noodles at the beginning of this chapter.

Egg Noodle Dough

2 large eggs.
½ teaspoon salt.
2 cups all purpose flour.

Break the eggs and add the salt to them. Beat the eggs and then add the flour. Use more flour if necessary to form a stiff dough. Knead about 5 minutes until the dough is soft and elastic. Roll out the dough to a very thin layer and transfer the sheet of dough to a clean cloth. Allow it to dry for about 20 minutes. At that time it will not be sticky or brittle. Start at one end and roll up the sheet of dough to form a cylinder or a flat roll. Using a single edged razor blade cut strips of dough either thin or broad as you prefer. Toss the strips to separate and then allow the strips to dry until they are quite hard and dry. *Do not try to make noodles during damp weather.* Noodles may be stored in a sealed glass jar.

If all we could do with this recipe was make noodles, I would not have included it in the book. When it comes to plain noodles, I usually buy them, but the recipe is versatile. There are many ethnic dishes that can be made with the aid of this dough. Almost every culture has developed this type of recipe. Ravioli is a good example. With an Italian sauce, it is ravioli, but in a Chinese restaurant it would be a won ton; in a Jewish delicatessen it is called a kreplach. If you were to ask for this dish in a German eating establishment it would be maultaschen (pockets).

The difference between these ethnic variations is usually in the sauce or in the filling. If you wanted to be innovative and different, there is no reason you couldn't serve Chinese ravioli or Italian kreplach. The doughs are similar to each other and to the basic egg noodle dough. A few of the dough variations are given and a choice of fillings. I have also included a few sauce recipes, but when it comes to serving these pockets of dough in a soup, you're on your own. I refuse to give the recipe for soup. Just remember that you don't have to do what everyone else does. Kreplach taste as good in split pea soup as they do in the traditional chicken soup. In fact, a bowl of pea soup and plenty of the Jewish ravioli make a complete meal.

When you get ready to make any of the filled squares of dough, it makes very little difference if you follow the Chinese, the Italian, the German, the Jewish, or any other noodle dough recipe you happen to have. There is one shortcut that works well if you're in a hurry. Ready made wrappers can be purchased in many shops. These are sold as won ton skins or egg roll skins. Won ton skins are squares measuring 3 inches per side. Egg roll skins are larger; they are 6 inch squares. The larger squares can be made into giant kreplach, ravioli or what have you, or they can be cut into smaller segments after filling with a pastry wheel.

Doughs for Filled Pockets

I. Basic Noodle Dough (see recipe on page 175)
II. Won Ton Dough
1 teaspoon salt
4 cups flour
2 beaten eggs
1 cup cold water

Sift or mix the flour and salt into a bowl. Add the beaten eggs and water. Mix the ingredients until a soft dough is formed. Knead in the bowl for about 5 minutes until dough is soft and smooth. If the dough is crumbly, add a little more water. *Do not work this dough too long or it will become stiff.* 5 minutes is maximum kneading time.

Divide the dough into 4 equal parts and roll each part into a ball. Take one ball at a time and with a rolling pin, roll out a square 14 inches on a side. Trim off the excess. The dough should be rolled very thin, about 1/16th inch thick. Cut the rectangle into 3½ inch squares with a razor blade. After the dough is cut, it can be used immediately or frozen in foil or in plastic wrap. If you do not fill your dough pockets immediately, cover the squares with a damp towel to prevent their drying out. Various types of fillings can be used.

Meat Filling

1 pound ground raw beef, pork or
   lamb, veal or 1 pound ground
   hash
1 egg
1 teaspoon salt
black pepper to taste
1 teaspoon onion juice
1 browned onion

Mix the meat, egg and seasonings together. Place the filling on the center of the dough square and fold it into a triangle. Seal the edges by pressing tightly. A fork or a pastry wheel can be used to make the seal. For smaller pockets use a 2 inch square. For larger items use a 3 or 3½ inch square. An even larger won ton, ravioli or kreplach can be made by using 2 squares. Place the filling on one sheet of dough and cover with the other; then crimp the edges. Boil the filled pockets in lightly salted water.

Rice and Cheese Filling

1 cup ricotta, hoop, farmer's or
   cottage cheese
2 cups boiled or fried rice
½ cup tomato sauce
Romano or Parmesan cheese to
   taste (optional)
salt and pepper to taste

Mix the rice, cheese and tomato sauce together. For an Italian flavor sprinkle Romano or Parmesan cheese over the rice mixture. Salt and pepper to taste. Stuff the dough pockets with the seasoned rice-cheese mixture.

The combination of rice and cheese is exceptionally tasty. Boil the filled pockets in lightly salted water.

Cheese Filling

1 egg
1 pound farmer's, hoop, feta or
   ricotta cheese
2 Tablespoons melted butter
½ teaspoon cinnamon
¼ teaspoon salt
1 teaspoon sugar or honey

Beat the egg with a wisk and mix the egg with the cheese. Add the melted butter, cinnamon, salt and sugar to the mixture and mix well. Stuff the dough pockets with the egg-cheese mixture. Cook by boiling in lightly salted water. This is a slightly sweet filling and goes well with either a tomato sauce or a butter sauce.

Chicken Filling

2 cups chopped cooked chicken
½ cup bread crumbs
1 cup bullion or consomme
Salt and pepper to taste
1 Tablespoon parsley (optional)

Instead of using raw ground meat, chopped, cooked chicken can be used as a filling. Other leftover meats can also be used as a filling if they are ground. Boil the filled pockets in lightly salted water or in soup.

Italian Filling

1 ten ounce package frozen
  chopped spinach (¾ pound of
  freshly cooked and chopped
  spinach can be used instead of
  the package of frozen spinach)
2 Tablespoons butter
¾ pound ground veal or beef
4 Tablespoons chopped onions
½ cup grated Romano or
  Parmesan cheese
a pinch of ground nutmeg
3 eggs
salt to taste

Melt the 3 Tablespoons of butter and fry the onions until they are cooked but not brown. This should take 7-8 minutes. Add the ground raw meat and brown it well. Transfer the meat and onions to a mixing bowl and after squeezing all the moisture out of the spinach, add it to the meat. Beat the eggs and add them, the grated cheese, the pinch of nutmeg to the meat. Salt to taste and use this to fill the squares of dough. Boil the filled pockets in lightly salted water.

Pork Filling, Chinese Style

¾ pound lean ground pork
4 teaspoons soy sauce
¾ teaspoon of freshly chopped
  ginger root
  or ½ teaspoon ground ginger
½ teaspoon salt
¾ pound fresh spinach or 1
  package frozen

Combine the pork, soy sauce, ginger and salt, mix and add the cooked, chopped, drained, squeezed spinach. Mix again and use to stuff the dough pockets. If you wish to substitute beef, veal or lamb, the soy and ginger will give you a Chinese flavor. Boil the filled pockets in lightly salted water.

Mass Production of Filled Pockets

Roll out 2 large sheets of dough thinly. Trim so that both are exactly the same size. Place 1 tablespoon of any filling at intervals along one sheet of dough leaving large unfilled margins. It is best to place the spoons of filling in even rows. After placing the filling in rows along the whole rectangle of dough, cover with the other layer and crimp the edges around the rectangle. You now have a large envelope showing many lumps. Take the pastry wheel and cut down the rows to form separate pockets around each lump. Allow the dough to sit for about ½ hour after using the pastry wheel. It will dry out and you can then separate each little pocket from the sheet. If you're not too steady in running a straight line with the pastry wheel, you can press the surface of the dough with the edge of a ruler and then follow the line with your wheel.

Cooking Dough Pockets

Regardless of ethnic origin kreplach, won ton, ravioli and all the others are cooked by boiling. They may be boiled in salted water or in boiling soup of any kind. Since the pockets are made of dough, cooking in soup will give the soup a floury taste. I prefer to cook them in boiling, salted water.

To Serve. In soup as dumplings: To each plate add a generous number of the filled pockets. It would be best to bring any extras to the table for you are sure to get requests for seconds.

Fried kreplach or ravioli are delicious side

dishes. Brown the pockets in butter or oil. For an Italian effect use olive oil with a clove of garlic crushed into the oil.

Filled pockets are usually served in a sauce either as a side dish or as the meal itself. When it comes to sauces, let your imagination soar. I will give a few sauces, but many others are possible.

Sauces for Filled Pockets

Prepared Sauces. There are several bottled and canned sauces that are excellent. Among these are various spaghetti sauces, sweet and sour Chinese sauce, canned gravies or even tomato sauce with added seasoning. Check your supermarket shelf. While you are there, you will also find packages of seasoning with instructions on how to make different types of sauces.

Homemade Sauces

Sweet and Sour Sauce with Bacon

This is a German sauce that is very tasty and goes exceptionally well with noodles and filled pockets.

5 slices bacon
1 large chopped onion
1/2 cup water or soup stock
1/2 cup wine
4 Tablespoons flour
salt, vinegar (lemon juice) and
    sugar to taste

Fry the bacon until crisp; drain on paper towels. Brown the chopped onion in the bacon grease to a golden color. Remove the onion and drain on paper towels. Put the 4 Tablespoons of flour in the bacon fat and saute it for a few minutes until the flour starts to turn a golden tan. Add water (soup stock) and wine to the pan with the flour, stirring as you heat and then put the onions back into the pan. Crumble the bacon and add it to the sauce. Simmer for twenty minutes and then add a dash of salt, sugar and vinegar. Taste to make sure you have a definite sour sweet flavor. Serve this over boiled or fried dough pockets. This is a delicious and different sauce.

Sweet and Sour Tomato Sauce

1/2 teaspoon salt
2 small or 1 large can tomato
    sauce or 1 can tomato soup
Mushrooms if desired
1 chopped onion
1/2 chopped green pepper
2 Tablespoons sugar or honey
2 Tablespoons lemon juice or
    vinegar
1/2 cup white wine

Saute the onion and green pepper in oil. Add the tomato sauce and wine and salt, then add the sugar and lemon juice. Allow to simmer for 20 minutes then taste. If you do not have a definite sweet sour flavor, add more sugar or lemon juice as required. Serve this sauce over filled dough pockets. If the sauce seems too thin, 2 Tablespoons of cornstarch or flour may be added.

Chinese Sweet Sour Tomato Sauce

2 small or 1 large cans tomato
　sauce or 1 can tomato soup
1/2 teaspoon salt
2 ounces chopped or sliced
　mushrooms
1 chopped onion
1/2 chopped green pepper
2 Tablespoons sugar or honey
2 Tablespoons vinegar or lemon
　juice
1/2 cup red or white wine
2 Tablespoons cornstarch or flour
1 teaspoon dried ginger or 1
　Tablespoon fresh chopped
　ginger *
1/2-1 teaspoon prepared dried
　mustard
2 Tablespoons soy sauce

Saute the onion and green pepper then add the wine, tomato sauce, vinegar, sugar and salt. Allow to simmer and stir in the cornstarch. When the sauce starts to thicken a little add the ginger, dried mustard and mushrooms. *For a hot sauce use 1 teaspoon of dried ginger or 1 Tablespoon of fresh ginger. For a milder sauce cut the amount of ginger in half. Dried mustard also makes a hot sauce. Use 1 teaspoon for a moderately hot sauce or half for a milder sauce. If you enjoy breathing fire, you can increase both the mustard and ginger. When this sauce is served over filled pockets, you have Chinese ravioli, or is it Chinese kreplach?

Italian Sauces

Several Italian sauces are given under Pizza in the next chapter.

Curry Sauces

A curry sauce is delightful with filled dough pockets. Although this type of sauce is usually eaten with rice, it is an innovative and tasty sauce for noodles.

　Simple Sweet and Sour Curry. Use either the Sweet and Sour Tomato Sauce or the Chinese Sweet and Sour Tomato Sauce recipes. Add 1 Tablespoon of curry powder for a moderately hot curry.

Tomato Curry. Omit the sugar and lemon from either of the Sweet and Sour Tomato Sauces. Add 1 Tablespoon of curry powder.

Curried Gravies. Beef and other gravies may be made into curry sauces by adding 1 Tablespoon of curry powder.

Indian Curry Sauce

This is a non-tomato curry.

4 Tablespoons butter or oil
1 chopped onion
1 Tablespoon curry powder
1 cup hot soup stock
1 cup hot milk
4 Tablespoons sour cream
4 Tablespoons cornstarch
1 cup apple sauce
1/2 cup white wine
1/4 teaspoon salt

Brown the chopped onion and then stir in the corn starch. Add the soup stock, milk and the curry powder. Allow the mixture to simmer for about 15 minutes. Add the applesauce, sour cream and white wine. Stir well and then add the salt and stir again. Allow to simmer for 15 minutes longer then serve over filled dough pockets.

Spaetzle

Not too long ago I didn't know the difference between a spaetzle and a spat. I learned the difference one night when dining at a German restaurant. I was so impressed with these Germanic noodles that I looked for the recipe and started to make them myself. Later I learned that the Italian gnocchi (pronounced yochi) were very similar to the German spaetzle. Some of the gnocchi recipes call for ricotta to be mixed in with the dough, but they are prepared in the same manner as the spaetzle. Spaetzle is boiled like a bagel and then fried before serving. I use them as a substitute for potatoes, but one of the big frozen food companies is selling a vegetable dish with spaetzle. I believe that theirs are boiled, not fried.

Gourmet shops that feature cooking utensils have special spaetzle graters. You can get along without one, but it is easier to grate a ball of dough than to roll it out and cut strips.

Spaetzle

3 cups all purpose flour
1 teaspoon melted butter
1 teaspoon salt
¼ teaspoon nutmeg (freshly
     grated if possible)
3 beaten eggs
½ cup milk

Stir the dry ingredients together and then add the teaspoon of melted butter and the 3 beaten eggs. Mix in the ½ cup of milk to form a heavy dough. If you have a spaetzle grater, roll the dough into a ball and let it sit uncovered for 20-30 minutes to partially dry out. If you do not have the grater, roll the dough out on a floured board to a thickness of about ¼ inch. Allow the sheet of dough to dry for about 20 minutes then cut the dough into strips. Divide each strip into portions ½ to 1 inch long and drop the pieces into boiling salted water.

Boil the pieces of dough for 6-8 minutes then remove from the water with a slotted spoon. Drain the spaetzle in a colander or on paper towels. Some cooks prefer to rinse the strips with cold water before draining.

The spaetzle are now ready for cooking. They can be kept in the boiled condition in the refrigerater for several days. Since this recipe makes enough to be a side dish for 8 or more people, I prepare for serving only what I need and save the rest for later.

To fry the spaetzle melt about 4 Tablespoons of butter or margarine in a skillet and saute the noodles until they are golden brown. The nutmeg gives this dish a unique but delicious flavor.

Spaetzle with Cheese

Prepare the spaetzle and fry them. Take a casserole dish and place a layer of spaetzle on the bottom. Sprinkle the noodles with Romano or Parmesan cheese then place a second layer of spaetzle on top of the first. Sprinkle this layer with the grated cheese too. I sometimes lay thin slices of Swiss cheese on top of the layers instead of using grated Italian cheese. The spaetzle casserole is ready to serve after heating it in an oven at 350°F. for about 30 minutes to melt the cheese.

Another variation of this dish is to serve it with fried onions. 2 large onions are cut and sauted in butter or oil. These are placed over the top layer of the noodles before the casserole is heated.

Rice

By no stretch of the imagination can rice be considered a bread, but rice is a grain similar to wheat. A large segment of the world's population lives on rice instead of wheat. In the Orient, noodles are made from rice flour instead of wheat flour. Noodles are not the only item rice flour is used to make; rice crackers, a sort of cookie are now imported into the United States from Japan. Still, even though I use cooked rice as a filling for some bread dishes the inclusion of a recipe for cooking rice seems a little out of place in a book on bread. I accept this fact but will include the recipe only because I feel that it should be included.

For most people, cooking rice is a difficult job. Rather than suffer rice boiled to mush, many people use either instant rice or cooking pouches of pre-cooked rice. Either of these methods is almost foolproof, but if you've managed to read this far, I will gladly certify that you are no fool. Instant rice costs too much and does not taste as good as regular rice. The stuff you get in the cooking pouches makes instant rice appear inexpensive.

Rice is used as a staple part of the diet throughout the Orient. There are many different peoples living in what we call the Far East. Although all of these groups cook rice, they do not all cook it in the same way. In Japan rice is served slightly on the soft side to make better balls of rice. Japanese rice is coated. My favorite recipe for cooking rice is an Indian one. A friend who was born and grew up in India learned this method from her Amah. She showed it to me. In this recipe rice is not added to boiling water. Cold water is poured on top of the rice. When cooked, it is not sticky. Each grain of rice is separate, but well done.

This recipe does not call for any measurements. It was given to me as it was used in India. Instead of measuring the amount of rice and water, I pick the size of the pot.

Indian Rice

Without measuring, cover the bottom of a pot with uncooked rice to a depth of 1 inch to 1½ inches. A large pot will take a large amount of rice, a small pot will take a lesser quantity. Pour cold water over the rice and pour it off to rinse the rice. Pour more water in to a depth about ¾ inch over the top of the rice. I use my index finger to measure. When the finger is touching the rice, the water is at the first joint.

Salt the rice using about ½ teaspoon for a 1 quart pot or more for a larger pot. Turn the gas on and bring the water to a vigorous boil. Boil until the water just barely covers the top of the rice then cover the pot and reduce the gas. Simmer for 2 minutes then turn off the gas but let the pot of rice sit covered for another 8-10 minutes. After the wait, check the rice. It should be perfect, but if you miscalculated the water level, heat it again for about 1-2 minutes covered and let it sit for another 8-10 minutes.

Using this method, I get good rice every time. I like not measuring, but one thing should be obvious. I am cooking more rice than I will use at one meal. To me this is not a drawback; I usually use a large pot to have even more leftover rice. I'm wild about leftover rice, but I don't eat it cold nor do I make rice puddings although I like rice pudding. I seldom reheat the rice to serve with a second meal. The reason I like to have leftover rice in my refrigerater is the dish known as Fried Rice. I think that Fried Rice is great for breakfast, wonderful for lunch and divine to serve along with dinner.

Fried Rice

½-1 cup (or more) cut up meat
   cooked ham, pork, beef,
   sausage, shrimp
about 1 chopped onion
½ - 1 chopped green pepper
¼-½ cup chopped celery
sliced mushrooms (optional)
bean sprouts. (optional)
rice to fill the frying pan
oil
Eggs. A minimum of 1 for a small
   pan or 2 or more for a large pan.
   After mixing in the egg, the rice
   should look moist.
Soy sauce, salt, pepper to taste

Chop the onion, celery, mushrooms, green peppers, or other vegetables. Brown them in the skillet with oil. Add the chopped meat and cook for a while. Turn off the gas and add the rice. Beat the eggs and work them into the rice with a fork. This will spread the cooked meat and vegetables evenly too. Add enough eggs that the rice looks quite gooey. It's hard to add too many eggs, easy to add too few. Turn the heat back on, sprinkle with soy sauce and salt and pepper. Allow the bottom to brown, then turn over the rice with a spatula to brown the other side. When the egg is no longer moist, the fried rice is ready to serve.

It is not necessary to have all the ingredients listed. I have at times used only rice and eggs. At other times I have thrown in any leftover I could find especially cooked peas, lima beans, zucchini squash and others.

Try this fried rice dish once and you too will cook your rice in larger quantities.

Cooking Rice (Other Methods)

Excellent rice can be cooked in a rice steamer if you have one. A crock pot can also be used to cook rice. It takes several hours but the results are similar to steamer rice. See your crock pot cookbook if you have a crock pot. I have never had much luck with recipes that call for rice to be fried first and then dropped in boiling water or with those that drop raw rice in boiling water. I prefer the method I have given to all of those.

Man does not live by bread alone, but bread can be used to prepare special dishes. These entrees are baked into or on top of bread dough. The best known of these dishes is the pizza.

Pizza

The recipe that follows was inspired by **Super Pizza** of Manhattan Beach, California. This is not their recipe, but is as close as I can come to duplicating it by taste. **Super Pizza** is a rather unique establishment that does not sell hot pizza. They prepare deep dish pizzas with the most filling I have ever seen. These are taken home and baked whenever you are ready to serve the pizza. My recipe is for the same type of pizza. You can prepare one of these when going to a party as a gift, or as a contribution to a pot luck dinner. Heat it there and have everyone tell you what a great pizza chef you are.

The dough used for this pizza can be any white or wheat bread dough made with either yeast or starter. I prefer to use either a French Bread dough or a Sourdough French recipe, but any bread will make a great pizza crust. Do not make your crust with baking powder or with biscuit mixes. Yeast is used because the action of yeast can be stopped at the point you prefer. If you like pizza that tastes more like bread or biscuits, go ahead with the baking powder, but you won't duplicate a pizzeria pizza.

Take enough dough to make one loaf of bread. Most of the recipes in this book will make two loaves. Roll the dough out to a rectangle. Select a large or small baking sheet or a pan with low walls. Round pizzas can be made in pie plates or in frying pans. Cast iron skillets are particularly good for making small, round pizzas. Roll the dough out until it is about ⅛ inch thick. Measure the dough against the pan you select and transfer it to the pan. The dough should be larger than the pan. Trim the edges. When using a pan with sides, allow the dough to come up on the sides of the pan to make a very deep dish pizza. After the dough has been fitted to the pan, allow it to rise to the thickness of pizza you prefer. I usually allow 20-30 minutes. If you like a very thin crust, bake the pizza shell immediately. After rising, bake the empty pizza shell at 350°F. for about 20 minutes. The heat will kill the yeast and prevent the dough from rising higher.

Now that the dough has been shaped and baked, you are ready to make the pizza. There is no definite recipe for a **Super Pizza.** You add what you want and the sky is truly the limit. This is the Dagwood of Pizzas. To start, brush the baked pizza dough with olive oil or salad oil and then pour in enough sauce to cover the bottom. Several sauce recipes will follow. Do not pour sauce over the various layers or you will have a sloppy, drippy pizza.

Start to build the pizza by putting a layer of one of the ingredients over the tomato sauce. Add as many layers as you wish. I once made a pizza that stood eight inches above the dough. Listed below are sample ingredients. You do not have to use all of these. You can add other ingredients not listed. Make the pizza the way you will like it.

Take coin shaped, thin discs of pepperoni and lay them over the sauce. The pieces should touch each other covering the entire dough with a layer of the sausage.

Chop an onion or two; I use a Veg-O-Matic, but you can use any method of chopping. Cover the layer of pepperoni with the onions.

Lay Genoa or other salami slices over the onions. Be sure to use only a single layer and let the slices touch each other to make a carpet of salami.

Layer sliced olives over the salami.

Spread a layer of Canadian bacon or sliced ham over the olives.

Top the ham with a layer of sliced green peppers.

You can keep adding ingredients or you can even repeat some of the layers. When you have a tall enough pizza, it is important to top your creation. Some people use a grated cheese such as Romano or Parmesan and sprinkle this between the layers.

The topping is made from grated mozzarella cheese. Spread this over the top of the pizza to a depth of at least ½ inch. More will not hurt. For a small pizza, one baked in a pie pan or skillet use 2-3 ounces of the grated cheese. A large pizza will take up to ½ pound of cheese; a giant pizza will use close to 1 pound of the grated cheese.

After the topping is put on the pizza pie, keep it refrigerated until you are ready to bake it. If you plan to transport the pizza, wrap it in aluminum foil or in plastic wrap. Remove the wrapping before baking.

To prepare the pizza for the table, bake in a 375°F. oven for about 30 minutes. If the pizza is very tall bake it for about 40 minutes. The edges of the crust should appear brown, if you can see them. The mozzarella cheese should be melted.

The only important thing to remember when baking this pizza is to put only 1 layer of sauce on the bottom and to put the mozzarella on the top. What goes in between is up to you.

Pizza Sauces

Thick Sauce. Some people like a very thick sauce. Take a can of tomato puree and add 1 Tablespoon of grated Romano or Parmesan cheese for every cup of sauce. Add oregano, basil and garlic to taste.

Another thick sauce can be made from tomato paste. This is almost too thick, but for every 2 ounces of paste add ½ ounce of tomato sauce or water. Stir and add the grated cheese and the spices. These thick sauces are best spread over the dough with a rubber spatula.

Prepared Sauces. Any bottled or canned spaghetti sauce can be used.

Sauces made by following the recipes on packages of sauce mix are excellent. Many years ago, I was given a scratch recipe for a spaghetti sauce by an elderly Italian friend who made the best sauce I had ever tasted. Everyone who ate at our home asked for the recipe. After enjoying this homemade sauce for several years, Lawry came out with a sauce mix package. To my surprise and annoyance, their recipe tasted so much like ours that I lost the original recipe. All sauce mixes make a decent tasting sauce, but my favorite is the one that comes so close to my original recipe.

You will use only a portion of the sauce for a pizza. Reserve the rest of it for spaghetti. Sauce can be frozen. I prefer to freeze it in heat sealed plastic bags, but empty milk cartons can be used after they have been washed out. I seal the cartons with a stapler before freezing. The use of bags or milk cartons avoids the cleaning of plastic containers which are particularly difficult to clean after holding sauce.

Spaghetti and Pizza Sauce (from Scratch)

1-2 chopped onions

1½ pounds ground meat (Sausage can be used instead of beef. Italian sausage is particularly good in this recipe)

4 ounces sliced mushrooms

1-2 sliced green peppers

sliced zuccini squash (optional)

½ to 1 cup chopped celery

1 cup red wine

11-12 ounces tomato sauce (If fresh tomatoes are used, use 3-4 pounds of tomatoes. Either cut them up and put them into the pan or puree them in the blender. It will take longer to simmer the sauce to the proper thickness using fresh tomatoes)

½ teaspoon basil (dried) or 1 tea spoon fresh basil

1 Tablespoon oregano

½ teaspoon powdered garlic or 2 cloves crushed

Grease a skillet and brown 1-2 chopped onions. Add the other vegetables and saute them too. Add the ground meat and brown it well. Add the spices, the tomato sauce and the wine and let the sauce simmer until it is thick. If flour or cornstarch is used, the sauce will thicken with less simmering. Some cooks like to add 2 Tablespoons of grated Parmesan cheese directly to the sauce. This is optional. The sauce made from this recipe is a marinara type sauce, different than those made from most sauce mixes.

Knishes, Pirogen, Piroske, Filled Pies

Every ethnic cuisine produces delectable dishes made of dough filled with meat, cheese or vegetables. These are for the most part tasty, nutritious dishes that deserve a place not only in this book but also on your table. Not all such dishes are listed in this section. I find the Cornish pastie too difficult to handle so it is omitted.

The dough used for these little pies can be either a special dough, a regular bread dough, or for the absolute tops use either a Brioche dough or a Challah dough. If you're in a hurry a recipe for a special quick dough is given below; if you happen to be baking bread the day you make these filled meat pies just use a portion of the bread dough.

Quick Dough for Knishes and Other Filled Pies

2 cups flour
1 teaspoon baking powder
2 ounces water
½ teaspoon salt
1 Tablespoon oil
2 beaten eggs

Mix the ingredients together to form a smooth dough. Add more water or flour if necessary then roll the dough to a thin rectangle about ⅛ inch thickness. If you are using a regular bread dough instead of the quick dough, allow it to rise, punch down and then roll it out to a ⅛ inch thick rectangle. Cut the dough into squares or rounds. A 5 inch square is a nice size to work with when making knishes. Place filling on the square of dough and fold over to form either a rectangle or a triangle. See illustrations. Rounds of dough are folded to make half moons. The triangle form is easier to seal than a rectangle when working with a square. After folding, pinch the edges to seal and then brush the surfaces with a beaten egg or egg yolk diluted with a Tablespoon of water. Larger pies can be made by placing the filling on one square or round and covering with another. Use twice as much filling for these bigger knishes. Bake filled dough on a greased sheet at 350°F until browned. This will take about 20 minutes.

If you use a regular bread dough, a yeast dough, you can make brown and serve knishes, Piroske or whatever you wish to call them. After filling the dough squares, let them rise for 20 minutes. If you are going to serve them direct from the oven, bake at 350°F. for 20 minutes or until they are brown. For brown and serve bake at 250°F. for 20 minutes to inactivate the yeast. Cool the meat pies and then freeze them. To serve place the frozen pies on a greased baking sheet and bake at 350°F. until they are hot and browned.

Fillings

Rice and Cheese Filling

2 beaten eggs
2 cups cooked rice
1 cup ricotta, hoop, or farmer's cheese
1 sauteed onion (optional)
1 sauteed green pepper (optional)
2 Tablespoons tomato paste or 4 Tablespoons tomato sauce

Mix the cheese, rice, and tomato sauce or paste and eggs together. If onion and pepper are to be used, saute them in butter or oil and then mix them into the rice.

Variation

½ cup of grated provolone, jack cheese or swiss cheese can be substituted for the ricotta type cheese, or be added in addition to the ricotta.

Fried rice can be used instead of cooked rice. Fried rice usually contains some form of meat which makes an excellent filling.

Spoon the filling onto the dough squares and fold. Bake at 350° F. for 20 minutes.

Potato Knish Filling

This Jewish dish tastes more traditional if chicken fat (schmaltz) is used, but any shortening including corn oil can be used instead.

3 eggs
4 cups mashed potatoes (instant may be used)
½ cup Matzo meal or corn meal
2 teaspoons salt
½ teaspoon pepper
3 onions
4 Tablespoons oil or schmaltz

Mash the potatoes and then mix them with the beaten eggs, meal, salt, pepper and oil. Spoon this mixture onto the dough and fold. Bake at 350°F. for 20 minutes.

Ground Meat

2 cups ground beef or lamb (left-overs may be used)
½ cup mashed potatoes
2 Tablespoons oil or other shortening
1 chopped onion
½ teaspoon salt
¼ teaspoon pepper
1 beaten egg
½ teaspoon dried mustard

Brown the onions and meat and then combine the ingredients. Spoon onto the dough squares, fold and bake at 350°F. for 20 minutes.

Beef, Egg and Onion Filling

1 pound chopped beef
2 sliced or chopped onions
3 hardboiled eggs
salt and pepper to taste
1/2 teaspoon dried mustard
1/2 teaspoon ground ginger
1/4 teaspoon dried basil

Brown the onions and meat. Chop the boiled eggs and mix them into the meat and onion mixture. Season and fill the meat pies. Bake at 350°F. for 20 minutes. This is very similar to the Argentinian empanada.

Chicken Filling

2 cups chopped, cooked chicken
1/2 cup bread crumbs or corn meal
1 cup chicken gravy (available in cans)
salt and pepper to taste

Combine the ingredients. Spoon onto the dough and fold. Bake at 350°F. for 20 minutes.

Rice and Mushroom Filling

1 cup cooked rice
1/2 cup sliced fresh or canned mushrooms
1 onion

Saute the onion and mushrooms in butter. Mix them into the rice. Season to taste and spoon onto dough squares. Fold and bake at 350°F. for 20 minutes.

Regular Style Cheese Filling

1 pound ricotta, fetta, farmer's or hoop cheese
1/2 cup sour cream
2 Tablespoons bread crumbs
2 Tablespoons melted butter
2 Tablespoons sugar
2 Tablespoons raisins (optional)
2 beaten eggs

Mix the ingredients and spoon onto the dough squares. Fold and bake at 350°F. for 20 minutes.

Black Bread

Sweet Cheese Knishes

These are special knishes; use a brioche dough or the special dough given.

To prepare the dough, sift the flour, baking powder and salt into a bowl. Add the eggs, sour cream and melted butter. Knead into a dough adding milk if there is not enough moisture from the sour cream to handle the flour. Roll out to a thickness of 1/8 inch and cut into squares or rounds.

Filling. Spoon the filling onto the dough squares, fold and bake at 350°F. for 20 minutes.

Dough:
2 beaten eggs
4 cups flour
2 teaspoons baking powder
1 teaspoon vanilla extract
½ teaspoon salt
1 Tablespoon melted butter
1 cup sour cream

Sweet Cheese Filling:
1 pound ricotta, farmer's, feta or
   hoop cheese
2 Tablespoons melted butter
½ cup sour cream
1 teaspoon vanilla extract
3 Tablespoons sugar or honey
2 beaten eggs
2 Tablespoons or more of raisins

A few of the more traditional recipes have been given, but there are many more possible. Use your imagination. Any of the Pirogen, Piroske, Knish type dishes can be filled with whatever filling you can conjure out of leftovers. See the fillings listed under Ravioli, Kreplach or Won Ton or make up new exciting fillings of your own. I will give a few examples I have never seen in any book for a knish filling. I'm sure that you can top me.

Chinese Piroske

Sauté the onions and brown the pork. Mix with the chestnuts, ginger, soy sauce and salt and pepper. Fill dough squares by spooning the meat out and folding the squares. Bake on a greased sheet at 350°F. for 20 minutes.

2 cups ground pork
1 chopped onion
1 can of water chestnuts
1 teaspoon ginger or dried
   mustard
1 Tablespoon soy sauce
   salt and pepper to taste

Mexican Knishes

This one is a sort of Jewish burrito.

Mix the salsa with the refried beans and then make the knishes by spooning the beans onto the dough squares. A hot salsa will give a hot, Mexican taste to the knish. If you do not use the salsa, mix a little tomato sauce in with the beans. Meat can be mixed in too. If raw meat is used, brown it first. Fold the dough over the filling and bake at 350°F. for 20 minutes.

1 can refried beans.
1 jar salsa.

Bagels and English Muffins

Scrambled Egg and Onion Pirogen

This pie was inspired by a burrito available here in Los Angeles. Instead of using a flour tortilla I bake my own envelope.

1 chopped onion
3 beaten eggs

Saute the onion and then scramble together the eggs with the onion. Ham, sausage or salami can be added to this dish. Spoon the filling onto the dough squares, fold and bake at 350°F. for 20 minutes. Serve hot.

Leftover Fillings

When I was young, they told me that it was a sin to waste food. This lead to a guilt complex over leftovers. Fortunately, I had this problem resolved for me when I dined at a Chinese restaurant. My fortune cookie read, "Man who has no leftovers get fat." Don't be guilty about having leftover foods. You can use these to fill knishes. Knishes can be frozen and eaten later. When the leftover is a roast, grind it into a hash and use it as if it were ground meat. If the leftover is a meat in a sauce, allow it to stand in the refrigerator long enough for the sauce to congeal. Spoon it onto the dough and seal it extra well to prevent leakage. You'd be surprised at what can be used as a filling. I've tried wok vegetables, beef stroganoff, meat balls, Hungarian goulash, and even leftover hamburgers. A good cook or baker can improvise.

Braided Entrees

The braid form used to make desserts can also be used for entrees. Use a regular bread dough; for special dinners use either Brioche or Challah.

Braids are open at the top so use fillings that are not apt to leak out. The cheese and rice fillings and the meat fillings used for knishes will work well in braids.

Ham and Mushroom Braid

Filling:
1 small onion chopped
1 cup sliced mushrooms
2 Tablespoons shortening or drippings
½ cup bread crumbs
½ cup diced ham
¼ teaspoon dried mustard
½ teaspoon soy sauce
1 beaten egg
salt and pepper to taste

Fry the onion in the shortening for 1-2 minutes. Add the mushrooms and ham and saute them, Remove the pan from the heat and add the breadcrumbs, soy sauce and seasoning. Mix in the beaten egg and allow the mixture to cool.

Take a portion of a bread dough and roll it out to a rectangle measuring 9 x 12 inches. One loaf of bread will produce 2 such rectangles. Place the rectangle of uncooked dough on a greased baking sheet and brush the dough with oil or melted butter. Spread the filling down the center leaving about ¼ of the dough uncovered by filling on either side. Cut diagonal slashes in the dough with a razor. The slashes should be about 2 inches apart. Fold a strip from alternate sides over the filling to give a braided effect. After a 20 minutes rise bake in a 375°F. oven for 25-30 minutes. Cool on a wire rack and serve. Finish the braid by brushing with egg or milk before baking.

Pigs in a Braided Blanket

For those who think that pigs in a blanket are the ultimate in haute cuisine, do not bother to read this section. The dish I wish to present here is related to pigs in a blanket, but is much more sophisticated. It blends eye appeal with taste appeal to make a dish you would not be ashamed to serve to company.

To increase the taste appeal, it is suggested that simple hot dogs are not used to prepare this dish. Recommended are Polish and other sausages including brown and serve links. There is a wide choice of ethnic sausages that will make this dish a culinary delight.

Prepare a bread dough, a yeast bread. If you have followed a two loaf recipe, take a portion of the dough and roll it out to a rectangle measuring 9 x 12 inches. Enough dough to make 1 bread will make 2 such rectangles. Lay the sausage along the center of the rectangle. When using fat polish sausage, I usually use 2 sausages side by side. If your rectangle is 12 inches long, 2 pairs of Polish sausage will fit. Trim off any any excess sausage and make the braid as described in the recipe preceding this. You may wish to spread prepared mustard down the center of the rectangle before putting the sausage on the dough.

Some sausages are long enough to fit the rectangle while others are so small that you will use three abreast and more than two deep. Mexican chorizo sausage comes in moderately hot, very hot and too darned hot. This type sausage should be split and the loose filling placed on the dough. Italian sausage should also be split and the loose filling used for the braids. It would be best not to put mustard on these before baking.

The use of a better tasting dough can also improve this dish. I recommend Challah dough but any yeast bread dough will make a tasty dish.

A Meal on a Bun

If a meal on a bun means a hot dog with all of the trimmings, take yourself out to the ball game and dine al fresco. If on the other hand you are looking for interesting entrees based on bread the recipe that follows is explicitly for you. The king of the meal on a bun series is Beef Wellington, but if you get out your gourmet cookbook, you'll only put it back on the shelf frustrated. Beef Wellington is too complicated a dish, too expensive for most people. It can be modified to where anyone can afford to turn out a good, no make that a great dish, but since it isn't the original Beef Wellington, I will call it Beef Waterloo.

Beef Wellington is for those people with Champagne (imported Mums®) appetites. It uses beef tenderloin and a hard to handle pastry shell. Between the beef and the pastry shell one usually finds a layer of *fois gras* (chopped liver to most of us.) When making Beef Waterloo, Lamb Waterloo, Ham Waterloo and Pork Waterloo, we substitute a less expensive cut of meat. If your appetites are in the domestic champagne category, the ideal meat is a standing rib roast. For those of us with beer pocketbooks, I suggest a rolled roast, either rump or clod, that has been marinated for 2 days in a fresh pineapple juice and vinegar marinade. If you can't get fresh pineapple use frozen or a commercial tenderizer. Canned pineapple juice must not be used; the heat of canning kills the enzyme, papain, that tenderizes meat.

The dough for the Waterloo dishes can be any bread dough, but Brioche and Challah dough are closer to the pastry dough found on the Wellington. If you prepare enough dough for 2 loaves of bread, you should have enough dough left after covering the meat to bake 1 loaf. Instead of *fois gras* (chopped liver) a variety of fillings to come between the dough and the meat will be given.

Beef, Pork, Ham or Lamb Waterloo

2-4 pound roast of ham
  ham may be pre-cooked variety
  other meats should be uncooked
Dough-(See Brioche or Challah
  recipes)
Vinegar-white or wine 2 cups
2 cups water
3 ounces fresh or frozen pineapple
  juice
2 sliced onions
3 bay leaves
½ teaspoon pepper
1 teaspoon salt

Place the meat, other than ham, in a large bowl and cover with a mixture of vinegar, water, onion, bay leaves, salt, pepper and pineapple juice. Ham need not be marinated in this manner. Leave the meat in the marinade for 24 to 36 hours turning it at least twice a day.

After the marinade has had a chance to work, place the roast in a small pan. If you have a roasting rack, use it. Cook the meat (beef, pork or lamb) for 4 hours at 325°F. If you have a meat thermometer it will be helpful to use it. If you are preparing Ham Waterloo, take the ham without using the marinade and bake it for 2 hours if it is a fully cooked ham. Glaze the top with honey or your favorite glaze before baking. Allow the roast to cool. The pan drippings may be skimmed and reserved for a sauce.

Make the dough according to the selected recipe. Brioche and Challah doughs are rich in eggs and oil; they are easy to work and give a special taste to the finished dish. After kneading the dough allow it to rise until it has doubled. Test with a finger. If the rise is complete, punch down the dough. If you are using a recipe for 2 loaves of bread, cut the dough in half. If you have selected Brioche dough, use the recipe in this book to avoid having to leave the dough in the refrigerator overnight. Place the portion of dough on a lightly floured board and roll it out to a rectangle ¼ inch thick. The other half of the dough can be used to bake a bread. Measure the length and diameter of the meat and then trim the rectangle of dough so that it is 2 inches longer than the roast and 2 inches wider than the diameter. Reserve the scraps; they can be incorporated with the dough for the bread, used to make rolls, or used to trim and decorate the envelope.

Beat an egg for an egg glaze. Brush the egg onto the outside edges of the rectangle. You should cover about 1-2 inches of the outside edges with egg. Place the filling in the center of the dough and spread it in a strip about 4-5 inches wide the length of the dough. Take the cooked meat and place it on top of the filling. Bring up the sides to come together at top center. Press the edges of the dough firmly together. The pinching and the egg glaze will hold the dough envelope together. Now fold in the ends and pinch them to make a seal. Take the pastry brush and brush the entire surface of the envelope with beaten egg.

Place the envelope containing the meat seam down on a greased baking sheet and sprinkle it with poppy seeds if you would like that touch. Allow the dough envelope to rise for 15 minutes in a warm place. Bake at 350°F. for 1-1¼ hours. It is best to serve this dish directly from the oven. If you get the envelope ready too soon, it can be placed in the refrigerator until you're ready to put it into the oven.

To serve, cut across the width of the envelope in thick slices. A sauce may be served with the dish.

Fillings

Chutney Filling. Spread chutney directly from the bottle over the dough.

Mushroom Filling. Melt 4 tablespoons of butter in a frying pan and add 1 pound of sliced or chopped mushrooms. Saute the mushrooms and add ¼ cup sherry, ½ cup chopped onion, 1 teaspoon dry mustard. Simmer until liquid is reduced almost completely. Cool in the refrigerator and when cool spread this filling over the dough.

HEALTH FOODS

Like a teenager maturing into an adult, as I grow older, I am beginning to have a genuine respect for some health food theories I once scoffed at. It isn't senility, atrophy of the brain or even age that has changed my mind. When I read about D.B.C.P. pesticide residues found in vegetables, I start to worry. I worry even more when I know that these chemicals have been found to cause sterility in the workers who made the produce and have been found to cause cancer in test animals subjected to low concentrations of these chemicals. When they tested sacchrine, the testers used unnaturally high concentrations of the chemical on the test animals, but when they tested the pesticides, the levels were comparable to the levels humans are exposed to in industry.

Pesticides aren't the only chemicals that make me worry. Chemical caponization of poultry can introduce a high level of estrogen into the diet. "Auriomycin"® used in cattle feeds to fatten cattle more quickly is passed on the consumer along with the steak or hamburger. Preservatives, artificial sweeteners, artificial coloring agents like Red Dye #2 are found in foods of every description. As a microbiologist, I have experimented on bacterial growth where the medium was altered by adding such ingredients. A series of genetic mutations occurred in some cases. I have no desire to become a test animal.

Years ago when a person interested in natural foods preached organic farming to me I dismissed him as a "health food freak." I laughed when they praised organic fertilizers for organic fertilizers cannot be used by plants until soil bacteria breaks the organic compounds into inorganic chemicals. At that time when asked if I preferred my strawberries to have manure or chemical fertilizers on them, I tried to be funny and said, "I prefer them with whipped cream." Simple inorganic fertilizers work well and will cause no problem with foods grown with their help, but if these compounds are used, can we be sure that no harmful chemicals have been mixed in with them? I now choose to consider the expression "organic fertilizer" to refer to a farming philosophy which rules out the use of pesticides and chemical additives.

I recently read a book about the use of horses in modern farming. There are a few farmers who still plow, rake and reap using horse drawn machinery. Unlike the diesel tractor, the horse's waste products can be returned to the soil in the shape of a rich manure that is an excellent fertilizer. There is no use of foreign oil and no pollution.

To be totally honest, I should mention that horse droppings are the prime infectious source of tetanus, but there is now a vaccine against this disease.

The recipes that follow are free of most chemicals. The shortening is cold pressed, polyunsaturated oil instead of saturated vegetable fats or animal fats. Greasing is done with cholesterol free lecithin. The flours recommended are either whole grain or are fortified by the addition of healthful substances. Use these recipes or the suggestions on how to convert any recipe to a more healthful product.

Health Food Breads

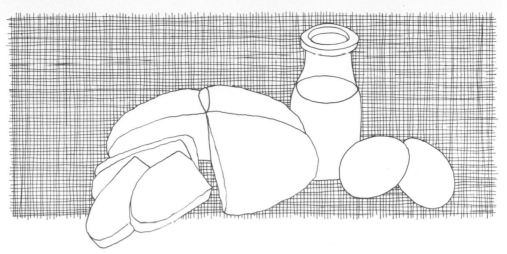

Many people are concerned with the quality of the food they eat. Others are forced to follow special diets for medical reasons. The recipes in the first section of this book do not meet the requirements of these people, but I offer no apology for this lack because most of the recipes in this book and in every other book on baking bread can be converted to health food standards if a few simple rules are followed.

There was once a song that told us to , "Accentuate the positive, eliminate the negative." This is the principle that converting an ordinary recipe to a health food recipe follows. Breads can be a wholesome addition to most diets, but with a few exceptions, most commercial breads add little to nutrition and may even contain substances harmful to good health. Bad as these breads are today, they are not as injurious to health as some of the breads sold during the eighteenth century, back in the good old days. There is one exception that seems a direct throwback to those good old days when a baker could put anything into a bread. I am referring to a high bulk bread that contains ground sawdust. In my opinion, that is as barbaric a practice as putting chalk into a white bread to make it whiter. The chalk was used in the eighteenth century. The sawdust you can get today.

Bread is basically flour and water with some shortening, salt and sweetener added. Since the bulk of the finished bread is flour, selection of the correct flour is of prime importance. Most of the flour sold in supermarkets has been degerminated, bleached and sometimes bromated. Wheat is our most important flour. In search of a light bread of dazzling whiteness, wheat flour has been stripped of the wheat germ, that portion of the wheat berry that contains most of the vitamins, enzymes and the nutrients. The flour that remains has been bleached to make it even whiter. This theft of the wheat germ has resulted in a flour that will produce a high, light, airy bread filled with empty calories and devoid of much of its nutritional value. White flour does have an additional advantage to the makers of the flour; since the wheat germ contains oil, whole wheat flour can turn rancid on the shelves. White flour has a longer shelf life.

Despite the fact that whole wheat flour does have more nutrition than white flour, too many people today are bad mouthing white flour. They should have their facts straight before they do this. Wheat is made up of three parts. The bran, which is excellent roughage makes up about 5% of a whole wheat flour. If the bran is removed the flour left is called whole meal flour and is a flour of 95% extraction. This extraction figure is used in the milling business to show how much of the flour is left after milling. The wheat germ is about 10% of whole wheat flour. After removing both the bran and the wheat germ the flour left is a flour of 85% extraction. It is called white flour. For those who are opposed to eating white flour but rave about how good whole wheat is, let them consider that 85% of whole wheat is white flour.

White flour does not have the nutritive value of whole wheat, but other than a decrease in nutrition it is not bad. White flour is easy to work with and produces breads that rise better. For certain breads it is impossible to substitute whole wheat. Brioche and Challah would be entirely different breads if wheat flour were used. Some white flours are better for you than others. An unbleached flour that is not bromated has not received chemical treatment. The wheat germ and the bran have been removed. If your diet were dependent on bread for the major source of protein the loss of the wheat germ would be serious. If you eat a normal diet a small loss of nutrition in the bread will not be significant.

Unbleached flour can be made more nutritious. Wheat germ may be substituted for part of the flour in the recipe. This will allow you to bake delicate breads like the Brioche and the Challah and still have good nutrition. Other enrichment can be added to bread where maximum nutrition is desired.

When baking with 100% stone ground wheat flour, you will run into certain problems. Wheat flour does not rise well. In the recipes that follow, I will offer certain methods to increase the rising ability of the wheat flour.

A 50% stone ground wheat bread where the other 50% is unbleached white flour will rise better than a bread made from 100% stone ground whole wheat.

Before coming to the recipes, it would be helpful to make some comments about the use of 100% whole wheat in baking bread. I have already said that there can be a problem with making such a bread rise. There are several ways of improving the rising ability of a whole wheat bread. The first of these is to use more yeast. Rather than go to the expense of buying more packages of yeast, we will grow the extra yeast ourselves by using the sponge method every time we bake a whole wheat bread. When the sponge is set up, the yeast cells are given a chance to multiply.

To set up a sponge, combine all of the liquid called for in the recipe with the dried yeast and a little honey. Add a part of the flour. After sitting in a warm place for a couple of hours, the mixture of flour, water and yeast will be filled with bubbles and will have risen in the bowl. It will look just like an ocean sponge that has absorbed water. As the yeast cells multiply in the sponge, they blow bubbles of carbon dioxide gas. More yeast cells produce more gas which helps the bread rise better.

The use of Vitamin C was described in the chapter on shortcuts. Vitamin C acts as a catalyst for yeast growth. When it is added, the time of generation is shorter. When baking with whole wheat flour, the addition to the sponge of a 50 milligram tablet of Vitamin C will produce more yeast more quickly and help the bread rise higher. Be sure to crush the tablet.

Whole wheat breads rise better if they are baked as pan breads instead of hearth loaves. The sides of the pan support the bread as it rises. This produces a higher, better textured bread.

Other whole grain flours than wheat are available. Most rye flour is whole grain, but if you purchase rye flour, check the label to make sure that it hasn't been degerminated or bromated. Corn meal is usually sold as degerminated corn meal. If your market doesn't carry whole grain flours, check your health food stores. A word of caution regarding health food stores is necessary. Since any flour with the germ left intact can turn rancid on standing, it is important to find a store that has a good turnover of the product to make sure that the flour is fresh when you purchase it. Once you have it home, store whole grain flours in the refrigerator and always smell the flour before baking. If you detect a rancid odor, discard the flour and purchase fresh. Some health food stores grind their own flour.

They sell you the grain and grind it after you make your purchase. Like a specialty coffee store that grinds the beans for the patron, you know that freshly ground flour is fresh for whole grain stores well. It only becomes rancid after it is ground into flour. The grinder at the health food store I patronize grinds too fine; it makes flour not meal. I like finer ground corn meal because it makes a lighter corn bread, but when I want rye meal, I want an extra coarse grind. A food processor would do the job on rye grain, but most health food stores sell rolled rye flakes for use as a cereal. These flakes are flattened out whole grain and contain all the nutrition and goodness of a kernel of rye. Rye flakes are about the same price as the whole grain. I buy the flakes and chop them in a blender at low speed. This makes an extra coarse meal that is ideal for baking.

Flour is the basic ingredient of all breads. For maximum nutritional value use whole grain flours. If you want to use a white flour for special baked goods use only unbleached flour and consider enriching the flour with wheat germ, soy flour, skim milk powder, eggs or high gluten flour.

The other ingredients found in bread need little discussion. Shortening is used in small quantities in some breads; other breads like the French bread do not use any shortening. Recipes in many books call for saturated animal fats like butter, lard or suet. Other recipes call for hydrogenated vegetable oil, a solid shortening. Whenever a hydrogenated vegetable oil or a saturated animal fat is called for in a recipe, oil can be substituted. Some oils are better than others for they are less saturated. Safflower oil, sunflower oil and corn oil are usually considered to be the best oils for human consumption, but olive oil, peanut oil and sesame oil have their fans. If the oil is prepared by the cold press technique any enzymes present in the oil will not be destroyed by heat when the oil is pressed. Look at the label; all cold pressed oils are labeled as such. The use of a cold pressed oil is not recommended for baking. The heat of baking will destroy any of the enzymes present in such oil. Cold pressed oils can be used, but they cost more than oils made in the conventional manner. Be sure to use a polyunsaturated oil instead of animal fat.

Shortening is also used to grease baking pans and sheets. DO NOT USE LIQUID OIL FOR GREASING. The molecule size of the oil is small because unsaturated chains make smaller molecules. Oil will be absorbed from the pan into the bread where it is not wanted or needed. For greasing use liquid locithin or even saturated fats. See the section on greasing (page 239).

Sweeteners. Sugar, cane sugar, barbados molasses and many other sweeteners offer only empty calories. The ideal sweetener to use on bread is honey which can be substituted spoonful for spoonful for sugar. Honey is a natural sugar containing a six carbon sugar called fructose. Sucrose, table sugar, contains one fructose combined with one dextrose in every molecule. Honey is not only good for you, but it enhances the freshness of bread, for honey is a natural preservative. Blackstrap molasses is rich in Vitamin B and in iron. It too can be substituted in equal volume for sugar. Blackstrap will darken the color of bread and is used by many commercial bakeries to make dark rye breads and pumpernickels. Bakeries use other coloring additives too, but the use of blackstrap molasses is a natural way to provide color.

Pure fructose in crystalline form is available in many health foods stores. This is the refined sugar that is found in honey. It has the advantage of being twice as sweet as either honey or table sugar. When using fructose, use only half as much. Since you use only half, the calories from the sweetener are reduced in half. With the crackdown on artificial sweeteners, one Los Angeles soft drink company is making fructose soda to reduce calories.

The last of the common ingredients in bread is salt. Before adding salt check the label on your box. If it contains strange ingredients, you can buy natural sea salt that contains nothing but a mixture of sodium and magnesium chlorides.

To Supplement Your Bread's Nutrition

To accentuate the positive, you can add ingredients that will increase the nutritional value of the bread. Protein is the ideal supplement. This can be added in several different ways.

1. Nonfat Dried Milk Nonfat dried milk, whole milk or liquid skim milk can be added to the recipe. When liquid milk is used, substitute it for part of the water. Milk powder can be added directly without making any substitution. There are two types of nonfat skim milk powder sold. One of them is the instant nonfat milk sold in supermarkets. This is dried by a high heat process which destroys some of its nutrient ingredients. The other milk powder is spray dried, low heat non fat milk.

For baking use either one. If you are purchasing for baking buy the less expensive instant milk. In the process of baking the heat will destroy any enzymes that would be destroyed in the instant powder. You will pay less and dissolve the milk more quickly with no loss in nutrition.

While talking about milk and dairy products, it might be a good idea to discuss the raw milk—

pasteurized milk controversy. There are those who believe that raw milk contains certain enzymes valuable to nutrition that are destroyed by pasteurization. The other school of thought looks back to before the Civil War when milk carried many diseases. Joseph Bordon's canned milk saved the lives of many infants at that time, but that was before certified herds were kept to provide safe raw milk. If properly controlled, certified raw milk is usually sold with a lower bacterial count than pasteurized milk. The milk must be checked regularly and the herds checked too. If the inspectors do their job, certified raw milk should be as safe as pasteurized milk.

All of this information should be interesting, at least from a historical point and from a public health viewpoint, but what about baking? When it comes to baked goods there is no difference between raw milk and pasteurized milk. The heat of baking is higher than the heat of pasteurization. If you start with raw milk, all enzymes will be inactivated by the heat. At the same time all bacteria will be destroyed by the heat. The best dairy product for baking is the least expensive.

Yogurt or sour cream can be used to replace a portion of the water in any recipe. The addition of either of these products adds the protein of the milk and gives a rich texture to the dough.

2. High Gluten flour is very rich in protein. I have seen 75% protein high gluten flour in some health food stores. If ½ cup of high gluten flour is substituted for ½ cup of whole wheat flour in a 100% whole wheat bread, you not only increase the protein, but increase the gluten too which will make the bread rise better.

3. Soy flour is another source rich in protein. Unfortunately, soy flour contains no gluten at all. To get the best results, I usually substitute ½ cup soy flour and ½ cup high gluten flour for 1 cup of whole wheat flour when making an all wheat bread. If you desire to have even more protein, a two bread recipe, one that calls for about 8 cups of flour will take up to 1 cup of soy flour and 1 cup of high gluten flour.

4. Eggs are another good source of protein. Most breads can be enriched by adding eggs. For use with whole wheat do not add more than 2 eggs to the recipe. Special egg breads like the Brioche and the Challah should not be baked with wheat flour. They are baked with unbleached. If you wish to make one of these, add 1 cup of wheat germ as a substitute for 1 cup of unbleached flour and 1 cup of skim milk powder to enrich the recipe. The recipes for Challah and Brioche will be found in the chapter on ethnic breads. When adding eggs to a bread, avoid using only yolks. The egg albumin, the white part of the egg contains a chemical called lecithin that helps metabolize the cholesterol found in the egg yolk.

5. Nuts and nut flour. Protein can be added to bread by the addition of nuts or nut flour. Nut flour is a rather tricky item to use. First you have to grind the nuts in a blender to a flour. This poses a problem because the nuts have a natural oil content. If blended too well, you will wind up with a nut butter instead of a flour. Hazel nuts (filberts) are the easiest nuts to grind into a flour. Nut flour will absorb water but at a different rate than wheat flour. Nut flour should be substituted for wheat not added, but even so, the water to flour ratio will be upset. The substitution is made on a cup to a cup basis. Never use more than 1 cup of nut flour in any bread recipe making two loaves of bread. In kneaded breads the ratio of flour to water is adjusted during the kneading by adding more flour if necessary. Never add nut flour to a batter bread where you cannot adjust the flour to water ratio.

It is far easier to use slivered or chopped nuts in a bread recipe. Since these do not take up water, they are added to the recipe rather than used as a substitute for flour. Slivered or chopped nuts can be added to any breads including batter breads. The nuts add character and crunch to any bread in addition to being a good source of nutrition. Add up to 1 cup of chopped nuts to any double bread recipe. Nuts can be added to a batter bread without upsetting the flour to water ratio.

When using unbleached flour, add wheat germ to restore some of the nutritional qualities of whole wheat. This may be added in addition to skim milk, soy flour or eggs. For a super high nutrition bread add nuts, soy, eggs, and milk.

Now that you know the ground rules, you can convert any recipe to a more healthful bread. On the following pages I have given a few such recipes that I have already converted to good nutritional standards. Before listing them, I want to make a few remarks about treats. I'm not advocating health food doughnuts, but even those can be made. As I pointed out in the regular recipes, the same dough can be used to fry a doughnut, boil a bagel, bake a roll or a bread. If you must have doughnuts, I have given a recipe for a baked doughnut to avoid deep frying in fat.

Health Food Bread Recipes

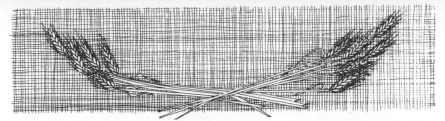

Fortified Basic 50% Wheat Bread

This bread may be baked with either starter or yeast. If a starter is used, decrease the recipe by 1 cup of water and 1 cup of flour. Add 1 cup of starter and allow the sponge to stand overnight. Even when yeast is used, bake by the sponge method to get a better rise from the whole wheat flour used. The addition of Vitamin C will decrease the sponge time; if allowed to go the full time, the Vitamin C will increase the number of yeast cells working.

50% Wheat Sponge:

50 milligram tablet of Vitamin C (crushed)

3½ cups warm water

1 package (1 Tablespoon) active dry yeast

4 cups whole wheat flour or 3 cups whole wheat flour plus 1 cup wheat germ

½ teaspoon honey

1 cup of instant non fat dried skim milk

The Second Step:

about 4 cups of unbleached flour

1½ teaspoons honey

1 Tablespoon salt

3 Tablespoon oil

Sponge. Crush the Vitamin C tablet in a bowl and add about 2 ounces of warm water and ½ teaspoon of honey. Swish the spoon in the water to wash the honey off. Add 1 package of active dried yeast and allow the mixture to stand in a warm place for about 10 minutes to prove the yeast. When the yeast becomes frothy, stir in the wheat germ and whole wheat flour. Cover the bowl and let it stand for an hour to 1½ hours. If Vitamin C is not used, the sponge should stand a little longer. When the sponge is ready, it will be filled with bubbles and have risen in the bowl.

The Second Step. Stir down the sponge and add ingredients. Work in the flour 1 cup at a time until a dough is formed. Sprinkle about ½ cup flour on the bread board and scrape the sponge onto the flour. Add more flour over the top of the sponge. Knead, working in more flour as necessary. Remember that a wheat bread dough should be slightly damp and sticky on the inside. When the dough no longer clings to your hands, you have added enough flour. Knead about 10 minutes until the dough is springy. The surface should be dry.

This recipe will make two large loaves. Wheat bread rises higher when baked in a pan for the walls of the pan support the dough and prevent it from spreading out. Hearth loaves can be baked, but they will be lower than breads baked in a pan. When baking hearth loaves, do not let the bread rise too much before baking or it will start to spread and produce a wide, low loaf.

After kneading, place the dough in a greased bowl and allow it to double. Depending on the temperature of the room, this should take about 1-1½ hours. Punch down the dough, divide into 2 portions and shape the loaves. Pan loaves can rise for 30 minutes after shaping, but hearth loaves should be baked 10 minutes after they are shaped. If the day is cold, you can let the dough rise after kneading in the oven. A pan filled with boiling water placed on the oven bottom will warm the oven.

Bake at 400°F. for 45 minutes. Test with a thin knife and cool the finished loaves on a wire rack.

Since wheat flour rises poorly, do not skip the rise after kneading unless you like bread with the texture of a brick.

A 50% whole wheat bread, particularly one baked with added wheat germ is high in nutritional value yet is a lighter, more delicate bread than one baked from whole grain flour.

Variations

Blackstrap molasses can be used instead of honey to give a darker color to the bread and to add iron.

Since a 50% wheat bread does contain some unbleached white flour, ½ cup of soy flour can be substituted for ½ cup of the unbleached flour to increase the protein.

Wholemeal Breads

Several of the recipes given in the ethnic bread section are wholemeal breads. To convert them to the highest nutritional standard, it is only necessary to substitute honey for the sugar listed in the recipe.

Maslin Bread page 133

German Beer Bread page 134

Welsh Barley Bread (Haidd) page 135

Ukrainian Rye Bread page 137

Vollkornbrot page 148

100% Black Rye Bread page 149

The Pita Bread, page 147, can be baked with whole wheat and honey instead of unbleached flour and sugar.

High Fiber Rye/Wheat Bread

Sponge:
50 milligram tablet of vitamin C
   (crushed)
4½ cups warm water
1 package (1 Tablespoon) active
   dry yeast
1 cup whole bran
3 cups rye meal or rye flour
1 Tablespoon honey
The Next Morning:
1 Tablespoon salt
2½ cups stone ground whole
   wheat flour
2 Tablespoons oil

Sponge. Crush the vitamin C tablet in a bowl and add about 2 ounces of warm water and 1 Tablespoon of honey. Add 1 Tablespoon of active dry yeast and allow the mixture to stand in a warm place for about 10 minutes to prove the yeast. When the yeast becomes frothy add the rest of the water and then stir in the bran and the rye flour. Allow the sponge to stand for at least 3 hours, or overnight.

The Next Morning. Sprinkle the salt over the sponge, add the oil and stir down. Start adding the flour mixing to form a dough. When dough is formed, turn it out on a floured board and knead, adding more flour if necessary. Knead 10 minutes. The dough should be firm, but moist on the inside. Place kneaded dough in a greased bowl and allow to rise in a warm place until dough has doubled. Punch down dough and shape into round or cigar shaped loaves. Allow the dough to rise again for 15 minutes on a greased baking sheet and then bake at 400°F for 45-50 minutes.

Before baking, you may use an egg wash, egg yolk or egg white to glaze the loaf, but if you omit this step you will still have a fine tasting bread. When glazed, sesame seeds add a nice touch.

The bran gives this bread a slightly different flavor than the plain maslin bread and also gives more roughage for our diet. This is a coarse textured bread that is delicious when hot. If you're cutting down on butter, try the turn of the century European way of eating this bread. Lightly crush a clove of garlic and then rub the bread with the crushed garlic. If you're expecting company, make sure they indulge too.

Recently I saw a commercial health food bakery product that startled me. They were baking whole wheat bagel. I tried this concept out by using whole wheat flour in the bagel recipe on page 130. As far as I'm concerned these aren't bagels, but they are good. Most of the bread recipes in the first section of the book can be made with either 100% whole wheat or with 50% wheat. The exceptions are the Brioche and the Challah.

Regular Wholemeal Bread

This is an European recipe which is not enriched. It produces a large loaf of bread which is traditionally baked as a hearth loaf, but it can be baked in a pan. European recipes use less liquid and produce a chewier type of bread. Do not use skim milk powder in this recipe unless you want a softer type of bread. In England and on the Continent they prefer breads baked with water. Originally this bread was baked with wholemeal flour (95% extraction.) I prefer to use 100% stone ground wheat. The bran provides roughage. If you want 2 loaves of bread, you may double the recipe but do not double the Vitamin C.

Wholemeal Sponge:
2 cups stone ground 100% whole wheat flour
1 Tablespoon honey
1 crushed 50 milligram Vitamin C tablet
1 teaspoon active dry yeast
2 cups warm water
The Second Step:
1 Tablespoon salt
1 Tablespoon oil
About 2 cups stone ground 100% whole wheat flour

European Style Wholemeal Bread

Sponge. Crush the Vitamin C tablet in a mixing bowl and add 2 ounces of warm water, the Tablespoon of honey and the teaspoon of yeast. Allow the mixture to stand in a warm place until the yeast becomes frothy. Add the remaining water and stir in 2 cups of whole wheat flour. Cover the bowl and allow the sponge to work for about 1½ hours.

The Second Step. Sprinkle the salt over the bubbly sponge and then all the oil. Stir down the sponge and start adding more flour. When a dough is formed, scrape the sponge out onto a floured board and work in more flour. This dough should be moist on the inside. When the dough no longer clings to your fingers and the outside feels dry, you have added enough flour. Knead for 10 minutes until the dough is firm and elastic.

Place the kneaded dough in a greased bowl and allow it to stand for about 1½ hours in a warm place to double. The oven with a pan of boiling water at the bottom is an ideal place to rise the dough. Finger test the dough to make sure the rise is complete. When you poke a finger into the dough, the hole should not fill quickly. Shape the dough into a round hearth loaf and place it on a greased baking sheet sprinkled with cornmeal. Allow the loaf to rise for 10-15 minutes then bake in a pre-heated oven at 450°F. for 35-40 minutes. Test with a thin knife and cool on a wire rack. The crust can be glazed with beaten egg, egg yolk or butter. Cracked wheat or sesame seeds can be sprinkled over the top of the loaf.

American Style Enriched Whole Wheat Bread

This bread, like the preceding recipe, uses only stone ground whole wheat flour, but it has a softer crumb because it uses more liquid and is enriched with milk. If whole milk is used instedad of dry, substitute milk for water. Again we will use the sponge method to increase the amount of yeast cells blowing bubbles of carbon dioxide gas which makes the bread rise. The use of Vitamin C is optional, but it does make the bread rise better.

Enriched Wholemeal Sponge:

1 crushed 50 milligram Vitamin C tablet

4 cups stone ground whole wheat flour

3 cups hot water

1 Tablespoon (1 package) active dry yeast

3 Tablespoon honey

2 Tablespoons blackstrap molasses

1 cup instant non fat dried milk

The Second Step.

2 Tablespoons cold pressed oil

1 Tablespoon salt

2½ - 3 cups whole wheat flour

3 Tablespoons oil

Sponge. Crush the Vitamin C tablet in a mixing bowl and add 4 ounces of hot water. Dissolve 1 Tablespoon of the honey in the water and add the package of dry yeast. Allow the mixture to stand in a warm place until the yeast becomes frothy then add the rest of the water. Stir in the other 2 Tablespoons of honey and 2 Tablespoons of blackstrap molasses. Add the dried milk and mix it into the liquid. Mix in the 4 cups of whole wheat flour and cover the bowl. Allow the bowl to stand in a warm place for about 1½ hours to form a sponge.

The Second Step. Sprinkle the salt and oil over the sponge and stir down. Work in about 2 cups of the flour and turn the sponge out onto a floured board. Knead, using more flour as necessary for about 10 minutes. The dough after kneading should be dry on the outside, but will be slightly moist on the inside. The texture will be firm and elastic. Allow this dough to rise in a warm place until it has doubled. Finger test to make sure that the rise is complete. The dough should rise in a greased, covered bowl for about 2 hours. If the day is cold it should rise in the oven with a pan of boiling water at the bottom of the oven. The water can be replaced with fresh boiling water after 1 hour's rise.

After the dough has risen, punch it down and knead for about 1 minute to remove any gas bubbles. Shape the dough into 2 loaves. Pan loaves will rise better than hearth loaves. Bake hearth loaves with a 10 minute rise after shaping. Pan loaves can rise longer if you wish. If you are in a hurry, the rise after shaping can be eliminated completely. Bake at 375°F. for 40-45 minutes. Test with a knife to make sure the bread is done. Cool the bread on a wire rack.

Variations

This bread with its sweet nutty flavor and coarse texture, so like a peasant bread makes a wonderful raisin bread. Large raisins that have not been sprayed or treated with sulfur are available at most health food shops. Raisins are an excellent source of added nutrition. Raisins are fermentable and should not be added to the bread until the sponge is formed. Should they be added in the first step, a semi-sourdough effect will be produced by the fermentation of the dried fruit. Use ½ cup to 1 cup of raisins with this recipe.

High Protein 100% Whole Wheat Bread

This bread is practically a meal in itself. Eaten in the European peasant style which means a bite of onion an a bite of bread, you will ingest proteins, energy, vitamins and the aroma of onion. Another way the peasants ate bread was to rub it with fresh garlic before eating. Bread at the time was the staff of life, the chief source of protein. I prefer eating the breads with onion to rubbing with garlic for fresh onions are brimming with Vitamin C. This bread is a useful adjunct to any diet, particularly a vegetarian diet. Raisins can be added to this recipe as can nuts to make it even more nutritious.

Sponge:
1 crushed 50 milligram Vitamin C
  tablet
½ teaspoon honey
1 Tablespoon (1 package) active
  dry yeast
3 cups plus 2 ounces of warm
  water
½-1 cup non fat dried milk
4 cups of stone ground whole
  wheat flour

The Second Step:
2 Tablespoons honey
½ cup soy flour
1 Tablespoon salt
2 Tablespoons cold pressed
  vegetable oil
2-3 cups whole wheat flour

Sponge. Crush the Vitamin C tablet in a large mixing bowl and add the 2 ounces of warm water. Stir in the ½ teaspoon of honey and the package of yeast. Allow this mixture to sit for about 10 minutes in a warm place. When the yeast is frothy, add 3 more cups of warm water and the non fat dried milk. Work in the 4 cups of flour and cover the bowl. Allow it to stand until a bubbly sponge is formed in about 1½ to 2 hours.

The Second Step. Mix in the honey, soy flour and oil, then stir down the sponge. Stir in about ½ cup of the whole wheat flour. When a dough is formed, scrape the sponge onto a floured board and knead adding more flour as necessary. Knead about 10 minutes. The dough will be firm and elastic, dry on the outside, but slightly moist on the inside of the ball. Place the kneaded dough in a greased bowl and allow it to rise until doubled. Finger test to be sure that the dough has risen completely.

Punch down the risen dough and divide into loaves after kneading for 1 minute to remove gas bubbles. Pan loaves are best with this type of dough, but hearth loaves will make a coarser, heavier bread. Allow the loaves to rise for 10 minutes after shaping. Bake at 375°F. for 40-45 minutes. Test with a knife and turn out to a wire rack to cool.

Variations
Add ½ cup to 1 cup of raisins.
Add ½ cup to 1 cup of nuts.
Add both raisins and nuts.
Increase the soy flour by substituting 1 cup of soy for 1 cup of whole wheat instead of ½ cup in the recipe. If you increase the soy flour and have high gluten flour available, decrease the whole wheat flour by 2 cups and add 1 cup each of high gluten flour and soy flour. The use of the high gluten flour will make a better rising bread.

Mixed Whole Grain Breads

To get the essential goodness of a whole grain bread, it is not necessary to limit yourself to whole wheat. Mixed grain breads, if all of the flours are not degerminated, provide a change of taste and texture. Any change prevents too much of the same thing.

Corn and Wheat Bread

The corn mentioned in the Bible is actually our wheat. The corn I refer to is maize. If Indian corn is ground into a 100% meal it retains the nutritional content of the corn germ and the roughage of the corn bran. Mixing this cornmeal with wheat flour will give a bread with a coarser texture than one made entirely of whole wheat. The texture approaches that of an old time peasant bread made with rye meal. If only 1 cup of cornmeal is used in this recipe the wheat taste is practically unchanged. Use 2 cups and you get a slight hint of cornbread. Use 3 cups and you know that corn is present.

Sponge:

1 crushed 50 milligram Vitamin C
   tablet
1 Tablespoon (1 package) active
   dry yeast
3½ cups warm water
3 cups whole wheat flour
2 Tablespoons honey
1 cup whole grain cornmeal
   If 2 cups cornmeal used,
   decrease wheat flour 1 cup
   If 3 cups cornmeal used,
   decrease wheat flour 2 cups

The Second Step:

1 Tablespoon salt
3 Tablespoons oil
2-3 cups whole wheat flour

Sponge. Prove the yeast in ½ cup of warm water containing the 2 Tablespoons of honey. When the yeast becomes frothy, add the rest of the warm water. Mix in the cornmeal and then stir in whole wheat flour. Remember if you increase the cornmeal to decrease the amount of wheat flour added in this step. Cover the bowl and allow the sponge to sit in a warm place for at least 1 hour for bubbles to form and the sponge to rise.

The Second Step. Sprinkle the salt and oil over the sponge and then stir it down. Add about 1 cup of flour to form a loose dough and scrape the sponge onto a floured board. Sprinkle more flour over the sponge and start to knead. Knead for 10 minutes adding more flour as necessary. This dough should be dry on the outside and moist on the inside. It should be firm and elastic after kneading. Place the kneaded dough in a greased bowl, cover and let it rise until doubled. Check the rise by the finger test. If the hole does not close quickly, the rise is finished.

Punch down the dough and knead again for 1 minute. Shape the loaves. I personally favor round hearth loaves for this bread. Hearth loaves can be baked on a greased baking sheet that has been sprinkled with cornmeal. The cornmeal enhances the bottom crust. A six inch skillet makes a nice sized loaf, one that weighs about 26 ounces after baking. I make 3 loaves from this recipe, two of them in 6 inch skillets, the other in an eight inch skillet.

After the dough has been shaped and placed on the sheet or in the skillet, glaze the top by brushing on an egg wash and then sprinkle poppy or sesame seeds over the wash.

Variations

The same basic recipe will serve to make other whole grain breads.
1. Use half whole wheat flour plus half rye flour.
2. Substitute barley flour for the cornmeal, but do not use more than 2 cups of barley flour.
3. Substitute buckwheat flour for cornmeal, but do not use more than 2 cups of buckwheat flour.
4. Make a 3 or 4 grain bread. Fifty percent or more of the flour in this bread should be wheat flour. The remaining flour can be a mixture of rye, barley, buckwheat and cornmeal in any combination.

Coarser Grained Wholegrain Bread

If the remains of a previously baked wholegrain bread are toasted and ground into breadcrumbs, these can be used instead of cornmeal in the recipe. The bread crumbs will give the bread a coarser texture. Toasted breadcrumbs do not mold quickly, but if you plan to keep them, it is suggested that you store them in the freezer.

No-Knead Whole Wheat Bread

This is a rather special recipe. It produces a whole wheat bread, a 100% whole wheat bread without kneading and takes less than two hours to go from opening the flour bag to hot bread.

2 Tablespoons (2 packages) active
   dry yeast
¼ cup honey or blackstrap
   molasses
1 Tablespoon salt
2 cups warm water
2 eggs
2 Tablespoons cold pressed oil
4½ cups whole wheat flour

The method given is the direct method, but if you wish to economize on the yeast, a sponge can be set up by mixing 1 Tablespoon yeast with the 2 cups of warm water and the ¼ cup of honey. Add 2 cups of the flour and let this sit for about 1 to 1½ hours for a sponge to form and then continue with the rest of the recipe.

The direct method calls for the 2 Tablespoons of yeast to be dissolved in the water. Add the sweetener, and the salt. Follow with the oil and the 2 beaten eggs. Mix in the 2 cups of flour as you would for the sponge and beat until the mixture is smooth.

Stir in 1 more cup of flour and beat very hard for 3 minutes. Do not skimp on the time; this beating takes the place of kneading. If you get tired, you may rest, but the total beating time must be at least 3 minutes if you beat by hand. If you have a mixer, you can beat for only 1 minute.

Work in 1 more cup of the flour and beat vigorously for 1 minute then follow with the last ½ cup of flour.

Grease 2 loaf tins either 8½ or 9 inch tins. This is a batter bread and must be baked in tins. Pour the batter into the baking tins, but do not more than half fill either tin. Bounce the tin hard on the counter to settle the rather thick batter. If bouncing does not fill the corners, poke the batter into them. Allow the batter to rise for 20 minutes. Placing the pans in a tray of hot water will insure a good rise.

Bake the bread at 200°F. for 12 minutes, then increase the temperature to 375°F and bake about 25 minutes longer. Test with a knife, If done, turn the breads out on a wire rack to cool.

Variations

To increase the nutrition you may add ⅔ to 1 cup of nonfat dried milk powder to the water.

Add ¾ - 1¼ cup raisins for one of the best tasting raisin breads you have ever eaten.

Sprouted Whole Wheat Bread

Sprouted wheat breads are a rather new innovation. Only a few commercial bakeries have this available, yet it is not too difficult to make at home. To bake this bread, you must first sprout the wheat; to get wheat to sprout is much easier than you think and the results well worth the small amount of bother involved.

To Sprout Wheat:

1/3 cup whole, not cracked, wheat
    kernels—these are also called
    wheat berries
1 cup water
1 mason jar, 1 quart size complete
    with lid

Soak the wheat for about 12 hours in the water. Drain, discarding the water and transfer the wheat berries to a 1 quart mason type jar. Discard the flat disk of metal that makes up part of the lid, but keep the band. Cover the jar mouth with nylon mesh or several layers of cheese cloth and screw the band on over the mesh to hold it in place. Take the jar with the wheat and place it in a cupboard. Sprouting works better in the dark. It will take about 2 days for the wheat to sprout. When the sprouts are ready, they will be about 1/2 inch long. The wheat berries must be kept moist during the sprouting. Rinse the berries with tepid water 3 or 4 times each of the 2 days it takes to sprout. You can run the water through the mesh into the jar and then drain it out again through the mesh. 1/3 cup of wheat berries will make about 1 1/4 cups of sprouts.

Sprouted Whole Wheat Bread

Sponge:

50 milligrams Vitamin C (optional)
2 cups stone ground whole wheat
    flour
1 Tablespoon yeast
1 teaspoon honey
1 Tablespoon blackstrap molasses
1 1/2 cups warm water

The Second Step:

about 2 1/2 cups whole wheat flour
1 1/4 cups sprouted wheat
1/2 cup wheat germ
2 ounces sesame seeds
1 Tablespoon salt
2 Tablespoons oil

Sponge. Crush a 50 milligram tablet of Vitamin C in a mixing bowl. Dissolve the honey and blackstrap molasses in the warm water and then add the yeast. Allow the yeast to prove for 10 minutes. It should be foamy at that time if the yeast is good. Stir in 2 cups of whole wheat flour and then cover the bowl and allow it to stand for about 1 1/2-2 hours for the sponge to develop.

The Second Step. Sprinkle the salt over the sponge and stir it down. Add the sesame seeds, oil and the sprouted wheat and beat them into the sponge. Mix in the wheat germ and then start to work in more flour until a dough is formed. Turn the dough out on a floured board and knead for 10 minutes working in more whole wheat flour if necessary.

Place the kneaded dough in a greased bowl and allow to rise until doubled. This will take about 1 hour. Punch down the dough, remove it from the bowl and knead again for 1 minute. Divide the dough into 2 portions and shape into loaves. Pan loaves are good, but I prefer the crunchier crust of a hearth loaf.

To finish the crust spray with water if a crunchy crust is wanted or use an egg wash. With an egg wash you may sprinkle more sesame seeds on the crust. For pan loaves, butter will soften the crust.

Bake at 375°F. for about 40 minutes. Test with a thin knife and cool on a wire rack.

Hi-Fiber Bran-n-Honey Wheat Bread

This is an excellent, good tasting bread that is crammed with nutrition and high in fiber. Anything that tastes as good as this should be bad for you, but this must be the exception that proves the rule. A good health food bread should taste good and this one does.

Sponge:

2 cups warm water
1 cup nonfat dried milk powder
1 Tablespoon honey
1 Tablespoon (1 package) dry yeast
2 cups whole wheat flour
1 cup whole bran (not cereal)
¼ cup honey

The Second Step:

about 2½ cups stone ground whole wheat flour
3 teaspoons salt
4 Tablespoons cold pressed oil

Sponge. Prove the yeast by dissolving 1 Tablespoon of yeast and 1 Tablespoon of honey in ½ cup of warm water. When the yeast gets frothy, add the 1½ cups of warm water and ¼ cup of honey. Stir in 1 cup of bran and then stir in 2 cups of whole wheat flour. Cover the bowl and allow it to stand in a warm place for about 1½ hours for a sponge to form. Vitamin C may be used to speed up the process if you desire. Crush 1 Vitamin C fifty milligram tablet and add it to the yeast water before proving the yeast.

The Second Step. Sprinkle the salt over the sponge and add the oil. Stir down the sponge and start to work in more whole wheat flour. When a dough is formed, scrape the dough onto a floured board and start to knead, adding more flour as necessary. Knead for 10 minutes until the dough is firm and elastic. Place the kneaded dough in a greased bowl, cover and allow it to stand for about 1½ hours to double. Finger test the dough to make sure that it has completed the rise.

Punch down the risen dough, knead for 1 minute and divide into 2 portions. Shape into pan loaves or hearth loaves. Finish the bread with 1 egg white mixed with 1 Tablespoon of water and beaten. Sesame seeds may be sprinkled over the crust before baking. Allow the shaped loaves to rise for 10-15 minutes before baking. Bake at 400°F. for about 40 minutes. Test with a knife and cool on a wire rack.

Cracked-Wheat Bread

For those who like chewy, crusty loaves.

Preparation of the Cracked Wheat:

2 cups water
½ teaspoon salt
1 cup cracked wheat

The Sponge:

1½ cups warm water
1 Tablespoon honey
1 Tablespoon (1 package) dry yeast
3 cups stone ground whole wheat flour
½ cup bran

The Second Step:

1 cup cooked cracked wheat
3 Tablespoons cold pressed oil
1 Tablespoon salt
About 3½ cups stone ground whole wheat flour

Pour 2 cups of water into a sauce pan and add the salt. Bring the water to a boil and dribble in the cracked wheat. Stir and allow the water to come to a simmering boil. Simmer the grain for 5 minutes, stirring occasionally to prevent burning. Allow the wheat mixture to cool.

The Sponge. Prove the yeast in ½ cup of warm water with 1 Tablespoon honey. When the yeast becomes frothy add the other cup of water and 3 cups of whole wheat flour and ½ cup of bran. Cover and allow this to stand in a warm place for about 1½ hours for a sponge to form.

The Second Step. Sprinkle the salt over the sponge and then the oil. Stir down the sponge and then stir in the cooked cracked wheat. Add the flour 1 cup at a time stirring until a dough is formed. Scrape the dough out of the bowl onto a floured board and knead, adding more flour as necessary. Knead 10 minutes. Place the firm, kneaded dough into a greased bowl and cover. Allow it to rise until doubled.

About 1½ hours after the dough starts to rise, punch it down, knead again to force out gas bubbles and divide the dough into either 3 or 5 portions for shaping. This dough should be shaped into cigar shaped loaves or baguettes. Roll each portion out to a rectangle and then roll up the rectangle into a cylinder. Round hearth loaves or pan loaves can be made if preferred. Sprinkle a greased baking sheet with cornmeal and place the loaves on the sheet.

Like a French bread, these loaves should be slashed with a razor in several places. They may be finished with cold water or beaten egg white.

Allow the shaped loaves to rise for 10-15 minutes then bake at 375°F. for about 40 minutes.

Doughnuts

Health Food Desserts

Coffeecake

The thought of making sweet rolls, dessert rolls and other dishes as part of a health food diet may seem heretical to some purists, but each of the following recipes are made up from good, healthful ingredients with no additives or harmful components.

Everyone has the urge to backslide occasionally. If these desserts are available, no backslider will dash out to the nearest bakery or doughnut shop and gorge on food filled with refined sugar and lard. It should be remembered that these dishes are not part of the basic diet and as such need not have all the nutrition packed into them that would be conferred by using 100% stone ground wheat flour. Most of the recipes use unbleached flour enriched with wheat germ, but whole wheat flour can be substituted.

The basic dough recipe for making most of these desserts is only slightly sweet, but lends itself to many dessert dishes. Honey is used in this recipe because the dough is a yeast risen, kneaded dough that is adjusted for flour to water ratio in the kneading.

Basic Health Food Dessert Dough

Sponge. Warm liquid milk to take the chill off. Dissolve the yeast and the ½ teaspoon of honey directly in the milk and let it stand until it becomes frothy. Stir in the wheat germ and then the unbleached flour. Cover the bowl and let it stand in a warm place for 1-1½ hours to form a sponge.

The Second Step: Add the oil, honey, beaten egg and salt to the sponge; then stir down. Work in the remaining flour until a dough is formed then scrape the dough out with a rubber spatula onto a floured board. Knead for 10 minutes, working in more flour if necessary.

Place the kneaded dough in a greased bowl, Cover and let it stand in a warm place until the dough has doubled. Finger test to be sure that the rise is complete. Punch down the dough and knead it again for 1 minute. The dough is now ready to use.

Sponge:

1 cup of liquid nonfat milk or
   regular milk
   A cup of instant dried nonfat
   milk dissolved in 1 cup of water
   may be substituted for liquid milk
   or ½ cup evaporated milk plus
   ½ cup warm water
1 teaspoon active dry yeast
1½ cups unbleached flour
½ cup wheat germ
½ teaspoon honey

The Second Step:

¼ cup cold pressed vegetable oil
3 Tablespoons honey
1 beaten egg
1 teaspoon salt
about 2 more cups unbleached
   flour

An entire series of desserts is modeled after the jelly roll. Of course we do not use jam or jelly unless it is a special honey based jam or jelly, but the procedure of handling the dough is the same. For all of these desserts, roll the punched down dough out to form a rectangle measuring 8 x 16 inches. Trim if necessary. The rectangle should be about 1/8 inch thick. Save any excess dough for a second rectangle or for other uses.

Poppy Seed Rolls

Filling:
1 cup poppy seeds
1/2 cup water
1/2 cup instant nonfat dried milk (optional)
1/4 cup of honey
1/3 cup chopped dates
1/3 cup raisins
1/4 cup chopped walnuts or almonds
nutmeg and cinnamon to taste
Glaze:
2 ounces of honey
2 ounces of orange or lemon juice
1 teaspoon of grated orange or lemon peel

Soak the poppy seeds in boiling water for ten minutes. Grind the poppy seed or crush them in a mortar if possible. Combine the poppy seeds, water, milk powder, honey, dates, raisins walnuts and spices in a saucepan. Cook over a low flame for about 5-10 minutes. When the liquid has evaporated the mixture is ready. Stir occasionaly while simmering. Cool from hot to warm before using. Do not use the mixture cold for it will be hard to spread.

Spread the poppy seed filling over the dough rectangle and then roll up the dough like a jelly roll. Roll the long side away from you towards you. Pinch the ends as you roll. Place the roll on a greased baking sheet and bake at 375°F. for about 35 minutes. For a sweeter pastry, brush honey over the dough before spreading the filling.

After baking this roll can be glazed with an orange or lemon glaze.

Prune Roll

1 pound dried prunes
2 teaspoons grated lemon peel
2 teaspoons lemon juice

Soak the prunes overnight and then cook until they are soft. Pit the prunes and chop them. Add the lemon juice and lemon peel, simmer until the water is driven off. Use this instead of the poppy seed filling to make a Prune Roll.

Stewed Fruit Roll

Cook fresh fruit (apples, apricots, peaches, etc) using honey as a sweetening agent. Use very little water and 2 Tablespoons of honey to each cup of fruit. Simmer until the water is driven off. Roll out a rectangle of dough and brush honey over the dough. Spread the stewed fruit over the rectangle and then roll up and seal like a jelly roll. Bake at 375°F. for about 35 minutes. This may be glazed with the lemon or the orange glaze described under poppy seed roll.

Cinnamon Roll

Brush the rectangle of dough with honey, Sprinkle ground cinnamon over the honey and then roll up like a jelly roll. Bake at 375°F. for about 35 minutes. This roll may be served glazed. For a sweeter roll sprinkle a little fructose over the cinnamon.

Cinnamon and Apple Roll

After spreading the dough with honey and sprinkling it with cinnamon, place thin slices of raw apple over the cinnamon. Roll up, pinch shut and bake at 375°F. for about 35 minutes. Glaze after baking if you wish.

Variations

Both the cinnamon and the cinnamon and apple rolls can be made with ½ cup of raisins sprinkled over the rectangle. Dried apricots can be used instead of apples. If apricots are used, soak them in boiling water for 20 minutes. Drain the water and chop the apricots before sprinkling over the dough. Apple sauce, if homemade or sugar free can be used as a substitute for fresh apples if they are not available. Soaked dried apples can be used too. Other variations are possible. It is suggested that you consult the chapter entitled Good Things From Bread. If you use any of the recipes there, substitute honey for sugar and enrich the flour with wheat germ or use whole wheat flour for maximaum nutritional value.

Health Food Doughnuts

The very name of this dessert seems a contradiction. Doughnuts are the acme of junk food. Doughnuts are fried in oil making them the spiritual equivalent of French fried potatoes. If baked doughnuts are made instead of fried, they can have a decent level of nutrition.

1 portion of the Health Food Dessert Dough described in this chapter

Raised Doughnuts

Divide the dough into 16 equal portions and roll each up into a ball. Punch a hole through the center with a finger and then work the dough to give a smooth rounded shape. Place on a greased baking sheet and bake for 15-20 minutes at 375° F. Glaze if desired.

1 portion of the Health Food Dessert Dough

Filled Raised Doughnuts

See the making of doughnuts (page 87). Use the poppy seed filling or prune filling (page 228). The other fillings described can also be used. Place on a greased baking sheet and bake for 15-20 minutes at 375°F. Glaze, if desired.

Please note that the dessert dough can be made with whole wheat flour if you prefer.

Whole Wheat Applesauce Doughnuts

These are quick, baked doughnuts.

1 cup applesauce
3½ cups whole wheat flour
3 Tablespoons honey
1 beaten egg
1 teaspoon salt
1 teaspoon baking soda
2 teaspoons vinegar

Sift the dry ingredients into a mixing bowl and then add the beaten egg, the applesauce and the vinegar. Stir well to a firm dough. More liquid or flour may be added if necessary. Knead for about 5 minutes and then form into doughnuts. See the preceding recipe. Bake the doughnuts at 375°F. for 15-20 minutes.

Finish with cinnamon or a carob frosting.

Other Health Food Desserts

See the recipes for regular desserts and convert them to health food standards. Recipes calling for baking powder may use baking soda and vinegar or lemon juice instead. Use 3 teaspoons of vinegar for each teaspoon of soda. Use 1 teaspoon of soda for each teaspoon of baking powder called for in the original recipe.

For recipes calling for large quantities of sugar substitution of honey works well for kneaded doughs. For batter doughs, the liquid to flour ratio would be upset. Use fructose instead of honey to substitute for sugar. Remember, use only ½ as much fructose as you would sugar. If you must use honey, decrease the liquid by 6 ounces for every cup of honey used or increase the flour by six ounces for every cup of honey used.

Special Diet Breads

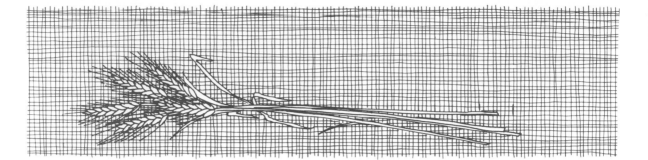

Many people are forced to follow a restricted diet for medical reasons. One such diet is popularly known as a "salt free diet," but should actually be called a "low sodium diet." Salt, which is sodium chloride, is the main source of sodium ingested by man, but it is not the only source. If, for reasons of health, sodium is restricted all sodium rich foods must be avoided. Many people on low or no sodium diets are allowed to substitute lithium chloride to make up for the lack of salt. The option to use this substitute is entirely up to the physician who restricted the diet.

The general rules to follow on a low sodium diet are: 1. Do not use table salt. 2. No baking powder or baking soda is allowed in the diet. 3. If sodium is severely restricted low sodium or sodium free water must be used.

To apply these rules to the baking of bread is not difficult. Bake without any salt unless the doctor allows lithium chloride. Only yeast breads are allowed for other methods of leavening require baking soda which is sodium bicarbonate or baking powder which contains baking soda. Tap water may be rich in sodium. Use only bottled low sodium water for baking. Butter and margarine are sold unsalted. Check with your physician to see if unsalted margarine and butter are allowed. Read the labels, for some margarines may contain sodium in the form of preservatives. When buying oil, check the label to make sure that it is free of preservatives and sodium. Do not use biscuit mixes or self rising flour, for these contain baking soda. Check milk sources with the physician or the American Heart Association to see if they are free of sodium.

Most recipes for yeast breads can be converted to low sodium breads by omitting the salt and using low sodium water. Eggs are essentially sodium free as is flour. Check the other ingredients before using them. One sample recipe for a low sodium bread will be given. Use it as a guide in adapting any other recipe.

Salt Free Bread (Direct Method)

½ teaspoon sugar. (If the diet is restricted in sugar also, put 1 Tablespoon of flour in the water when you are proving the yeast. If a sweeter bread is desired add 1-2 more Tablespoons of sugar)
1 Tablespoon active dry yeast
1 teaspoon lithium chloride salt substitute. (If allowed by physician)
1½ cups warm water
4 cups unbleached flour
1 Tablespoon salt and preservative free oil

Place the yeast in a bowl with the ½ teaspoon of sugar and add 2 ounces of warm water. Allow the yeast to stand in a warm place until it becomes frothy. Add the rest of the warm water, the salt substitute if it is allowed on the diet, the oil and start to work in the flour one cup at a time until a dough is formed. Turn the dough out onto a floured board and knead for 10 minutes adding more flour if necessary. Place the kneaded dough in a greased bowl, cover and let stand in a warm place until the dough has doubled. This should take from one to two hours. Punch down the dough and then knead for about 1 minute. Shape as either pan or hearth loaves. After shaping allow the bread to rise again for about 15 minutes. Bake at 400°F. for 45 minutes. Test with a knife and cool on a wire rack.

Variations

Other flours may be used. Wheat germ may be substituted but do not use more than ½ cup of wheat germ to replace ½ cup of flour. Dinner rolls, baguettes, baguette rolls or a bubble loaf can be made instead of the usual pan and hearth loaves.

Gluten-Free Bread

Many children and some adults are on gluten-free diets. This means that they cannot eat ordinary breads. Gluten-free breads are baked with gluten-free flour. In England they use a gluten-free baking powder for these breads, but a careful reading of American baking powder labels does not show any source of gluten. Not having an English baking powder tin handy, I can't be sure why they worry about gluten in baking powder, but they might use flour instead of corn starch in their baking powder. I prefer a gluten-free yeast bread, but I will give both types of recipes.

Breads baked without gluten stale quickly. This problem is lessened because a lack of gluten limits the rise of the bread. Bake in special small pans and freeze what you do not require immediately. Freezing will protect the freshness. Because gluten-free breads rise poorly special recipes are required.

Gluten-Free Yeast Bread

1½-2 teaspoons active dry yeast
5 ounces warm milk
5 ounces warm water
1¾ cup gluten-free flour
1 teaspoon salt
1 Tablespoon oil
½ teaspoon sugar
⅓ cup non fat milk powder

Dissolve the yeast in about 2 ounces of warm water and add the ½ teaspoon of sugar. Allow to stand in a warm place until the yeast is proved by becoming frothy. Add the remainder of the warm water and the warm milk. Stir in the non fat dried milk then the oil, salt and flour. Mix well to form a batter and then cover the bowl and let the batter rise in a warm place for 20 minutes.

While the batter is rising, prepare a pan. Gluten-free flour will stick to a pan, so it is necessary to line it with greased wax paper before the batter is poured. This recipe will fill one 4½ x 2½ x 1½ inch pan.

After allowing the batter to rise, stir it down and then beat it thoroughly with a spoon. Pour the batter into the pan. Cover the pan and let the batter rise again in a warm place. If the pan is placed in hot water, the heat will speed the rising. When the batter has risen to about ½ inch from the rim of the baking pan, place the bread into a hot oven and bake at 425°F. for 30 minutes. Test for doneness with a knife and if done cool on a wire rack. The bread will stale quickly. Store in a plastic bag and if necessary, freeze part of the loaf.

Variations

Gluten-Free Cheese Bread

Use the same recipe but reduce the milk and water to 4 ounces each. Add ½ cup of grated Cheddar cheese. Beat the cheese into the batter before you let it rise the first time. The baking time and temperature remain the same.

All gluten-free breads including those baked with yeast are not kneaded. Kneading in regular breads is done to strengthen the gluten. Since these breads do not have gluten, they are baked as batter breads. In any batter bread the liquid to flour ratio is critical for it can't be adjusted. Follow the recipes exactly. The Fruit Bread recipe requires a different liquid to flour ratio than either the Cheese Bread or the regular Gluten-Free Bread.

Gluten-Free Fruit Bread

1 Tablespoon (1 package) active
   dry yeast
3 ounces warm milk
3 ounces warm water
1½ cups gluten-free flour
2 Tablespoons sugar
¼ teaspoon salt
2 Tablespoons oil
½ cup mixed dried fruit

Place 2 ounces of warm water in a mixing bowl and add the Tablespoon of yeast and the 2 Tablespoons of sugar. Allow the mixture to stand in a warm place until the yeast becomes frothy. Add the remaining liquid then sift the flour and salt together into the bowl. Mix well. Cover the bowl and allow the batter to rise for 20 minutes. Beat the batter with a spoon and pour into a small pan lined with greased wax paper. Allow the batter to rise again in the pan until it is ½ inch from the rim of the pan. Bake at 375°F. for 35 minutes. Cool on a wire rack. Remove the wax paper while the bread is cooling.

Gluten-Free Quick Bread

To bake a quick bread that is gluten-free, you must use gluten-free flour and a gluten-free baking powder. American baking powders are gluten-free, but check the label to make sure that your powder contains cornstarch instead of flour.

2 cups sifted gluten-free flour
4 teaspoons baking powder
2-4 Tablespoons sugar or 1-2
   Tablespoons fructose
1½ cups whole milk
¼ cup oil

Line a small pan with greased wax paper. The recommended size pan is 4½x2½x1½. Sift the dry ingredients into a mixing bowl and add the oil and milk. Stir into a thick batter and turn the batter into the prepared pan immediately. Bake at 425°F. for 30 minutes. Test with a knife and cool on a wire rack. This bread stales quickly. Freeze what is not needed to keep it fresh

Baking for Low Calorie Diets

There are two types of low calorie diets. One to lose weight. The other to hold you at your new lower weight. Bread is restricted in quantity on both diets and dessert-type baked goods are also restricted.

The number of calories due to sugar in baked goods can be cut in half by substituting fructose for sugar. Remember, you only use half as much fructose. Replace every Tablespoon of sugar with a teaspoon of fructose. Despite reducing the sugar used, only in very sweet desserts do you reduce the calories drastically. Calories in baked goods come from the flour.

There are times, even if we're dieting, that a dessert will do more good than going without. When you are reduced to a trembling wreck by the craves, use good judgment in how you satisfy yourself. Limit the amount of sweets you eat and if you eat a baked dessert, chose a semi-sweet one instead of one with a heavy sugar content. Fructose would help you reduce the calories even more, so consider this sugar as a way of making sweet baked goods that do not contain as many calories as those made with sugar or honey.

Miscellanea

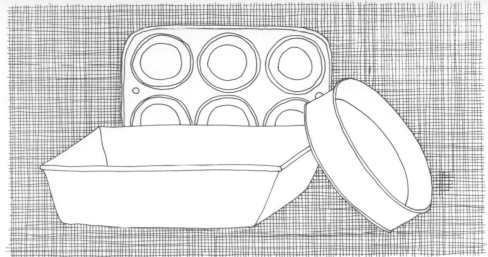

Greasing

All recipes call for pans and baking sheets to be greased before they are used. If this step is omitted, the bread will stick to the metal or glass and tear. It's almost heartbreaking to try to turn a loaf out of a poorly greased pan only to have part of the bread remain in the container while the other part comes out on the rack.

Grandma used a liberal application of animal fat to prevent sticking. Some people still use lard, suet or butter to do the job, but others prefer not to use animal fat which is highly saturated and filled with cholesterol. Vegetable shortenings and oil are available to use instead of animal fat, but oil will seep into the bread and give it a strange taste. Hydrogenated vegetable fat is a saturated fat.

If you are using any fat for greasing, look at the label. Some shortenings contain preservatives. I have found hydrogenated vegetable shortening that is marked "Pure vegetable shortening". This contained no preservatives. I have found other solid shortenings with preservatives. This includes a mixture of vegetable and animal fats put out by a major national company and many brands of margarine. Natural margarine, pure butter and many brands of oil are free from chemical additives. The only way to tell is to read the label carefully. By law all ingredients must be listed on the label.

For people who would rather bake without using saturated fats to grease there are two ways to go. Teflon® pans allow breads to bake without sticking. This coating must be treated gently or it will go bald and bread will stick to the bare spots. Some observers have suggested that this tendency of the plastic coating to peel means that a portion of the Teflon® is ingested into the diet. I have no scientific facts to either prove or disprove this claim.

If it is true, the material is inert and should cause no clinical problems. I think that it is only a rumor similar to the one that originated in the 1920's about aluminum pots or to the foul canard once circulated by the manufacturers of Cuban cigars. They spread the word that Philippine cigar tobacco was picked by lepers. The story was a lie, but it effectively killed the sale of Philippine tobacco in the United States for over forty years. Tales like this do get created. I wouldn't be at all surprised if I found that the makers of aluminum pots once spread the story that cooking in cast iron pots caused the ingestion of rust. Weight the merits of the story on your own scale, but remember that the new miracle coatings will work without grease until they go bald.

Several years ago, some products using soy lecithin came onto the market as a subsitute for greasing. One such product is sold under the trade name of Pam®. I'm not too fond of using aerosols, so I've never bothered to read their label. The product works, but I don't know if it is pure lecithin or not, but it is thin enough to spray. If you are interested in the product, read the label and see if anything is added to the lecithin. I recently found a rather thin liquid lecithin preparation made by "Iris." This product contained lecithin, oil and preservatives. I think it was meant for frying because the presence of oil with its short molecular chain might cause problems with baking. Oil is absorbed into the bread.

There is a less expensive way to go that is guaranteed to contain no additives of any type.

Pure liquid lecithin is found in health food stores in pint bottles. A pint should be good for a decade of baking. Very little is used each time. This unrefined type lecithin is viscous and dark colored, but just a few drops will coat a big baking sheet and like that famous coffee, it is good to the last drop. Liquid lecithin contains absolutely no cholesterol. It is relatively low in calories and the fatty acids present are not saturated. It is the ideal grease for baking and works well for frying the greaseless way too.

Making and Baking with Yogurt

Many recipes in this book call for buttermilk or sour cream. In any of these recipes, yogurt can be used as a substitute. If you decide to make your own yogurt you can control the caloric content because yogurt can be made with either whole milk, lowfat milk or nonfat milk.

The acidic content of either homemade or store purchased yogurt is high enough to react with baking soda to release carbon dioxide gas for leavening.

It is also possible to substitute yogurt for sweet milk or cream in baking, but it will lend its own distinctive flavor to the finished product. There will be a slight sourness, which can be increased if desired, similar to that produced by a sourdough starter. In the section on sourdough breads, a recipe is given for a sour yogurt bread. If made with an overnight sponge, this bread will come close to a sourdough bread in flavor. When baking plain or vanilla yogurt works best unless the fruit flavor will blend in with what you're baking.

Making yogurt at home is simple and a good way to cut the cost of this handy ingredient. No only will you reduce the price to a fourth or less of what the grocer charges, but you also eliminate additives and preservatives. You do not need a yogurt machine to make great yogurt. You probably already have the equipment needed in your house.

To make yogurt you do need three things. The first is milk and you have your choice of regular, lowfat or nonfat. The second is a starter. Getting the starter is a simple task. Just go into your local market and purchase a cup of commercial yogurt. For the starter you can use a flavored yogurt or a plain one. Buy the brand you prefer. Remove 3 Tablespoons of yogurt from the cup and place them in a bowl. Liquefy them with a whisk or fork. Your starter is ready. You can eat the rest of the cup before going on or you can place it back in the refrigerator for later.

Plain Yogurt

1 quart of regular, low fat or non fat milk
3 Tablespoons yogurt (starter)

Heat the milk just to boiling and then allow it to cool to about 100°F. Skim any scum off the top of the milk and pour it into the mixing bowl with the liquefied yogurt starter. Mix well and transfer to individual cups. Cover each cup and incubate the milk for about four hours at 100°F. Actually any temperature between 85°F. and 110°F. will work but at lower temperatures, a longer incubation will be necessary to set the yogurt. When ready, the yogurt will have the consistency of a custard, but it will firm up more after refrigeration.

Sweetened and fruit yogurts are made in the same way. Add 1 Tablespoon of honey or sugar for each cup of milk. If you are using fructose, add only 1 teaspoon per cup. If you want to make vanilla yogurt add 1 teaspoon of vanilla extract per quart of milk. Stir the sugar and extract in to dissolve before dispensing. Fruit yogurt is made by putting the fruit in the cups and then filling with the milk. You may use 1-2 Tablespoons of fruit preserves, canned fruit, fresh fruit or jam in each cup before the liquid is added.

Incubating Yogurt

A thermometer is essential. Do not use a fever thermometer because it will not show a drop in temperature. The following ways will provide the necessary heat to incubate your yogurt.

1. Take a rectangular baking dish and fill it with hot water from the tap. Check the temperature; it should be very close to 100°F or 39°C. Place the dish on a hot water bottle and cover the dish, bottle and yogurt with a heavy towel. Check the temperature every half hour. If it is dropping add more hot water to the bottle and the pan. This is primitive, but if you keep a close eye on it, it will work.

2. A better method than #1 is to use an electric heating pad instead of a hot water bottle. Set the control on medium and watch the temperature. You may have to set it on high or even cover with a towel. My pad works beautifully on high without the cover.

3. A heated hostess tray can provide the source of heat. You will have to check the settings to see which provides the proper temperature.

4. A crock pot type of slow cooker can be used to incubate the yogurt. Place about 2 inches of hot water in the pot and then set the jars into the water. Watch the temperature. Some pots will work on low, others require high. It may be necessary to use the cover. Each cooker is a rule unto itself.

5. An electric frying pan can be adjusted to hold the correct temperature. Place 2 inches of water in the pan. Use hot water at a temperature of about 100°F. Turn the thermostat control until the red light winks on to show that you are heating and then back off until the red light goes out. Check the temperature at frequent intervals with a thermometer.

6. I have heard that placing yogurt in an oven with the pilot on will produce the proper temperature. It may, but it doesn't work in my oven. You can check the temperature of your's with a thermometer. If it works, you do not have to set the yogurt cups in water. They will work directly on the rack.

Types of Yogurt

Wholemilk yogurt. This is rich and creamy and makes a good substitute for sour cream in cooking and baking. The butterfat content is 4%.

Lowfat yogurt. This tastes almost as rich as that made with wholemilk, but the butterfat is only 2%. I like this one as a base for salad dressings and on baked potatoes as well as for baking.

Non-fat yogurt. This is made with skimmed milk and contains absolutely no butterfat. It sets up as firmly as the richer yogurts and has a good sour, tangy flavor but does not taste as rich and creamy. If you're counting calories this is a great way to go.

A word of warning. Since yogurt is dependent on being incubated at a certain temperature, do not use heat resistant cups like styrofoam to incubate.

To cover cups without lids, use plastic wrap and a rubber band.

CONVERSION TABLES

American Measure	Metric Measure	English Measure
1 teaspoon	7 grams	1 coffee spoon
1 Tablespoon	14 grams	1 soup spoon
2 teaspoons	14 grams	1 soup spoon
2 Tablespoons	28 grams	1 Tablespoon
¼ cup	57 grams	2 ounces
1 cup	227 grams	8 ounces
2 cups	454 grams	1 pound
½ cup liquid	150 ml.	4 fluid ounces
1 cup liquid	300 ml.	8 ounces or 1 pint

2 teaspoons	equal	1 Tablespoon
2 Tablespoons	equal	1 ounce
16 Tablespoons	equal	1 cup

Pan Size	Bread Weight	Cup Measure
9 x 5	2 pounds	3 cups
8½ x 4½	1½ pounds	2 cups
7½ x 3½	1 pound	1½ cups
5½ x 3	½ pound	1 cup

Some older cooking and baking books tell us to use a moderate oven or a hot oven instead of giving a temperature. The oven temperature table shows these settings with the temperature in both Fahrenheit and Celsius (Centigrade.)

Oven Temperature

	Degrees F.	Degrees C.
Cool	300	150
Warm	325	165
Moderate	350-375	175-190
Mod. Hot	375-400	190-205
Hot	425	220
Very Hot	450-500	230-245

Temperature Conversion Formulas

European cookbooks list the temperature for baking in degrees Celsius (Centigrade). It is convenient to be able to convert these to degrees Fahrenheit because American ovens are marked only for Fahrenheit. The formulas for conversion are easy to use.

To convert Celsius to Fahrenheit:

$$\frac{\text{Degrees C.} \times 9}{5} + 32 = \text{degrees F.}$$

To convert degrees Fahrenheit to Celsius:

$$\frac{\text{Degrees F.} \times 5}{9} - 32 = \text{degrees C.}$$

Index